AF541898

AUTOCRATS

Also by the author

Where Borders Bleed: An Insider's Account of Indo-Pak Relations

Durand's Curse: A Line Across the Pathan Heart

Second Night

India's World: How Prime Ministers Shaped Foreign Policy

Wartime: The World in Danger

AUTOCRATS

Charisma, Power, and Their Lives

RAJIV DOGRA

RUPA

Published by
Rupa Publications India Pvt. Ltd 2024
7/16, Ansari Road, Daryaganj
New Delhi 110002

Sales centres:
Bengaluru Chennai Hyderabad
Jaipur Kathmandu Kolkata
Mumbai Prayagraj

P-ISBN: 978-93-6156-009-5
E-ISBN: 978-93-6156-384-3

First impression 2024

10 9 8 7 6 5 4 3 2 1

Printed in India

To my brave daughter Radhika Swarup,
my inspiration and my sunshine.
And to my son Ram Dogra, a man without malice.

CONTENTS

Part 1: THE BACKDROP

1

BRAINWASHING

In the dark times, will there also be singing?
Yes, there will be singing. About the dark times.[1]

—Bertolt Brecht

People choose their own icons and, in most cases, they get it wrong.

This is not our only complaint with the world. An often-asked question is: why are dictators so cruel and uncaring about the consequences of their actions?

One way of explaining—but not excusing—their conduct is to point out that a dictator's world is made of winners and losers. What the dictator prefers to talk about is winning. The public good is something only people like to talk about, but sadly, it is they who always end up as losers. Yet, they do nothing about it. Had they not been complicit, the authoritarian leader could never have grabbed power.

And so, this follow-up question is posed frequently: why do people submit?

There is no uniform answer. Because all dictators do not fit into a single mould—the one size that fits all. Despite this, a common thread binds the way they maintain their hold over people. Fear is the universal key. To cite an example, while living in Romania in the late 1990s, almost a decade after its dictator Nicolae Ceausescu was deposed, I noticed that people were afraid of their shadows. They still looked over their shoulders to see if they were being followed. While strolling in a park, they looked around suspiciously to check if the person sitting on the nearby bench was holding a newspaper in front of his face. They would then discreetly check if there was a hole in the newspaper. It was a sure sign that the person keeping a watch through the hole was the regime's spy.

Gradually, some people started to loosen up and set themselves free from fear. They, and a few of those who were in positions of power during Ceausescu's time, were willing to talk. The former wanted to relive that nightmare one last time, and get it off their chest. The latter were mostly people who were known to have collaborated with the dictator. They were eager to open up because they wanted to erase the blot of having been facilitators of the dictator's regime.

The story I pieced together from them, of cruelty under Ceausescu, is typical of what happened in East Europe in the second half of the twentieth century. The dictatorial methods varied, as did the extent of harshness, but the fear and the brutality were uniformly pervasive. Its beastly dimension in Romania was revealed to me by Ion Caramitru, a famous film and theatre actor who became the Minister of Culture after the revolution. He had occasionally dared the Ceausescu regime through innuendos during stage performances. One of these was noted by the secret police and, soon thereafter, Ion was picked up for re-education.

Ion's account was the answer to my question: what makes a dictator oppressively powerful and heartlessly uncaring?

> 'We were monitored all the time,' Ion began in a slow, theatrically low voice. 'Every single act of ours was

controlled. The State decided who you could meet and who you couldn't, who you could talk to and for how long, what you could eat and how much, what you could buy and what you could not.'

'Really?'

'The State determined what was good for you and how much of it was good for you.'

'You are talking in riddles,' I said. 'You have to tell me in simple words what actually happened and describe the way it happened. Only then will I get the right picture.'

'All right,' Ion said gruffly. The impatience in my voice must have surprised him, but he continued. 'Nicolae Ceausescu had a brutal method of dealing with his opponents. It was called the re-education programme.' Ion added, drawing in a huge breath, 'This was meant to correct those who had strayed from the designated path. I was one of the chosen ones because I had been critical of Ceausescu during a stage performance. The next morning, I was driven all the way to Sibiu to be put in a correction centre. There, my re-education began in stages.'

'Stages?' I echoed.

'On the first day, I was told that my education could take place only in a clean environment. I thought that was good news; after all, who can object to cleanliness. Actually, I was eager to begin. I didn't suspect anything even when they gave me a wet rag. But when they asked me to hold the wet rag between my teeth, I hesitated. At this, their tone changed. They started to shout and roughly shoved me about. One of them caught me by the arm and ordered me to clean the floor with the rag.

'After I finished one round of cleaning, they hit me

on the back and asked me to carry on with my job. It then became my routine to clean over and over again. Sometimes, another prisoner, someone who had been re-educated, would be asked to sit on my back, so that with his weight pressing me even closer to the ground, I could clean the floor better.

'This went on throughout the day. I cleaned that same floor from early morning till late at night, without a break, without food and water. At night, I was told I could sleep on the wet floor that I had cleaned so well.'

'So you slept.'

'I was about to sleep, out of sheer exhaustion. Just then another inmate came and started lashing at the soles of my feet with a wet rubber hose. It was as bad as being beaten with a thick metal rod.

'This went on all through the night. The moment my eyelids drooped, the hose came down viciously. By early next morning both my feet were covered with blisters.'

'That was awful.'

'It was just the beginning. Next day, the second stage of my education started. The jailors called it "brainwashing", because in this phase I was required to dip my head repeatedly in a bucketful of urine.'

'It can't be true,' I protested. 'This is disgusting. Don't tell me anymore.'

'This kept happening routinely,' Ion carried on, wanting to get it off his chest. 'The form and the number of my other punishments varied—from sweeping the floor with a rag in my mouth to being beaten by a wet hose in the night. But I had to start each new day by dipping my head in a bucketful of urine. That was a must. By the tenth day, I didn't need anyone to push me towards the bucket. I crawled on my own towards it.

Urine was my early morning baptism, my brain coolant, my therapy.'

'You said a point came when you stopped caring. You weren't afraid any longer. When did that happen?' I asked in a voice far louder than normal.

'I don't remember the precise moment when the limits changed for me, but I must have crossed the rubicon in that bucket of urine. At some point when my head was deep in other people's piss, I got the ability to realize what was always there within me. The feeling that it was up to me to be in charge of my life, you know the kind of sensation one gets after smoking pot—the freedom to float, the freedom to do as you please; to eat what you want, whenever you want and as much as you want.

'It gave me the freedom to think the impossible, the freedom to talk, walk and dream. I learnt to dream in a bucket of piss. I began to dream every drowsy day and each wakefull night. I was at peace, without boundaries, without restrictions.'

Ion paused to draw deep at his cigarette. Then he said in an even voice, 'Ceausescu did me a favour.'

'How?'

'You resist physical torture with anger, and so you hate the system even more. But the bucket of urine was my liberator. It set me free from fear. This ultimate humiliation gave me the confidence that nothing worse can follow even if I were to rebel. That is how I joined the Revolution of 1989.'

Ion's account is typical of the way people suffer and of the way tyrants act. Only the methods vary. If the Central Intelligence Agency (CIA) prefers water-boarding, the Inter-Services Intelligence (ISI) resorts to mind-altering drugs and crippling the body to a vegetative state. China takes the extreme path by imprisoning a million Uighurs, torturing men and raping their women to change the progeny.[2]

If these are the methods of dictators, how should people react to them? Isn't there some way of opposing a dictator? There isn't a lot to go by, but Nelson Mandela had a suggestion: '*I learned that courage was not the absence of fear, but the triumph over it.*'[3]

Sadly, courage is not a common commodity and not many can conquer fear. Like the quest for nirvana, transcending fear is tough. Therefore, the vast majority takes the easier route by opting to play it safe. It submits. This lack of challenge suits the dictator. It was as true of the way we behaved in the past as it is now in this age of the internet. A Freedom House report of 2021 confirms this:

> The long democratic recession is deepening. The impact...has become increasingly global in nature, broad enough to be felt by those living under the cruellest dictatorships, as well as by citizens of long-standing democracies. Nearly 75 per cent of the world's population lived in a country that faced deterioration last year.[4]

It is the lives of 75 per cent of the world's population that should worry us. How do they live caged in the vast autocratic prison of our world? Sadly, they rarely have the small consolation that Harry Belafonte talked about: '*You can cage the singer but not the song.*'[5]

WORLD AT AN INFLECTION POINT

A complete history of the world's political experiences, its triumphs and tragedies, its periods of agony and the interludes of ecstasy, is yet to be written. When it happens, that tome might conclude there has been more pain than pleasure, more control than freedom and that the dark times have largely been history's signature tune. This brutal reality means dictatorship was the default condition of humanity from the dawn of civilization.

This is a pity because if democracy is the story of beautiful impossibilities, dictatorship is the destroyer of everyone's everyday delight.

It is about the malice and treachery in people and it is about all that is dishonourable in society. Alas, dictatorship is also about the unreal times when people are their walking images: weak, afraid, cowardly and fearful. This has to be so because the fundamental assumption of most authoritarian regimes is that man is intrinsically evil. The only way to keep this evil in check is by constant supervision, and through periodic application of force.

The twentieth century experience is a cruel case in point because this was one of the bloodiest of all centuries. This can be attributed to Hitler, Stalin and Mao who killed more of their own citizens—by some estimates close to 170 million—than they killed foreigners. As in the past, in more recent times too, dictators have been directly or indirectly responsible for poverty, refugee flows, cruel repression and wars.

This eternal face-off between the brave, striving yet vulnerable people and a hulking, violent dictator is seldom subtle. It always resembles a long-running film noir narrative about good and evil that truly belongs to the era dominated by mythological characters, where good ultimately triumphs and evil dies. Over centuries, the script has varied and the characters have changed, but the suffering has been uniform and the result never certain till the very end.

Let me take some recent cases where an autocratically inclined politician gains power. To keep himself in power, free of challenge, he breaks every rule in the book to arrest political opponents and civil society activists. For instance, Serbia's president Aleksandar Vučić insisted that the country needed to rid itself of 'lying and treacherous journalists that act as foreign mercenaries.'[6] Or as Poland's Law and Justice party did over several years by replacing judges who deemed the party's policies unconstitutional.[7]

The list can go on to include Putin, Erdogan and many more. Then there are others like Imran Khan whose autocratic rule was short-lived; it was cut short because Pakistan's bigger autocrat, its army, wanted him removed. Still, so long as he was in power, he followed the autocrat's script and relied successfully on communication skills:

- He never spoke down to people.
- He appealed to their deepest moral instincts and aspirations in ways that they could easily grasp.
- He made up for a lack of verbal dazzle by speaking directly to his audience in a simple, unadorned manner.
- He understood the power of repetition. Every speech was broadly the same speech. He constantly hammered home the same themes—national self-respect, honesty in public life, the importance of Islamic values. It wasn't scintillating, but it was effective.

However, an autocrat can be effective only up to the time he has an audience. Once the army stepped in and deprived him of followers, he began to sound nervous, hollow and without messianic zeal. There were still Imran Khan addicts amongst the population, but the Khan phenomenon had been punctured.

One of his autocratic predecessors was General Zia-ul-Haq. He is still remembered scornfully in Pakistan as one of its severest dictators. His long, seemingly endless iron rule made people wonder if they would, in their lifetime, taste freedom. It provoked some poetic angst as well. One of the more recalled couplets of that time by Habib Jalib applies, almost without exception, to dictators everywhere:

Tum se pehle vo jo ik shakhs yahan takht-nasheen tha
us ko bhi apne khuda hone pe itna hi yaqeen tha

(The person who occupied this throne before you,
He too was certain that he was God.)[8]

Dictators are not the only ones with complex personalities. Democracies, too, have their share of them. Charles De Gaulle, for instance, was regarded even in his lifetime by his peers as egotistical, with delusions of grandeur, and perpetually aggrieved over slights real and imagined.

This confusion is not new. Far back in time, Plato believed that democratic forms of government created a licentious and undisciplined population who fell easy prey to the smooth-talking politician.

The President of the United States Joe Biden is unlikely to make it into any list, made by a modern-day Plato, of the smooth-talking stereotype. But he is credited with occasional reflection and, in one of those special moments, he maintained that the world is at an 'inflection point' in a battle between 'democracy and autocracy'.[9]

However, it is not the first time this argument has been made, nor is it the first time the world finds itself at such an inflection point. Machiavelli pondered over it in two of his celebrated works. If *The Prince* remains a guidebook for dictators, his equally great, perhaps more deliberated, work *Discourses on Livy* is a vigorous defence of democracy.

In *Discourses*, Machiavelli wanted to understand how Rome rose from a small city-state to dominate the entire Mediterranean region and some of the world beyond it. His conclusion was clear—Rome achieved glory because of its republican form of government. With Rome's experience as his guide, he asserted that democracies were better able than autocracies to harness the energy of a society towards greatness.

Yet, it was the same Machiavelli who settled the argument by maintaining, in *The Prince*, that '*...since love and fear can hardly exist together, if we must choose between them, it is far safer to be feared than loved.*'[10]

As he said then, so now the world seems to be opting for strongmen, those it can fear. And going by current global trends, Biden's wish is at best minority wisdom. This is so even in Europe where governments are increasingly being led by right-wing political parties.

In this new phase, Europe seems not to have learnt from its darkest moments in history. Its post-World War II resolve of 'never again' lasted just over two generations, almost for as long as Europe was cushioned by plenty and prosperity. The war in Yugoslavia shattered the illusion that Europe was war-proof; the one in Ukraine is further proof that the continent has ridden out its luck.

It is not just the continent's peace that lies wounded. Europe's democratic 'firewall' is also starting to crack. How did it happen? In part, it was due to growing economic insecurities and inequalities. These plus resentment against immigrants provided ample material for far-right parties that offered scapegoating as an answer.

As increasingly in Europe, so too in the rest of the world. Democracy has been reduced to a label under which the rulers are elected. Once a strongman is elected, the democratic process is discarded in favour of absolute rule.

But this rule does not end with his reign. It goes on even after the dictator has been removed. Those ugly memories, and their bad taste, linger because the system that sustained the dictator does not die with him. For a brief while, though, there is hope of a new dawn; people begin to think that maybe this time there could be a new beginning. Therefore, in the post-autocrat days, people's lava of angst and anger begins to cool, and a new hope moves in.

Alas, that hope and those dreams die young.

2

POMERIUM

Can people not take preventive action and mark out a potential dictator in advance? Is it not possible to tell a dictator from a democrat by looking at a leader's face? After all, it is often said that a face provides the truest reflection of a person's character. For instance, Hitler and Erdogan would stand out as typical models of a dictatorial face—grim, dour and scowling.

But some faces can be deceptive and their severity cannot be the sole indicator of a person's disposition. As the Chilean dictator Augusto Pinochet said, '*I'm not a dictator. It's just that I have a grumpy face.*'[1]

On the other hand, some cruel dictators have a deceptively pleasant face. Kim Jong-Un of Korea looks amused most of the time. He would probably be smiling even when ordering a kill. It is the same with Xi Jinping of China. His is an inscrutable face; looking at him it is hard to guess his thoughts.

Still, and generally speaking, it will be fair to say that the face reflects the man. Since democracies value justice, openness and transparency, people prefer a politician whose face conveys warmth and likability. But dictatorships are different. They operate through subordination of population, deception and tyranny. It is to keep this absolute control that dictators keep a distance from people and therefore seem cold, aloof and harsh. Some suggest that like bad karma, the scowl lines on their faces are a consequence of their actions.

Despite the negative warnings people get from looking at the face of a potential dictator, they submit and dictators spring up fairly regularly. They do not always need an excuse, or an occasion, to grab power. In most cases, a dictatorship arrives without warning. It is simply there, when just a day before it was not. Sadly, this pattern has repeated itself over and over again.

Along with it, and throughout history, the antihero has engaged people's imagination. This has been the enrapturing theme in ancient Indian epics, Greek dramas and folklore. Later, when the printing press began to amplify the written word, the antihero became a literary staple. In due course, films brought in an entirely new dimension of raw emotions. Thus, the negative in human character, the villain, was a constant through the centuries. It vicariously kept us in thrall.

The resistance to it should have been equally consistent. Alas, this was not so. The human mind is fickle and human beings are risk-averse. We opt to fume and raise our fists in the safety of our homes rather than gird up to challenge the oppressor on his turf.

But it wasn't always so. There were occasional exceptions to the rule. Arjun, the great warrior, picked up arms and was ready to join the battle in the *Mahabharata*. But on seeing relatives and friends ranged against him, he laid down his arms in despair. How, he wailed to Krishna, could he kill his own? The dialogue that followed between his enquiring mind and the infinite wisdom of Krishna is distilled in the *Bhagavad Gita*, the Song Divine.

Krishna then reveals to Arjun the reason behind his manifestation in human form:

Yada yada hi dharmasya glaanir bhavati bharata
Abhyutthaanam adharmasya tadaatmaanam srijaamyaham
Paritranay saadhunaam vinaashaay cha dushkritaam
Dharma sansthaapanaarthaay sambhavaami yuge yuge

(When there is decay of righteousness, O Bharata [Arjun], and there is exaltation of unrighteousness, then I manifest Myself for the protection of the good, for the destruction of evil-doers, to establish righteousness, I come from age to age.)

At this, Arjun takes up arms again. Lord Krishna's role is pivotal in ensuring the triumph of the righteous. It was an enormous victory against formidable odds, but Krishna had promised much more—that he would come 'from age to age' to 'destroy the evil doers'. Sadly, this part of Krishna's promise has remained just that, words in wind. But to be fair, even a God fatigues; how often can he help those who do not themselves resist?

In the centuries since the *Mahabharata*, tyrants and despots have ruled regularly. Instead of letting people float free, they have repeatedly shackled them in disciplinary chains. In all this, the dictator forgets that there is inevitably a sequel. As Juvenal, the Roman poet, warned, '*Few tyrants go down to the infernal regions by a natural death.*'[2]

As a result, the spectacle of a power-hungry dictator receiving his comeuppance has played out innumerable times in history. Hitler, at the height of his power, was a phenomenon; what he eventually became—the cornered man in a bunker—was a psychologically commonplace creature.

Let's recall also the case of Byzantine emperor Andronicus-I Comnenus. He was beaten and dismembered by a mob, his handsome face was burned with boiling water, and his hair and teeth were pulled out. Centuries later, in 1996,

Najibullah, then the President of Afghanistan, was castrated and dragged through the streets before he was hanged. More recently, Gaddafi's death was as elemental as the wild scenes from Biblical times. In its gore, it seemed a replay of the deaths of King Ahab and Queen Jezebel of Israel, who were thrown off a palace balcony and whose blood was licked off the street by dogs.

These incidents should be a warning for potential dictators and for people as well. But people have short memories. As time goes by, they begin to accommodate the past, rationalising the bad bits as inevitable and remembering the happy times with a nostalgic smile. Consequently, over and over again, dictators succeed because people yearn for everything and believe everything. In that state of innocence, they forget the age-old caution of Marcus Aurelius:

> Everything we hear is an opinion, not a fact. Everything we see is a perspective, not a truth.'[3]

Despite this truth, we tend repeatedly to be taken in by embroidered words. Sadly, and going by current trends, dictatorship and authoritarian rule seem to have become normal to human existence. The autocrats of the second half of the twentieth century were, at least, concerned about their image abroad. Today, the authoritarian leaders don't care much if they and their countries are criticized. They are willing to accept economic collapse, to see their country enter isolation and mass poverty if that's what it takes to stay in power. Assad applied this model in Syria. The Taliban leadership in Afghanistan did not care that financial collapse was looming, nor were they worried about global criticism when they began arresting and murdering Afghan officials and civilians.

In sharp contrast, democracy is a place for ideas, for

breathing free, for solace and refuge. But democracy took a long time to arrive.

Otherwise, for centuries, the authoritarian type has prevailed. This has been so ever since the first groups of people began to form. At first an informal arrangement, it got steadily more formalised as an institution when societies and then states came into being. Even the epics and folk tales held us in a fearful grip with accounts of power and misdeeds of the cruel among kings.

As the world progressed, it added more variations to the same theme: how to keep groups of people in a restricted state; the *pomerium* they should not cross. At school it was the class monitor, outside it was the bully who forced discipline after his fashion. The pattern kept repeating itself as assemblies of men got larger until, at the State level, a single man or a limited group established control. This remained the norm for centuries the world over.

LIBERTY OF REPUBLICS OVERTURNED

All along, and despite his many shades, the ruler has mostly been authoritarian. To be a strongman is the operational mode, and the deception follows a standard script.

In the beginning, dictators have almost every citizen's wish on board.

The long night of despair starts when it is already too late for the dictator to change his ways and for citizens to change him. Even those leaders who at first seem liberal take the opposite turn in power.

This pattern of pretention before grabbing absolute power has been perfected over centuries. We are consequently at a stage where now, more than ever before, the games of power defining modern societies are rigged in ways that favour tyranny. It is about this trap that Alexander Hamilton had warned:

> Of those men who have overturned the liberty of republics, the greatest number have begun their career by playing an obsequious court to the people; commencing demagogues and ending tyrants.[4]

This script has seldom changed. When a dictator grabs power, everything changes: his behaviour, his feelings and his relationships.

But people are slow to notice. At first, they are seduced by the illusion, ignoring what is in plain sight. Their expectations swirl around him. But these do not last long as he begins to rewrite rules. Despite the absolute power he thus accumulates, he is not at peace with himself. He becomes a habitual fretter; at the height of his power, a recurring stress dream haunts him that one day it will all come crashing down.

The funny thing is the dictator knows it and so do people; just the timing of it eludes them.

Till then, until the time the first faint voice of protest is heard, the citizens live a life of nightmares. The dictator's conduct till that protest is so incomprehensible that people end up looking bewildered. On the rare occasion when they smile, it does not mean they have accepted dictatorship. It only means they have reconciled to living under it.

This period is rarely short. In most cases, it leaves societies deeply polarised, with one section consisting of blind followers who refuse to see any wrong in the dictator and his rule. They are the ones whose voice prevails as long as the dictator reigns. The silent majority sulks and bides its time in the hope that this too shall pass.

As time passes, public memory fades. Even the most horrible phase of dictatorial atrocities becomes a hazy blip.

This is especially so with the second generation—people born after the terrible tenure of a dictator. Their remembrance of things past, of the cruelty of everyday life under a dictator, is largely anecdotal. There is just the lingering curiosity among them about what it is like to live in a dictatorship. As George Orwell wrote in *1984*, *'Everything faded into mist. The past was erased, the erasure was forgotten, the lie became truth.'*[5]

But what about the dictator? While he is ruling, how does he feel?

Is someone like Kim Jong Un of North Korea comfortable living with lies and doing what he does to people? Can he sleep well at night? What is he really like deep down in his heart? For years and years, I thought about it incessantly, and I asked the question of everyone I met. I listened carefully to their answers, to see if they were my answers too.

There were clues from historical accounts as well.

Sometimes, a spouse acts as a restraining influence. But when she is no longer by the dictator's side and her calming influence fades, his cruel streak knows no bounds. This was the case with Stalin. When his first wife Ekaterina Svanidze died, Stalin is said to have remarked at her funeral, *'This creature softened my heart of stone. She died and with her died my last warm feelings for humanity.'*[6]

Stalin was stating the obvious because there was no one else who could hold out a restraining finger and tell the dictator, 'You are going too far.' By and large, a dictator does not accept any limit to the exercise of his capabilities and power. He takes major decisions on his own and punishes at random. And worse still, every dictator surrounds himself with sycophants.

By then, society begins to choke. At that point, a question first begins to float. What is it that follows once a society has submitted?

Does it keep some wriggle room for itself? Does it have the luxury of an escape clause or the insurance of a return policy? Once installed in power, can a society then tell the dictator, 'Sorry boss, you are not the person we wanted!'

'Tough luck', mocks the strong man in response. History is witness that a dictator does not come with a warranty of satisfactory performance. When he grabs the top chair, he becomes a fixture.

Saddam, Gaddafi, Erdogan or Putin are not the type to leave power voluntarily out of the goodness of their hearts, or to give the next person a go at governance. Neither they nor many others, like the strongmen of the Stans, yield ground. They may be short on performance but they are convinced they are what the country needs. Take, for instance, the case of Indira Gandhi who was a strong leader but essentially a democrat. Yet, when a court verdict threatened to unseat her, she took to the logic of dictators:

> After my judgement in 1975 what could I have done except stay? You know the state the country was in. What would have happened if there was nobody to lead it? I was the only one who could, you know.[7]

People endure somehow the long, dark night the dictator envelops them in, hoping it is transient. This period of gloom varies in intensity, depending upon the whims of the strongman. Still, it is not all doom and gloom.

It isn't as if the dictator prowls the streets to pick up and put into his dungeon every passer-by. In fact, the average person is safe; the general experience has been that the common person may suffer deprivation but he is not likely to be punished for being sullen. For him life carries on as before; less happily and less comfortably but safely because the strongman ensures there is law and order in the State.

It is the intellectual, the politically ambitious and the rivals who fret and fume.

They wait in the wings, hoping the opportunity to rebel and revolt will strike sooner than later. The common man will then be tugged in somehow to provide the numerical strength. Till that happens, society plods on limply.

That mass suffocation does not happen suddenly. In fact, on his way to power a dictator usually makes extravagant promises.

WHEN THE GODS CEASED TO BE

At first the authoritarian leader is cautious; he does not snuff out democracy overnight. He does it methodically, chipping away at the democratic pillars one after the other. In this pursuit, he makes the masses his collaborators. He gradually persuades and manipulates them to relinquish their rights and give over that power to him. This mass brainwashing has led to some of the worst crimes against humanity. Eventually people find out that his offer of paradise is shackled to hell. This period of bitterness was so described by Thomas Paine: '*These are the times that try men's souls...Tyranny, like hell, is not easily conquered.*'[8]

In power, a dictator is likely to organize repression, order mass arrests, encourage routine torture and sanction summary trials. Mass murders are explained away as necessary for the defence of the State. A challenge to his authority is crushed promptly and often brutally. The pattern is largely the same the world over.

Juan Perón was the president of Argentina when he began to face opposition from four members of the Supreme Court. He did not have the patience to confront them legally or constitutionally. Instead, he used his majority support in the

Parliament to impeach three judges. The fourth judge took the hint and resigned before the impeachment proceedings against him could be initiated.[9]

The media, too, does not escape the dictator's attention. Ecuadorian president Rafael Correa won a massive $40 million defamation suit against the owners of newspaper *El Universo*, when the latter called him a 'dictator'.[10] Why and how this massive fine was imposed can only be explained by the fact that he had in place a compliant judiciary. Autocratic legalism is the technical term for this behaviour, and it is not just a Latin American phenomenon.

Let us take another example of extreme arbitrariness, this time from a different continent. A Zambian opposition leader Hakainde Hichilema was arrested in 2016 and charged with treason. What was his crime? As Hichilema found out to his horror, he had been charged with treason because he had not stopped for a motorcade carrying President Edgar Lungu. This 'endangered the President's life', the High Court charged. It was only to be so because the judges of the High Court had been hand-picked by the ruling Patriotic Front.[11]

To take a recent case, China President Xi's strike on the billionaire Jack Ma was just as shocking as its smothering completeness. It demonstrated that the government in China exercises a form of power that is as fine-tuned as it is total. Whether it is lashing out at a corporate critic or suppressing Uighurs, China's government under Xi has put in shape a new twenty-first century techno-totalitarianism. It combines many tools of classical control with new ones of mass suppression through technology.

As with China, many other authoritarian states exercise total control and comprehensive surveillance of its people. Once at a meeting in Uzbekistan, I inquired of the Secretary at the Ministry of Internal Affairs about the extent of their knowledge of anti-regime elements. He surprised me with his reply, '*I know exactly how many men in Uzbekistan did not sleep in their beds last night.*'

This reply exhibited a shocking intrusion into people's privacy. But his confidence was also proof that despite technological advances, the age-old practice of human intelligence remains unsurpassed. It is efficient and it instills fear, unlike faceless technological tools.

In despair, and as a last resort, people look to the justice system of a country to stand firm against tyranny. Sensing this, Turkey's Erdogan sacked thousands of judges after a failed coup attempt against him.[12] This resulted in a system where no judge dared rule against the president's political wishes. This pattern of emasculating the judiciary has unfortunately been repeated extensively by authoritarian leaders elsewhere.

These instances are merely representative. As a general observation, it will be fair to say that autocracy is insidious and there is as yet no instruction manual on how to survive under it. Still, if a quick prescription of coping was asked for by people, a start could be made with these:

- The State is afraid of people's thoughts. This is a huge advantage. The State can never reach into your brain if you don't let it.
- Humour is another weapon the State cannot counter. But humour and passive resistance have limits in the face of some of the most oppressive regimes.
- Mahatma Gandhi's instrument of choice was the inner strength of people to stand up to a dictator, '*Non-cooperation with tyrants is a duty.*'[13]

On a practical note, there is also the example of Sudanese-British billionaire Mo Ibrahim. He sponsors the Ibrahim Prize, which awards five million dollars to an elected African leader who promotes democracy, is honest and cedes power without a fuss. He has also the 'Ibrahim Index of African Governance', an evaluation of Africa's 54 governments. If a leader becomes oppressive and corrupt, his country's ranking falls. Ibrahim announces the rankings of this exercise in paid advertisements in African newspapers.[14]

Ibrahim's efforts are noble. He may even have succeeded in planting hope that one day democracy and rule of law might prevail. Whether he will continue awarding the prize is open to doubt. He will also do well to remember what the Greek philosopher Diogenes maintained many centuries ago. When asked why he was seeking alms from a statue, he said, '*I am practicing disappointment.*'[15]

Yet, we assume hopefully that efforts like that of Ibrahim's will be enough to pull a society out of the dictatorial trap.

3

MUSKETS ARE BETTER

The bad, the despised and the feared have existed from the time human interaction began. Only the nomenclature has changed. But even that changed nuance does not matter to the dictatorial type. Terms like 'demon', 'tyrant' and 'dictator' may be variations of the same theme, their significance too may have changed with use over the years, but none of this bothers the authoritarian ruler.

He also has an entirely different approach to truth. Whatever he says is the truth, any evidence to the contrary is irrelevant. And on this point, he ignores even Machiavelli's advice, '*It is not titles that honor men, but men that honor titles*.'[1] Taking this argument further, even the fear of karma and its consequence does not bother a dictator.

This sense of impunity is one reason why, from the earliest times, demons have existed in myths and legends.

FROM BENIGN TO BEASTLY

In ancient Greece, the word *tyrannos* carried no ethical censure. It simply referred to anyone, good or bad, who obtained executive power in a *polis* (city-state) by unconventional means. The support for tyrants came from a growing middle class and from the landless peasants in debt to wealthy landowners.

The negative use of the word began in fifth-century Athens, when the democrats created the tyrant as their anti-type. By Greek thought, tyranny was about the worst form of governance. Later, ancient Rome also had its share of tyrants. But Romans were wary of criticising them. This fear became more pronounced when the famous lawyer Cicero's head and hands were cut off and nailed to the rostrum of the Senate to warn people of the dangers of speaking out against tyranny. There has been no change in this pattern ever since; the tyrant has not mellowed and the people have rarely been emboldened enough to challenge him.

'Tyranny' and 'tyrants' were not merely the burden of the Western world. The East has had its share of tyrants. In China, its first Emperor Qin Shi Huang unified seven separate kingdoms into one nation. He built the Great Wall and was buried with an army of terracotta soldiers. In terms of achievements, his contribution was certainly considerable. But he was also a tyrant. That's why the Chinese continue to have mixed feelings about him. India too had them in plenty, both in its mythology and in reality. The Mughal King Aurangzeb was just one of them.

Regardless of where they rule, ruthless ambition is a common trait of tyrants. To them winning is everything; they must prevail, dominate, claim victory in every interaction by any means possible. In sum, a tyrant knows no laws but those of his caprice.

Both Plato and Aristotle speak of the king as a good monarch and the tyrant as a bad one. Both say monarchy or rule by a single man is royal when it is for the welfare of the ruled, and it is tyrannical when it serves only the interests of the ruler. Both make lawlessness a mark of tyranny. In a further elaboration, they defined a tyrant as a person who rules without law, using extreme and cruel methods against his own people and others. Aristotle, in particular, did not give a tyrant any benefit of the doubt and explained tyranny as '*that arbitrary power of an individual which is responsible to no one, and governs all alike, whether equals or betters, with a view to its own advantage, not to that of its subjects, and therefore against their will.*'[2]

Despite this list of negatives, everyone does not view tyrants as evil. They have had their apologists.

Thomas Hobbes was one such. He claimed in *Leviathan* there was no objective distinction between kings being vicious or virtuous. Instead, he faulted critics for their nitpicking and for being uniformly negative: '*For they that are discontented under Monarchy, call it Tyranny; and they that are displeased with Aristocracy, called it Oligarchy: so also, they which find themselves grieved under a Democracy, call it Anarchy...*'[3]

This was only to be expected from Hobbes. He, after all, advocated the survival of the fittest. And in *Leviathan*, Hobbes also argued, '*The state of nature was one in which there were no enforceable criteria of right and wrong. People took for themselves all that they could, and human life was solitary, poor, nasty, brutish and short.*'[4]

As against this rather extreme view, Dante viewed tyrants through a rigorous prism and described them as those who laid hold on blood and plunder in the seventh Circle of Hell (*Divine Comedy*), where they were submerged in boiling blood. He included in his list of tyrants Alexander the Great and Attila the Hun.[5]

Surprisingly, even Niccolò Machiavelli viewed tyrants through a wary eye. In *Discourses on Livy*, he categorized rule by a single person as 'tyranny' regardless of the legitimacy of that rule. In fact, he also issued a warning to the erring rulers, '*The best fortress is to be found in the love of the people, for although you may have fortresses, they will not save you if you are hated by the people.*'[6]

Edward Gibbon had a similar warning in *Decline and Fall of the Roman Empire*. Noting that Roman emperors were deified, Gibbon called the emperors tyrants and their rule tyranny. He added, '*The Roman Empire may be defined as an absolute monarchy disguised by the forms of a commonwealth.*'[7]

'Despot' is another example of how the usage of certain terms can change the way they are perceived. Initially, it was not regarded as a negative term. In ancient Greece, a despot (*despótès*) was a master who ruled in a household over those who were slaves or servants. On a societal scale, it referred to the absolute ruler of a subject people, those who were enslaved or otherwise held captive.

Far from having the pejorative connotation of our times, a despot was considered a legitimate title of office in the Byzantine court. This title was also bestowed on sons or sons-in-law of reigning emperors, and initially denoted the heir-apparent of the Byzantine emperor. The Pharaoh of Egypt was another example of the classical despot. Even today, in the Orthodox Liturgy, if celebrated in Greek, the priest is addressed by the deacon as a 'despot'. By around the sixteenth century, its usage became more broad-based and in the English language a 'despot' was a generic title for anyone in authority. So far so good. One could even say there was no major blot yet on a despot's cloak.

The transformation of the term, in France, started in the 1690s. The word 'despot', in its new negative meaning, was popularised by the opponents of Louis XIV, who used *despotisme* to describe their monarch's absolute power. Later, Montesquieu put a formal seal to the issue when he made a distinction between absolute monarchy and despotism.

He described monarchy as a system where a single person governed with absolute power by fixed and established laws, whereas a despot ruled by his or her own will and caprice.

But the real challenge, in Europe, to the idea of a despot began in England around the time Shakespeare began to write. Doubts grew whether despots were necessary and good for a country. How does a figure like Richard III or Macbeth ascend to the throne? Shakespeare asked such questions in tune with people's angst. Why did large numbers of people knowingly tolerate being lied to, he wondered? When a person ascends to power, there is still a chance the despot does not cross the red line to brute power. This is the point Shakespeare makes when Brutus cautions in *Julius Caesar*, '*Th' abuse of greatness is when it disjoins remorse from power.*'[8]

By the early eighteenth century, there was further regression due to feudal rule in Europe. The deterioration reached such a stage that during the French Revolution, the term 'despot' was derisively used by the revolutionaries to describe the government of Louis XVI. With that, 'despot' began to mean: *A ruler who governs absolutely or tyrannically; a tyrant, an oppressor.* So, what started as an idea to describe the oppressive behaviour of Louis XIV got formalised by the misdeeds of Louis XVI.

Despot is not the only term that has undergone transformation from benign to beastly. 'Autocrat' is another case in point. This coinage, too, traces its origin to Greece. In Greek, *autos* is used for 'self' and *kratos* for 'power'. In medieval times, the term *autocrates* was used for anyone holding the title *emperor*. As with some of the other absolute forms of governance, autocracy too was considered a positive concept for a long time. In its early sense, and use, it meant 'lack of conflicts of interests' as also an indication of grandeur and power.

The term 'autocrat' found particular favour with the Russian tsars for the form of dominance established in the mid-fifteenth century by Ivan the Great, who drove out the Mongols and established tight control over government. The term was given royal sanction in 1762 when Catherine the Great called herself an 'autocrat' in a manifesto: '*We, Catherine the second, by the Grace of God, Empress and Autocrat of all the Russians...*'[9]

In fact, until fairly modern times, the Russian tsar continued to be called '*Autocrat of all the Russians*'.

Beyond titles like this, and besides monarchies, democracies too have leaders who are autocratic in their behaviour. France's Charles De Gaulle, for example, could be cold, abrasive, petty and haughty in his dealings.

However, autocrats have also been known to accomplish great new things. In the business world, for instance, some autocratic leaders have been innovators who revolutionized industries. Henry Ford is the oft-quoted name in this list. This, of course, is the rare good side of the picture.

Otherwise, for a long time now, 'autocrat' has been a despised term because autocratic leaders impose their will and do not seek opinion or expertise from others. When they pretend to consult experts, it is largely for form's sake. In actual practice, the autocrat takes decisions as per his whims and this arbitrariness leads to extremes. Some successful autocrats like Attila the Hun, Adolf Hitler and Joseph Stalin were also maniacal tyrants.

Over time, the *kratos* part of autocrat began to acquire greater weight. It was only natural because of the concentration of power in a single centre, be it an individual dictator or a group of power holders, such as a committee or a party leadership. Gradually, 'autocrat' also came to mean the use of force to suppress opposition and to limit social developments that might lead to opposition. In this new form, autocratic power is not subject to control: it is absolute power.

RULE BY ROD

If the terms listed so far had Greek roots, the word 'dictator' traces its origin to ancient Rome. To begin with, it was used to describe a 'magistrate'—a legal appointment by the Senate with wide-ranging powers given for a limited period. The negative connotation the term acquired was after Cornelius Sulla's second civil war, when he made himself the first Dictator of Rome. Following Sulla's example, Julius Caesar was proclaimed *Dictator perpetuo* (Dictator in perpetuity). After Caesar's assassination, his heir Augustus was offered the title of dictator, but he declined it.

Yet another form of absolute control is described by the term 'totalitarian'. To begin with, it was not an English word. It sprang from the Italian term *totalitarismo*. This was first used by a critic against the fascism prevailing then in Italy. Ironically, however, the term was embraced enthusiastically by Mussolini who defined it as meaning, *'Everything in the State, nothing outside the State, nothing against the State.'*[10]

Exceeding the brutality of other forms of absolute rule, totalitarian regimes commit genocide with equanimity. The acknowledged theorist of totalitarianism Hannah Arendt held that totalitarians taught their followers to *'believe everything and nothing, think that everything was possible and that nothing was true.'*[11]

George Orwell's imaginative account in *1984* describes a world made up entirely of totalitarian regimes. That fictional foray apart, the world suffered enormously under Hitler and Mussolini. It was enough for people to start abhorring the term 'totalitarianism'.

Yet, there was a time when, in Germany and Italy, they were held in awe bordering on reverence. That aura lasted as long as they performed by taking the national destinies forward. To give this argument concrete shape, consider these facts about the conquests made by Germany and Japan during the Second World War. In that period both acquired large empires. Hitler's sway was over land masses larger than the US. These were more densely populated and more economically productive than anywhere else in the world. The Japanese Empire was larger still. It surpassed the German Reich in its geographical stretch and in the size of its population.

All along strongmen have dominated one unfortunate part or the other of the world—Mao in China, Ceausescu in Romania, Zia-ul-Haq in Pakistan, Saddam in Iraq, Gaddafi in Libya, Kim in North Korea, and the cruelly comical Idi Amin of Uganda. They were all dictators with absolute control over their societies. However, and fortunately for the world, their numbers were nowhere near Orwell's warning of the world being governed entirely by totalitarian regimes.

This desire for control is not peculiar to the totalitarian leader only. The East European regimes were communist in practice but in total control of society. It is also sometimes the case with the duly elected, democratically chosen civilian leaders who are constantly on the lookout for conspiracies against them from rivals within their political party and by the opposition. The big difference is that while they make the outward show of being benign, an absolute ruler can also be blunt. As Mussolini remarked, '*Words are fine things, but muskets are even better*.' [12]

He was not wide of the mark because all these terms ranging from tyrant to dictator signified, over time, the rule by rod. The names given to them differed, depending on the severity of the rule or the circumstances at the time. Therefore, every name conveys the nuance and essence of what its severity meant.

However, my broad purpose is to illustrate these different types without getting entangled in the nomenclature. Along with it, and for our current need, I will use the terms *authoritarian*, *autocrat* and *dictator* interchangeably without debating the dialectics of using one or the other while elaborating a point. Though 'authoritarian' is most often used in recent times, it does not quite convey the immense harm that the all-pervasive atmosphere of fear does to a society. 'Autocrat' conveys adequately that sense of oppression, and I employ extensively this term. However, 'dictator' is my preferred choice since it more fully conveys the state of suppressed societies.

There are at least five different types of dictatorship: monarchy, military dictatorship, single person dictatorship, hybrid dictatorship and party dictatorship. So far, in the modern age, all dictators have been male. One brief exception was the period of Emergency imposed by Indira Gandhi. In those very long nearly two years, she had acted arbitrarily, almost like a dictator. But that spell was an aberration.

Moreover, a civilian dictator is unlikely to have a pre-existing organization to rely upon. He picks and chooses from among the party cadre, the bureaucracy and his acquaintances to create an organization on the job. All he then wants is for it to act like a machine: one that ticks to his wishes and guesses his priorities.

While most features of strongman rule have remained the same over time, some aspects have undergone change. There is a significant difference between the modern authoritarian's cult of personality and that of the former monarchs, some of whom, like the Roman emperors, were deified. In contrast, the twentieth-century cult of political personality is more populist, like the cult of celebrity or a movie star.

Yet another difference is that large-scale violence is no longer used as a means to exterminate opponents. The new autocrats use violence sparingly. This is their key innovation. But when they cross the line, it is a sign bad days are about to begin for them. A tape of the former Ukrainian president Leonid Kuchma ordering the abduction of a journalist, Georgy Gongadze, who was later found dead, helped fuel the Orange Revolution of 2004.[13]

The enormous force of the State is now used as an instrument to keep people in check, to see that they do not deviate from the line drawn by the dictator. A dictator will imprison those who oppose him, while a tyrant will kill them. Salazar, Mussolini, Castro and Napoleon did evil acts, yet they also accomplished notable achievements for their respective countries in some fields. They were dictators, not tyrants.

For a dictator, winning is the be-all and end-all. This applies to elections, the rule of law as well as international relations, as witnessed in 1975, when a period of Emergency was about to be imposed in India by Prime Minister Indira Gandhi. One of her officers wrote in his diary, '*...A cloud of fascism and dictatorship is hovering over the country...the Prime Minister will not flinch from anything to maintain herself in power. This could prove to be a big danger to our democracy. Individual liberties can be quashed.*'[14] This is exactly what happened over the next 21 months. Gandhi regretted it later, but at that time she did all this to maintain herself in power. But neither this nor numerous other examples have deterred leaders from brandishing the rod and imposing their will on a population.

GOVERNMENTS WITH OVERLAPPING CHARACTERISTICS

Towards the end of F. Scott Fitzgerald's novel *The Great Gatsby*, a protagonist Nick Carraway remarks, '*The loneliest moment in someone's life is when they are watching their whole world fall apart, and all they can do is stare blankly.*'[15]

Multiply this sentiment a million times and it fits the condition of a population which finds that the leader elected by them has turned a dictator. One of the first things that people begin to notice then is that their political space, rather whatever remains of it, has become dark. Another shock follows quickly. As dark times close in on the population, people observe a transformation in their leader. The person who earlier seemed approachable and welcoming has turned broody, on the way to becoming brutish.

People then wonder whether the dark times have produced such a leader, or is it because of his rule that the times are dark.

This confusion is not unique to people. The states themselves are uncertain as to the category of the government they fit in during those dark times. Interestingly, such strongmen themselves do not like to call their government a dictatorship. Accordingly, a country's description of its form of government is not always transparent. For example, the former Soviet Union declared itself a democracy. Some others confound even more, either deliberately or brazenly. Article 1 of the Constitution of the People's Republic of China (PRC) describes it as '*a people's democratic dictatorship.*'[16]

Even otherwise, various forms of government are not always sharply defined. Rather they often have overlapping characteristics, as is the case with totalitarianism, authoritarianism and fascism.

To begin with the extreme, 'totalitarianism' as a form

of government lives up to its title in every sense. Under it, the State's power is unlimited and it controls virtually all aspects of public and private life. This includes all political and financial matters as also the attitudes, morals and beliefs of people.

A totalitarian government aims to replace existing political institutions with new ones and the supersession of the legal, social and political traditions with the ones it fancies. Totalitarian governments typically pursue a special goal, such as industrialization or infrastructure projects, or expansion of frontiers, intended to mobilize the population in its favour. All resources are devoted to achieving this special goal regardless of the economic or social cost.

However, the fall, when it happens, can be sudden and catastrophic for a totalitarian leader. In a totalitarian State when you lose power, you don't just lose your job; you lose your wealth and freedom. You probably lose your life and possibly your entire extended family as well. You are literally erased from history.

Fascism, like totalitarianism, also implies absolute rule. It combines ultra-nationalism with a widely held belief among people that the nation must and should be somehow saved or 'reborn'. Rather than working for concrete solutions to economic, political and social problems, fascist rulers divert people's focus by promoting the need for a national rebirth. For this, fascists encourage among people cults of national unity and racial purity.

Historical evidence tells us that the means of doing so is by exacerbating societal divisions, encouraging tribalism and the use of violence. None of these require well-pondered moves. Instead, they need just muscle power to maintain control. Therefore, lumpenism is essential to fascism.

An authoritarian State, on the other hand, is not so

all-encompassing. Russia and China are among the many authoritarian systems currently where decision-making power is concentrated in the hands of a small ruling elite, unchecked by free elections, autonomous legislatures or independent judiciaries. Neither provides protection for civil liberties or basic human rights and both impose control on speech, the press, political opposition and civil society. The mainstay of authoritarianism is populism, which by its very nature has a smoke-and-mirrors quality; a thin-centred ideology that divides society into two homogenous and antagonistic groups of 'pure people' and 'corrupt elites'. Authoritarian leaders, too, exercise power arbitrarily and without regard to existing laws or constitutional limitations. They cannot easily be replaced through elections.

In an autocratic system, people rise by ruthlessly carving their way up the hierarchy. This ruthlessness makes them aware that others may be even more ruthless, which leads them to become paranoid and despotic within their sphere. They also practice what scholars call 'negative selection' by not getting the best people to advise them. In consequence, the government suffers.

Generally, in autocracies, as in dictatorships, no one tells the top man what he doesn't want to hear. As a result, the information flows to the top are distorted. For instance, the Russian intelligence's initial failure about Ukraine was astounding. Putin was completely out of touch with the desires of the Ukrainian people, their methods of resistance or the extent to which his own military had been undermined by corruption.

The resulting failure is not unique to Putin's Russia. This example can be multiplied many times over, as it is an inbuilt feature of the draconian system. Zbigniew Brzezinski and Carl Friedrich put forward a theory to explain some of the differences in absolute rule. To them, the main element of authoritarianism is prohibitions, and understanding what people must not do, while totalitarianism includes both prohibitions and prescribed behaviour.[17] To put it differently, people have to know not only what they should not do, but also what they should do, at the command of the State. It is not just repression and control that are important, but also the mobilization of the already submissive masses.

In this transformation, the rights of a people get changed to their duties.

A principal cause for this is that a dictator is not answerable to anyone. A politician is concerned about the next election, a leader worries about the next generation, but a dictator is sharply focused on obedience. To make matters worse for the population, dictatorship is resistant to reason. Overall, everything is represented more aggressively under an absolute ruler because absolutism in any form—be it tyranny, totalitarianism, autocracy or dictatorship—is basically a crisis of masculinity.

Finally, it should be mentioned that authoritarianism or dictatorship is not limited to one stereotype or the other. A strongman from any part of society could usurp authority. It could be in the form of a military regime, an oligarchy, indirect military control, monarchy or a personalized regime.

But how do we tell if a regime is one such?

Often, the line determining the end of democracy and the beginning of absolutism in any form can be blurred. Still, if a rough litmus test is needed, an authoritarian government is one with strict rules that limit the freedom of its people to express themselves or choose their leaders through free and fair elections.

In the end, whatever the term used for exercising control—be it tyranny, fascism, dictatorship or authoritarianism—it is the result that matters. In that respect, there isn't much difference in the methods of control used by dictators. As Che Guevara said:

Cruel leaders are replaced only to have new leaders turn cruel.[18]

Part 2: THE SEED SPROUTS

4

BORN BAD

It is sometimes argued dictators act the way they do as the result of a dysfunction. This may not be a flawed assumption. Some deceitful, manipulative, even sadistic behaviour appears to be programmed genetically—suggesting that some people are born to be bad.

In fact, according to an Indian folklore, it should be possible to predict the type of adult a child would grow up to be. This Hindi saying '*Honhaar birwaan ke hoth chikne paat*' translates roughly as: 'Coming events cast their shadows before.' Others take a different view. They maintain that evil does not manifest itself early and cite this assertion by an ancient Chinese philosopher Mencius that '*man's nature is good, he is born good-hearted, but due to external influences he can become evil.*'[1]

History too is proof that most dictators do not turn ruthless from their childhood. If this is so, is it at least possible to divine signs? Can't we associate the time of birth with his dictatorial turn potentially?

This can only be speculative because there isn't definitive evidence yet that associates a dictator's birth with a particular date or month. But as a broad sweep, it is said that some of the world's worst dictators were born under the sign of

Taurus. This list includes Oliver Cromwell (25 April 1599), Catherine the Great (2 May 1729), Vladimir Ilyich Lenin (22 April 1870), Ho Chi Minh (19 May 1890), Ayatollah Khomeini (17 May 1900), Pol Pot (19 May 1925), Saddam Hussein (28 April 1937), and the inspiration for many dictators, Niccoló Machiavelli (3 May 1469).

Despite this compelling evidence, the zodiac sign under which a person is born should not be blamed for what he eventually becomes. It will be unfair to label Taurus or any other sign as the harbinger of evil, because people born the same day can turn out completely differently. Take the case of Adolf Hitler and Charlie Chaplin, born only four days apart in April 1889 in relatively poor families. Both rose to great heights in their chosen profession and both, in their distinctive way, have left a lasting impression on the world. One of these men would make the world laugh, the other would inflict misery. Therefore, it is not the evil stars that should be held responsible; it has to be something else. But this is where confusion confounds because a myth prevalent in folk tales maintains that evil stars are a reality.

All along, people have continued to wonder how 'evil' affects a child. Are the seeds of 'evil' ingrained in a child's DNA or do they develop them as a result of their childhood experience? The scientific fact maintains that our brain is not a finished product when we are born. The structuring of the brain depends on its experiences in the first hours, days and weeks of a person's life.

On the other hand, it is also asserted that a child does not arrive in this world as a clean slate. Every child comes with a history of the nine months between conception and birth; that their genetic print is inherited from their parents.

TRAUMA OF CHILDHOOD YEARS

The scientifically accepted formative period starts after birth and the environment a child finds itself in then. Eventually, a person's character depends on the love, protection, tenderness and understanding he receives in his early years. But if a child is forced to grow up neglected, emotionally starved, and is subjected to physical cruelty, it will forfeit the innate capacity for empathy.

For most people, the memories of early childhood consist of a series of impressions—some very clear, others hazy outlines. By and large, they cherish these childhood memories. But dictators remember only the bad parts where an abusive father, relative or friend had done them dirty. This pain persists as anger against the unfair world; it is a dialogue of revenge that goes on incessantly in his head.

Dictators like Hitler, Stalin, Ceausescu, Mao and Saddam had difficult childhoods.[2] These bitter experiences were unconsciously re-enacted by them later on the political stage. In his book *Hitler's Father: Hidden Letters – How the Son Became a Dictator*, Austrian historian Roman Sandgruber argues that Alois Hitler played a large role in shaping the psychology of his son.[3]

Adolf Hitler was born in Austria's *Braunau am Inn* in 1889 to Alois and his third, much-younger wife, Klara Pötzl. The family had once lived in a Jewish-owned property in Urfahr near the Danube river. This book also mentions that Hitler's mother, nearing death in 1907, was treated by a Jewish doctor who later escaped to America. Despite this, later in his life, Adolf Hitler became the scourge of Jews—a most evil, vile and detested anti-Semite figure in history.[4]

Hitler's own early years were hellish. When he was 10, he had already witnessed the death of a younger brother.

His father Alois, a drunk, used to beat him savagely. Alois died when Adolf was 13. Four years later, in 1907 his mother Klara succumbed to breast cancer and the teenaged Hitler became a virtual orphan. These experiences may or may not have been the fundamental reason for his cruel streak, but they must have been a contributory factor.[5]

Some characteristics of violent and authoritarian tendencies show themselves early. Take the case of Benito Mussolini. He was a difficult child prone to insolence and violence. In an effort to mellow him down, Mussolini was sent by his parents to a strict Catholic boarding school. But even there, the school staff could not discipline him. At the age of 10, he was expelled from the school for stabbing a fellow student with a penknife. By the time he turned 20, he had the dubious distinction of having stabbed some more youth, including one of his girlfriends.[6]

Meanwhile, in Russia, Joseph Stalin grew up as an only child in an impoverished family. In fact, out of three children, he was the only baby who survived. His father, a shoemaker, was alcoholic and would often beat him. He abandoned his family to work in a factory, when Stalin was just five years old.

As a young student, Stalin showed a contradictory mix in behaviour. He was studious as also wildly rebellious. He engaged in numerous acts of mischief, such as throwing lit fireworks in shops. In 1901, when he was 23 years old, Stalin joined the Social Democratic Labour Party and got involved in organizing protests and strikes against the monarchy. His ruthlessness during those strikes, often using extreme violence, and his ability to raise money for the party by kidnapping people, and through robbery, impressed Lenin. Around this time, he adopted the name Stalin which in Russian means 'man of steel'.[7]

At the other end of the globe, and in a different era, Idi

Amin was born in the small Kakwa tribe in Koboko, a village in north-western Uganda. His mother was a self-proclaimed sorceress. Amin was virtually abandoned by his mother when he was still a baby. He survived by selling snacks and doing casual labour work. Amin's childhood left him lonely, bitter and ruthless.[8] It was an accumulation of these experiences that must have influenced his beastly behaviour when he became Uganda's dictator.

A dozen years younger to Idi Amin, but equally brutal in his ways, Saddam Hussein's childhood was similarly trying. His misfortunes began even before he was born. His father walked out on Saddam's mother about six months prior to his birth. Since her husband had deserted her without leaving any financial support, her anger and anguish increased. She would repeatedly try to pull out clumps of her hair. On a couple of occasions she even tried to commit suicide. It wasn't just self-harm she was attempting; she would also regularly smack her stomach in the hope it would make her abort the unborn child. Shortly after Saddam was born, his elder brother died of cancer at just 12 years of age. This added to his mother's psychological issues.[9]

At that tender age, Saddam's uncle Khairallah took him under his care. Saddam stayed with Khairallah till he was three. He was sent back to live with his mother when she remarried. But this didn't improve Saddam's situation because his step-father, Ibrahim al-Hassan, routinely abused Saddam physically and psychologically. Al-Hassan would also make Saddam steal for the deeply impoverished family. Saddam became so frustrated with his unbearable circumstances that he ran away from home when he was just 10.[10]

Saddam's immense paranoia as a ruler is ascribed to his atrocious childhood. His suspicion of others and the constant feeling of being surrounded by enemies was due to the conditions he had lived through. The police State, therefore, defined his regime, where everyone was under surveillance and constantly being watched.

But a bruised childhood need not turn a future dictator into a monster. Russia's Putin too had an ugly childhood. He may be a strict ruler, and firm with those standing in his way, but he has not resorted to Hitler's horrific actions.

> Putin was a street kid in a city devastated by a horrific, three-year siege by the Nazis during WWII, a genocide described as the world's most destructive siege of a city. Most of the population of three million people died, one million starving to death. Putin's father was badly injured in the war, his mother nearly died of starvation. Living in a rat-infested apartment with two other families, the family had no hot water, no bathtub, a broken-down toilet, little or no heat. His father worked in a factory; his mother did odd jobs she could find.[11]

If he was brought up in miserable conditions at home, the streets did not offer him any comfort. Almost throughout his growing years, he was bullied by other youth. Yet, there is no conclusive proof that those scars continue to rankle.

There are, therefore, two sides to the argument with overwhelming evidence in support of the assertion that even if dictators are not born bad, the trauma of childhood years lingers as a hurt. Later, when that person acquires dictatorial authority, it magnifies into revenge against the world that had treated him badly.

EXCEPTIONS TO THE RULE

If these and many other dictators had an unenviable childhood, there are also cases of the other extreme. Early

Roman emperors like Nero and Caligula were brought up in luxury, yet they turned out to be monsters as rulers. Another example of this kind is the North Korean dictator Kim Jong-Un. He had a pampered childhood, and his father, Kim Jong-Il, favoured Kim over his older brothers due to his perceived suitability to lead the country.

As a child, he had on call 24/7 a team of dedicated staff and his playrooms boasted 'more toys than any European store'. The gardens of his home were filled with cages containing monkeys and bears for his entertainment. A personal chef was hired to cater to his whims. In school, he was notoriously brutish and would kick and spit at his schoolmates. He was called 'the little dictator' for his bullying ways with other students.[12] Despite all this pampering, Kim is just as insecure as other dictators and just as violent with his enemies.

Vladimir Ilyich Ulyanov (Lenin) was another exception to the rule. Unlike many other dictators, he was born in 1870 into Russia's minor nobility. His father held a senior position in the tsarist civil service. Consequently, he enjoyed an idyllic childhood. He wasn't at all interested in politics until his 18th year when a family tragedy—the execution of his elder brother—radicalized him. From then on, he was a highly emotional man who flew into tremendous rages.[13]

Despite his fierce faith in communism, Lenin was the product of his time and place: a violent, tyrannical and corrupt Russia. Eventually, the communist regime in the Soviet Union was largely shaped by his personality: intolerant, intemperate, secretive and suspicious. The revolutionary State he created was less the socialist utopia he envisioned, but rather a reflection of the Romanov autocracy into which he was born. But there was also a soft side to him. He was personally kind to people, and because of his upbringing he loved nature, hunting, shooting and fishing. He could identify hundreds of species of plants. The general impression makes him out as a distant and unfeeling figure, but that is a superficial view. In fact, his 'nature notes' and letters to his family reveal a side of Lenin that would surprise people.[14]

Since I am listing exceptions to the rule that dictators generally have a difficult childhood, let me also add a case of manufactured childhood.

The cult of personality around dictators like North Korea's Kim Jong-Il (the present Kim's father) is sometimes the product of a PR-style myth-making. Kim, for example, was supposedly born in a village in the shadow of a sacred Korean mountain where, according to this imaginative account, his arrival was foretold by a swallow and he took birth under a double rainbow. The reality, however, is disappointingly commonplace. Kim was born in a small town in the former Soviet Union where his father was leading a brigade of exiled Korean troops under Russian command.[15]

While these are some exceptional cases, by and large, most childhood accounts of people who grow up to become dictators reveal a pattern of deprivation and misery. As a rule, a future dictator is more likely to have missed the magic people normally associate with childhood. Instead, for a dictator, it is a period to be wiped off the personal slate. All he carries of it is the sense of hurt that he was treated unfairly.

But this feeling of grievance does not hinder their march to the top. Instead, they turn their story of woes into a legend of heroism—that they overcame formidable odds through sheer grit.

But dictators are not the only ones born poor. Some democrats are also born in poverty. But they do not carry it as a grudge against the world.

Moreover, in contrast to a democratic leader's clearer

vision generally, dictators are unable to distinguish the significant from the ordinary.

At the height of his power, when he is surrounded by supplicants and favour seekers, a dictator rarely has the time alone to reflect on his childhood. If given the opportunity, would his younger self be satisfied with the path he has taken or would it advise him to pursue a different career? Would the child express disappointment over the mass murders, brutality and corruption under his regime?

It is more than likely the dictator would be told things he would not want to hear. Children's innocence leads them to spontaneously speak their mind, which is why dictators avoid travelling back in time.

This is also why dictators do not talk about their hesitations and their regrets, or of the possibility of living a different life. To put it differently, the bitter childhood experience is certainly a factor, but that is the dictator's personal demon.

What matters to people is not so much his personal angst as his actions as dictator; these remain etched in public memory. Viewed in that mirror, most dictators look the same.

George Orwell transcribes just such a dilemma in the last lines of *Animal Farm*, where Pilkington and other human farmers come to have dinner with the pigs at the farmhouse. Watching this gathering through the window is an assembly of other animals who find they are unable to tell the pigs and the humans apart:

> The creatures outside looked from pig to man, and from man to pig, and from pig to man again; but already it was impossible to say which was which.[16]

5

DESTINY PLAYS A PART

Sometimes it seems higher forces, far above mere mortals, conspire in favour of a dictator.

They step in at the vital last moment, when the fate of a nation seems to hang in balance, to give the critical push in favour of a dictator. Some call it providence, others sigh resignedly to say it is divine design. Still others fatalistically shrug their shoulders to add it is a cycle and all nations go through it.

Simply put, destiny plays its part.

Adolf Hitler's improbable ascent to absolute power is as much a tribute to luck as a lesson in the vagaries of history. During his 13-year quest for the leadership of Germany, he had failed many times. His eventual success, despite multiple setbacks, shows how demagoguery can overcome challenges and profoundly change history.

All this while, even as fortune is pushing the future dictator up to great heights, people remain convinced it is a mirage, that it cannot happen in their country. A passage in Fred Uhlman's novella, *Reunion*, is worth recalling. A German Jewish physician, twice wounded in World War I and proud of his country, is convinced the Nazis are a passing aberration. Therefore, he berates a Zionist:

> Do you really believe the compatriots of Goethe and Schiller, Kant and Beethoven will fall for this rubbish? How dare you insult the memory of twelve thousand Jews who died for our country?[1]

Soon, Germans fell for that 'rubbish'.

A number of factors contributed to Hitler's rise. By 1933, Germany was in a dire situation: six million Germans were out of work, the unemployment rate was at 24 per cent.[2] At this juncture, a confident new government was needed—at least that is how the people felt. After a series of clandestine meetings by political players in a posh Berlin villa, Hitler emerged as the secret choice to be appointed chancellor by President Paul von Hindenburg. But this arrangement was delicately balanced on the unanimous agreement of a multi-party coalition that formed the cabinet.

A few hours before his swearing-in, Hitler said his prospective cabinet ministers should agree to new elections within six weeks. It was a shrewd move on his part because Nazi popularity was growing and victory in a new election would affirm its hold on power. On the other hand, an election after a year or two of their stay in power carried the risk of anti-incumbency. While others agreed to Hitler's proposal for immediate elections, a veteran leader Alfred Hugenberg, who was to be minister of economics and agriculture, demurred. Hugenberg was 24 years senior to Hitler. Marinated by experience, he distrusted the noisy Nazi and did not want to give him an even freer hand. But without Hugenberg, there would be no swearing-in.

The suspense continued even after Hitler and the cabinet members entered the chancellery. Sometime soon thereafter, the president's top aide rushed up to them to say, '*Gentlemen, you can't keep the president waiting any longer.*'[3]

It was a decisive moment for Hitler, for Germany and for the world. Hugenberg could have stuck to his stand and reiterated his disapproval to hold early elections. That would have been the end of Hitler's political ambitions. But Hugenberg was a man of the old school. He didn't want to be a spoiler. He got up from his chair and joined the rest in the swearing-in ceremony.

However, this did not mean the end of his reservations. The next day, Hugenberg confided in a friend: '*Yesterday, I did the stupidest thing of my life. I joined forces with the greatest demagogue in world history.*'[4]

He should have added, '*Luck was on Hitler's side.*'

Hitler was not the only one, luck has played favourites with others as well. Fortune played its part in Lenin's rise too. Though his family belonged to a minor branch of the royal family, it had fallen foul of the establishment. This happened after his brother was hanged for an assassination plot against Tsar Alexander III. After his brother's execution, Lenin's family was shunned by the liberal society in provincial Russia. It wasn't so much the frowns of society, but the hurt that his brother was hanged which made Lenin take to radical causes. As a result, he was jailed in 1895 and later exiled to Siberia. After completing his jail term, he moved to Western Europe. Lenin was in Switzerland in February 1917 when a series of strikes, bread riots, revolution and a mass army mutiny forced the abdication of the last Romanov emperor, Nicholas II. At this point, Germany helped Lenin and some of his supporters' return to Russia. The German hope was that after he seized power, Lenin would make a separate peace and take Russia out of the war.[5]

Had Germany not helped him, Lenin might not have got home in time to launch the revolution that transformed his country and a large part of the world. On his part, Lenin grabbed the chance and cleverly built further on that piece of luck.

Almost half a century later, Romania's Nicolae Ceausescu had greatness thrust on him. In 1965, when President Gheorghiu-Dej passed away, Ceausescu was the youngest member of the Central Committee of the Romanian Communist Party. He was selected as the new president because it was thought that a high school drop-out could easily be manipulated by the rest of the committee.

Ceausescu came across as a stern-looking man who seemed to have serious doubts about his abilities, even his identity. He was born in a family of seven children where two of them, one of his older brothers and he himself, were named Nicolae. People joked that his father was too drunk to remember that he had already named one older son Nicolae!

In the beginning, his political speeches were so bad and so grammatically incorrect that it caused great bewilderment among people. His TV appearances were comic, to say the least. He made nervous gestures with his right hand, and struggled and stuttered over every word.

Even ordinary Romanians thought that Ceausescu was a man of average abilities—his political vision was flawed, he was sometimes megalomaniacal, and often brutal in his conduct. Yet, he was the absolute ruler of Romania for 24 years because luck was on his side.

Luckier still was Pakistani Army Chief General Pervez Musharraf. Had it not been for his kindly stars, he would have been a dead man on Tuesday, 12 October 1999. It all started after Musharraf's misadventure in Kargil where Pakistan faced a military humiliation and PM Nawaz Sharif a major setback nationally and internationally. Ever since, Sharif and Musharraf were like two scorpions, circling each other, waiting to strike the final blow.

The denouement took place on a fateful Tuesday when Musharraf was returning by a commercial PIA flight from Sri Lanka. Sharif grabbed the chance to dismiss the airborne army chief and appoint another general in his place. Meanwhile, a side drama was in play between the Karachi airport control and the plane's pilot, whose desperate pleas that the plane was running short of fuel were met by the response that he should divert the aircraft out of Pakistan. Finally, with just 7 minutes of fuel left in the aircraft, the local army unit forced the air control to let the aircraft land. By a strange quirk of fate, the time in Karachi then was 19:47 p.m., coincidentally matching the year when Jinnah landed in Karachi to preside over a newly formed nation.[6]

If there are instances of success, there are many cases of hard luck also, including some instances where people got victimized because they happened to be friends of a dictator. One such account was told by Shakespeare in *Julius Caesar*. A few days after Caesar's assassination, his friend Cinna went to the Roman Forum to see his friend laid out for funeral. There, he joined a crowd of Caesar's mourning and angry supporters. Some in that multitude mistook the poet for a different Cinna, one of Caesar's assassins. These angry men tore the poor Cinna limb from limb. His plaintive cries, '*I am Cinna the poet, I am Cinna the poet*', were lost in the mob's frenzy for revenge.[7] It was a case of mistaken identity but this is what happens when luck deserts someone.

CIRCUMSTANCES LEADING TO EASY ASCENT

Let me, for the sake of argument, concede destiny plays a vital role in giving a dictator that critical push up. It should then mean conversely that destiny simultaneously dooms people to misery! It was perhaps with this cycle in mind that Victor

Hugo wrote, '*When dictatorship is a fact, revolution becomes a right.*'[8]

If only destiny played by rules and with some empathy towards people, that is how it would be. Sadly, this is not so in the real world. People suffer because they must—this is what is destined for them.

Even if it is their assigned part, isn't there some way to warn people of the coming events, of the ill destiny that awaits them? Can it be said with some degree of confidence that there exists a dataset about the circumstances which lead to dictatorship? Usually, a country's slide towards authoritarian rule begins with bad economic policies resulting in price rise, unemployment and poverty. What complicates the picture is wrong foreign policy choices leading to fractious relationships with other countries. In most such cases the existing leadership is seen by the people as weak, indecisive and incapable of taking the country out of the morass it has got stuck in. The consequent public resentment opens the window for an aspiring dictator to step in and demand arbitrary power to deal with the national emergency and restore order. In the grip of hard times, people are often willing to go along and support measures that would be unthinkable in good times.

The latest example of it is the Taliban takeover in Afghanistan. Despite mountains of money poured into it by a country that prided itself in promoting democracy, and despite the desire of the Afghani people themselves to preserve their freedom, the country caved in. It did so because it ticked all the boxes that speed-slide a country towards dictatorship—monumental corruption, uninspiring leadership and a demoralized army. The Taliban slid into the governmental crack that was wide open and declared Sharia as the law.

There are other reasons, too, especially the dictator's overwhelming conviction that he has the answer to all of the country's ills. However, considering this issue in light of practical experience takes us to a somewhat confusing and contradictory terrain. In the nineteenth century, Europe was at the peak of its power; its empires stretched over large parts of the world covering a land area larger than any other empire in history. Its wealth was the envy of the world and its culture set the standard for the world. All through the nineteenth century, there was enduring confidence that the European power structure was sound. Therefore, there was no reason to have thrown it all away.

Yet, by 1914, the Great War had begun to knock at that wall of invincibility. Slowly, it began to cripple France and sap British resources. In four grim years that followed, imperial Europe tore at each other. After the war the bitterness lingered, the riches began to dry up, and economic decline started. This, in turn, pushed in the totalitarianism of fascism, Nazism, communism and, eventually, yet another World War.

In contrast, and to begin with, the world was benign at the beginning of this millennium; the tense confrontation of East–West had calmed, the world was largely at peace with itself, and it was prosperous. For a while it was also thought democracy would prevail everywhere. However, all of a sudden, over the last few years, strongmen have appeared to control many national destinies. In this transition, people have been passive. Lulled, they have forgetten the cyclical nature of history—of it being merely a link that strings the future to its past.

Aldous Huxley might have been generalizing this complex issue, but he was not far off the mark when he said, '*So long as men worship the Caesars and Napoleons, Caesars and Napoleons will duly rise and make them miserable.*'[9]

Given the multitude of causes behind the rise of dictators, including some that are deeply personal, it is difficult to fix a pattern to them. In contrast, a civil war is relatively easy to predict. Like wind in a gathering storm, it happens because it begins to conform to a set of variables. However, there is one big difference between the probability of civil war overwhelming a country and a dictatorship striking it. A reasonably cohesive country is generally safe from civil war, but no country in the world can claim to be dictator-proof.

Ironically, however, if a country has been torn by a civil war, the next stage usually is the takeover by a strong leader. Countries like the US have charged their intelligence agencies to study governments across the world and predict two or three years in advance the chance of a civil war or the takeover by a dictator.

One result of these studies has been the doubt about the widely held belief that poverty leads a country towards dictatorship. Instead, it is the half-fulfilled hopes in a partial democracy that are likely to make way for a dictator. It is the 'half democracies' that create new openings; a fresh set of opportunities for the new winners and losers.

A recent addition to the list is chronological; since the beginning of this millennium the number of democratically elected leaders veering off course towards authoritarianism has increased. This has happened in Europe too, which, since the end of World War II, had prided itself in being one of the main bastions of democracy in the world. In Hungary, for instance, the government has silenced dissent and controlled the media through Kafkaesque regulations.[10]

But why do the otherwise democratic countries stray towards authoritarianism? A possible explanation is that they do so because institutional safeguards, meant to check just such trends, begin to crumble. They fail to put up resistance when they should. Consequently, people follow the line of passive acceptance and resign themselves to lifelong sadness.

The bigger question is: why do people let it happen to them when they know they would ultimately be deprived of their freedom? The one big answer is that they are taken in by the lies of an aspiring strongman, that their democratic leaders at that point are weak and corrupt. If they continue to govern, they are sure to lead the country further downhill.

The fault ultimately is of democracy and people enjoying the scope it offered to them to live a free life. They should have put their guard up at the first sign when they noticed that democracy was beginning to decay. Some of these signs are:

- Historically, unchecked centralization has been the enemy of liberal democracy.
- Ideology and '-isms' lead *ipso facto* to a strongman at the helm. Most communist leaders were and are in the dictatorial mode.
- Dictators carefully nurture a 'cult of personality'. They tend to portray themselves as humbly born, but endowed with special talents. Sadly, this triumphalist narrative of a dictator's exceptionalism is rarely contested, except post-event.
- When the economy begins to decline and a country is ruled by some ineffective and indecisive leader, a thought begins to take hold—wouldn't the country be better off under a strongman.

Geography is another factor. Some regions seem to be dictator-prone. The Gulf sheikhdoms are typical and most Gulf states are governed by sheikhs answerable to no one and who allow no dissent.

But geography is only a rough indicator. After the horrors of Hitler and Mussolini, post-war Western opinion makers began to bracket despotism with the tribal societies of Africa, the chaos of Latin America, the controlled states of the Eastern Bloc, and a section of Asia. It was the Western belief that their state of plenty would never again be buffeted by ill winds.

Along with it came another idea: while the West had prettified the world, the eastern part of Europe had irretrievably bound itself in authoritarian chains. It was an expedient feint, a handy political tool, a propaganda point promoted by Western ideologues. It helped push the Eastern bloc to the wall, but the idea itself was founded on defective knowledge. This confidence did not last long and soon there were right-wing governments in Europe. Besides, after Donald Trump, can it really be said America will never be ruled by an authoritarian leader?

On a somewhat similar note, a German theologian Dietrich Bonhoeffer, opposed to the Nazis, had wondered: how could a nation that had given the world Gutenberg, Goethe and Beethoven embrace Hitler? He was imprisoned and eventually executed for his mental exertions. While in prison, he wrote an essay *On Stupidity* where one of his observations was:

> In conversation with (a stupid person) one virtually feels that one is dealing not at all with a person, but with slogans, catchwords and the like that have taken possession of him. He is under a spell, blinded, misused, and abused in his very being. Having thus become a mindless tool, the stupid person will also be capable of any evil and at the same time incapable of seeing that it is evil.[11]

All autocrats may fall under this category, but all people may not be stupid. Then again, two things defy limits—man's stupidity and the universe. After all, only stupid people will submit, and often be satisfied, that as a society they are being whipped into shape by a strongman.

Unfortunately, it is people's limitation that they are not perfect. Otherwise, a simple test would confirm to them the charismatic new leader they are beginning to idolize is a potential dictator. It would have told them that a good leader is able to see the grand sweep of history, whereas a dictator is distracted by minor diversions.

That simple test would have also reminded the people of this great dilemma of history—a weak point of democracy is its moral self-applause and that of dictatorship, its imperial demeanour. But people rarely heed the warning signs. They forget that speaking assertively is not a substitute for thinking deeply. People also forget it is better to learn from complex thinkers than smooth talkers.

This, alas, is the general human condition. Therefore, dear reader, resign yourself to the regret that comes from being imperfect societies—societies that breed and bring to the fore men who are autocrats.

As for our destiny, let me give the last word to Shakespeare, who wrote in *Julius Caesar*, '*The fault, dear Brutus, is not in our stars, but in ourselves, that we are underlings.*'[12]

6

A FIRM HAND AND A CLEAR EYE

'To dig a well with a needle'

This lovely Turkish expression captures eloquently the huge task of investigating, understanding and then unravelling the phenomenon of tyrants, authoritarians and dictators. What is it that motivates some to be domineering, to want to be the overlord of others, to conquer foreign lands and to subjugate people, both foreign and their own? Comprehending all this is a Sisyphean task. You think you have reached the core when another layer pops up, further deepening the mystery surrounding the capture of power by the dictator.

This happens despite the fact that wise men like the Greek tragedian Euripides have warned, '*When one with honeyed words but evil mind persuades the mob, great woes befall the state.*'[1]

Alas, this warning has remained just that. Generations of people have admired his warning for its wisdom, and its cautionary note, yet people fall one more time for syrupy promises.

Indeed, how is it possible for an entire country to fall into the hands of a tyrant? It has been a recurrent theme in great epics around the world. Later, Shakespeare and many others have given their versions and interpretation. But neither those warnings nor the institutional safeguards have deterred dictators from grabbing power.

As for people, and why they submit to dictators, George Buchanan, a historian and humanist scholar, differed from Euripides in his interpretation, '*A king rules over willing subjects, a tyrant over the unwilling.*'[2]

Both these wise men may have explained why people submit, but this applies only to a section of people who are too timid to resist and raise their voice. There are others who blindly follow the potential dictator. My query is addressed to them. Why should people be drawn to a leader clearly unsuited to govern, someone dangerously impulsive, viciously conniving and indifferent to truth? It is also addressed to the intellectual class who are otherwise quick to analyse and see through the façade. Yet, they too become unquestioning followers of the strongman.

The question why some dominate and others submit has been an eternal mystery—one that has multiple shades. For that reason, we will keep addressing it at various stages of this book.

■

The school bully, the tyrannical parent, the domineering relative, the awful boss, the would-be dictator—how do people become like that? Is it biological or cultural? What makes a tyrant tick?

A cursory look at their behaviour shows that tyrants are generally slippery. They like to keep us confused about the essence of their being. Under their spell, we overestimate the extent to which a tyrant decides or chooses his demeanour.

The fact is that just like ordinary people, tyrants too don't choose their personality. They slide into it. A case in point is

Hitler. A list of his characteristics would be too detailed, but this representative selection from George Orwell's review of *Mein Kampf* should suffice:

> ...He is the martyr, the victim, Prometheus chained to the rock, the self-sacrificing hero who fights single-handed against impossible odds. If he were killing a mouse he would know how to make it seem like a dragon. One feels, as with Napoleon, that he is fighting against destiny, that he can't win, and yet that he somehow deserves to. The attraction of such a pose is of course enormous...[3]

In that larger-than-life manner, he had also promised greatness for Germany but that remained elusive. Instead, Germany under Hitler became a fantasy zone where nationalism drove ecstasy.

The term 'moral cretinism' was first used to describe the times of Hitler.[4] The term reflected dramatically the fact that the politics of fascism were immune to moral sensibilities; under its spell, the sense of compassion and decencies got immobilized.

It is also a fact that influence over others can take immoral forms such as the use of force, domination, coercion or manipulation. But everyone is not self-seeking or dictatorial. We can influence people in positive ways as well. While each of us has the ability to choose the ends we aim at and the means we use to attain our ends, what is not under our control is our desire for power. As German philosopher Friedrich Nietzsche explains in *The Dawn of Day*:

> Neither necessity nor desire, but the love of power, is the demon of mankind. You may give men everything possible—health, food, shelter, enjoyment—but they are and remain unhappy and capricious, for the demon waits

> and waits; and must be satisfied. Let everything else be taken away from men, and let this demon be satisfied, and then they will nearly be happy—as happy as men and demons can be...[5]

DARK TRIAD

For our current discussion, the pressing question is: how do we describe a dictator in the current times?

Once, it was fairly simple to answer this question. The telltale signs included a love of uniforms, a propensity to harangue interminably, and a short fuse with critics, who were more likely to be done away with.

Now things are more complicated.

For instance, is Viktor Orban of Hungary a dictator? Is Erdogan of Turkey one? Were Donald Trump as President of the US and Jair Messias Bolsonaro as President of Brazil not dictatorial while they were in office? Did they not whimsically discard democratic norms when it suited them? Were they not extreme when they directly or indirectly encouraged their supporters to rampage through their respective parliaments in defiance of the popular vote?

The follow-up question is: can all self-willed leaders be categorized as dictators? The answer to that is a clear no. It is not possible for anyone and everyone to be a dictator. The very first requirement is that a potential dictator must come of age when the political system of his country is unstable.

It also requires a confluence of many other events to ensure his rise. First, a person must be born with the potential to develop brutal personality traits. These include narcissism, paranoia and an overwhelming desire for control. A potential dictator is likely to have grown up in difficult times and he could have suffered physical and psychological abuse in his childhood. His youth may have been marked by anti-social behaviour.

What are the other signs to look for in such a person? An early indicator is a dictator's ability to inspire enthusiasm. Narcissistic leaders promise to achieve amazing results. They are great at presenting themselves and their ideas. Even more importantly, their speeches mesmerize people into believing that at last the messiah they were waiting for has arrived.

They know how to influence others. The methods may vary from one dictator to the other, but essentially they involve ingratiation, forming political alliances, horse trading and even threats. The dictatorial types are willing to make mistakes and take risks. They bounce back quickly from failure.

Besides these evident observations, the concept of 'dark triad' (it refers to a trio of negative personality traits—narcissism, Machiavellianism and psychopathy) has sometimes been used to explain a dictator's mindset.

Among its characteristics, the first is narcissism, which was grossly evident in Trump.

There is a dark side to narcissism. Despite outward bravado, deep down the narcissist is a nervous, insecure person because he knows he is not what he has made himself to be. As Freud pointed out, narcissists are emotionally isolated and highly distrustful. Perceived threats can trigger their rage, and achievements can feed the feelings of grandiosity.[6]

Over time, however, this Freudian view has undergone some change. Now, psychiatrists acknowledge we are all somewhat narcissistic. However, there is a big difference in terms of the degree or extent of narcissism. In most of us, it is a microscopic challenge limited in scope and effect to the individual and to his immediate circle. The ill-effect of narcissism is limited to them, like their bad karma.

That is not how it works in the case of a dictator. With him the canvas is large; the entire country and its population is at his mercy. Therefore, the ordeal for a country is far greater. The challenge for the people is to ensure such leaders do not self-destruct or lead the country to disaster. This is neither easy nor always possible because it is very hard for narcissistic leaders to work through their issues—and virtually impossible for them to do it alone.

Narcissists need colleagues and even therapists if they hope to break free from their limitations. But because of their extreme independence and self-protectiveness, it is very difficult to get near them. This is the dilemma for a country that has a narcissistic authoritarian as its leader.

When such a person is riding high, at the very top of the country's pyramid, who can dare suggest to him that he needs to consult a psychiatrist?

Yet, many of them need to. It will not be an exaggeration to assert that narcissism is normal among leaders. This must be so. Otherwise, they would not have the confidence to roughly elbow their way past others to reach the very top.

What then are the signs of extreme narcissism that border on personality disorder? It is difficult to make a definitive list, but if a leader has a majority of these characteristics, it should be taken as a sign of worry:

- belief that he or she is special and unique,
- lack of empathy for others,
- need for excessive admiration,
- obsessive sense of self-importance.

Nikita Khrushchev, a former premier of the erstwhile Soviet Union, thought Stalin was an example of this type. Accordingly, he denounced his predecessor's penchant for promoting his personality cult as evidence of unhealthy egotism. In his famous Secret Speech of 1956, he alleged Stalin had even rewritten party history around his own biography.[7]

It is too soon to fix a similar label on President Xi, yet his actions so far make him a perfect fit. He has centred all power in him, be it military, party or the executive. There is simply no one who can be considered as being within touching distance of the authority he has accumulated, and the myth of greatness that has been systematically built around him.

Xi's narcissism has also extended the illusion of his grandeur beyond national shores. He seems convinced Western democracies are in decline and that the future lies with his model of authoritarian governance. He is also increasingly veering Chinese foreign policy towards grievance-based nationalism. Asserting control over the so-called lost territories of China is central to this agenda. So is dismantling existing institutions of global governance. In short, Xi wants to mould his country and the world outside to suit his grand ambition.

GOAT

Like Stalin and Xi, other leaders, past and present, may have been narcissistic in the extreme sense. It was their good fortune that this fact, along with its adverse impact on their handling of policy issues, remained a dark secret limited to their immediate circle.

However, narcissism and personality peculiarity are not limited to dictators. The democratic world, too, has been burdened by some such. Richard Nixon would find a mention in a list about narcissistic presidents of the US. Lyndon B. Johnson is likely to be at the top of that list and one can only imagine the blunders he may have committed.

According to biographer Robert Dallek, *'Pres. Lyndon B. Johnson in addition to showing signs of bipolar disorder, was a man possessed by inner demons. He suffered from a sense of emptiness: he couldn't stand to be alone; he needed constant companionship, attention, affection, and approval. Johnson also had a compulsion to be the best, to outdo everybody, to eclipse all his predecessors in the White House and become the greatest president in American history.'*[8]

Dallek adds, *'He had insatiable appetites: for work, women, food, drink, conversation, and material possessions. They were all in the service of filling himself up—of giving himself a sort of validity or sense of self-worth. Additionally, Johnson had some famously exhibitionist tendencies, another mark of a narcissist.'*

A self-obsessed leader like Johnson generally equips himself with notions of grandeur, believing he is the greatest ever—the ultimate GOAT (greatest of all time). This is what drove Caesar, Genghis Khan, Napoleon, Hitler and many others to dangerous paths. While some among them have rightly been praised for their dare and genius, it is not the norm. We make a big mistake when we give all tyrants uniform credit for thinking through their strategy. In fact, their impulsiveness has, more often than not, brought disastrous consequences for people.

Sadly, these negatives are not limited to the economy or societal issues.

The effect of invasions, and the dictatorial restrictions an absolute ruler imposes, has historically also been detrimental to the progress of art and science. These declines last long because once a society is pushed down the slide, the recovery along the path up can take the effort of generations. India's is a case in point. The glory that India once was in the intellectual world gradually became a distant memory because of a thousand years of foreign occupation, and the resulting authoritarian order.

It is a little-realized fact that when the Western world was celebrating the glory of renaissance on the cushion of prosperity, a yoked India was mourning its near total absence. This happened despite the fact that India accounted then for a quarter of global trade. It was only natural because a people cannot be artistically alive under invaders and foreign rule.

At the end of the sixteenth century, well into this dark period, Abul Fazl was to mourn:

> The blowing of the heavy wind of taqlid (tradition) and the dimming of the lamp of wisdom...the door of 'how' and 'why' has been closed; and questioning and enquiry have been deemed fruitless and tantamount to paganism.[9]

Equally negative was its effect on practical matters. It was observed that:

> The Mughal Empire has produced not a single worthwhile text on crafts or agriculture, how many volumes of poetry or histories...it might have to its credit.[10]

The question then is: don't dictators realize the consequences of their actions? What motivates them to condemn a people for entire generations?

The short answer is: they don't care.

It is not just the arrogance of power that makes them immune to others' pain. Their physiological structure is wired to make them uncaring. The pain and death of people might be noted by the likes of a Genghis Khan, a Hitler, or the leader of the Taliban, but there is no evidence to suggest they lost any sleep over it. A fresh report of massacre becomes one more statistic for them.

A dictator is also nervous of expertise, so he surrounds

himself with lesser men, people of mediocre abilities. By this, he seals himself in an echo chamber of yes-men. Anticipating this failing among dictators, Machiavelli had warned, '*The first method for estimating the intelligence of a ruler is to look at the men he has around him.*'[11]

But this sage advice means mere words for a dictator. For him, words are devices to be put to use as convenient to him, and in the form they suit him. They have no sanctity and their truth is not absolute.

The other feature the 'dark triad' marks out is sociopathy. In a dictator, it means disregard for the rights of others and an inability to understand others' feelings. A dictator breaks rules and makes impulsive decisions without feeling guilty for the harm they cause. He may also use mind games to control friends, family members, co-workers and even strangers. The essential element of this characteristic is remorselessness.

Even so, dictators tend to be excessively concerned about how they are perceived. Is this a sign of insecurity or a contradiction that even as they don't care for the rights or sensitivities of people, they crave for their approval all the time? It could partly be put down to their anxiety that they should be able to anticipate challenges to their power well in time. But it is also an indication of their narcissism.

Gaddafi's case illustrates this narcissistic streak well. He considered himself a fashion icon and would say, '*Whatever I wear becomes a fad. I wear a certain shirt and suddenly everyone is wearing it.*'[12]

His face was visible in public works of art throughout Libya and it could be spotted in airports, on pens or even in pop songs. Libyans read his quotations from *The Green Book*, in which he described his political philosophy. As a narcissist, Gaddafi wanted everybody to know and love him.

Since many dictators are narcissistic, can we simply use

that trait to predict who is likely to become one? This is difficult to assert as an absolute confirmation because all dictators do not come to power in the same fashion or under similar circumstances. For example, Kim Jong-Un was raised in an extremely privileged, 'Western' childhood. When his father died, the younger Kim simply glided into his dynastic position. As against this, Saddam Hussein climbed the hard way through the Iraqi political system for years till he was able to strong-arm his way into power. If an audacious Idi Amin grabbed power by the barrel of a gun, a submissive Ceausescu was catapulted into it by wily politicians in the hope they would control the levers of power. Mao Zedong led the communist army through a long civil war before he assumed dictatorial powers over his country. Hitler staged many unsuccessful coups before he could come to power. All through, he undertook an intense propaganda campaign and used intimidation and violence against his opponents.

Despite these differences, a common trait among dictators is their enormous confidence in always being right, regardless of the subject or issue at hand. It is a different matter that hindsight has usually assessed them to be wrong each time, but for the moment their bluster prevails, as was this boast by Mussolini when he invaded Ethiopia, '*The present century is the century of authority, a century of the Right, a Fascist century.*'[13]

Yet, in many ways, they behave differently. Some dictators are reclusive like Ceausescu of Romania; others love a sense of drama, like Khrushchev of the Soviet Union who banged his shoe against a UN table to make his point.[14] He might have shocked the stiff-collared assembly of diplomats seated there, but the next morning his picture with a shoe in his hand dominated the news the world over. Still others want a larger-than-life projection of themselves. Gaddafi once had himself crowned the 'King of Kings' of Africa.[15] Each one of these dictators reflected a different personality trait, their mode of governance was not alike, but as a broad category they were all a carefully calculated act, meant to convey a message.

The public is invariably taken in by the theatrics and the form of the act. Dictators, especially those from an army background, appear to people as confident examples of fitness, as persons who pump iron. They also give the impression of being confident and quick with their decisions. But usually there is another side to them. In private many are uncertain of their authority, insecure about their image and plagued by self-doubt. These strong men, despite their sense of huge power, are known to suffer from severe anxiety.

One reason could be the fear of assassination by their enemies within and outside the country. There were 43 assassination attempts on Hitler's life. He survived them all, only to take his own life. Mao is known to have lived through an assassination attempt by high-ranking military officers. Fidel Castro was a frequent on his enemies' hit list. Among the many attempts on his life—some put the figure at over 600—quite a few of these were encouraged by the CIA.

THE CURIOUS CASE OF PUTIN

The CIA also played a leading role in providing personality profiles of leaders of a neighbouring country or some rival countries. Even though intelligence agencies around the world have been historically involved in this task, the CIA, in particular, has been prolific. In 1943, the Office of Strategic Services (OSS), the CIA's World War II-era predecessor, commissioned Henry A. Murray of the Harvard Psychological Clinic to evaluate Hitler's personality based on remote observations. In an unsparing assessment, Murray and his colleagues concluded that Hitler was an 'insecure, impotent, masochistic, and suicidal neurotic narcissist.'[16]

The CIA also profiled the then Soviet premier Nikita Khrushchev before his 1961 meeting with President John F. Kennedy in Vienna. This got JFK hooked on CIA personality profiles, particularly the 'salacious' bits about foreign leaders. In its profile of Khrushchev, the CIA described him as:

> An uninhibited ham actor, who sometimes illustrates his points with the crudest sort of barnyard humor...He is immoderately sensitive to slights—real or imagined, direct or inferred—to himself, his political faith, or his nation...Capable of extraordinary frankness... Khrushchev can also on occasion be a gambler and a dissembler expert in calculated bluffing.[17]

It is not just the CIA that spends considerable time studying profiles. Mossad, ISI, KGB and many other intelligence agencies around the world also spend hours researching the issue. But their labour is not a guarantee of its accuracy. One such study by the Pentagon concerned President Putin. After scrutinizing vast amounts of Putin's video footage, this 2008 effort concluded that Putin's defining characteristic is '*autism*':

> ...the Russian President carries a neurological abnormality...identified by leading neuroscientists as Asperger's Syndrome, an autistic disorder which affects all of his decisions.[18]

If this was not a Pentagon project, it would have been dismissed as a waste of resources, time, money and effort, and its findings would have been trashed as cynical nonsense. Instead of any disorder hampering his performance, Putin seems to have done very well health-wise. Despite criticism about his venture into Ukraine, he has, by and large, steered his country to reasonable prosperity, and on the international stage he has emerged as an astute global leader. If any certificate to this effect was needed, then the former Japanese Prime Minister Shinzo Abe provided it with this fulsome praise of Putin, '*President Putin's stance left a strong impression on me. While other leaders were calling for Assad to resign, Putin said that he did not care if Assad resigned. However, he asked who would govern Syria next? The G7 leaders said they had the Free Syrian Army, in response to which Putin asked if the Free Syrian Army had ever won a battle...if they were really ready to govern Syria. This was realism.*'[19]

Abe added, '*...President Obama severely criticized the Assad administration for the use of chemical weapons and pushed President Putin into a corner, saying that the United States had evidence. Putin countered, saying he had heard that line before. He said, "Iraq did not have weapons of mass destruction [WMD], did it?" Putin was never on his back foot against the seven other nations. Indeed, he appeared almost dominant.*[20]

'*...his ideas were based on a strong concept of power politics believing that in the Middle East, the ruthless and strong win...I think that...Putin had a good understanding of the reality in the Middle East.*'[21]

After reading this exchange among the world's most powerful, and noting Putin's coherent and dominant voice, can it be said he is autistic or has a malignancy that affects his decisions? In fact, Abe's comment should seriously put to question the validity of Pentagon's study and its recommendation.

So, after centuries of experience with dictators and tyrants, are we any closer to judging what personality traits mark them to be so? Though the degree of their fears, prejudices, violence and obsessive self-interest varies, some personality traits seem common. Naturally then, the opinion on the issue is divided, but the medical science seems to suggest a common clue.

James Fallon, a neuroscientist who had done some research on the issue, notes: '*Successful psychopaths are usually charming, charismatic, and intelligent. They brim with self-confidence and independence, and exude sexual energy. They are also extremely self-absorbed, masterful liars, compassionless, often sadistic, and possess a boundless appetite for power. These are just a few of the character traits present in a genuine psychopath.*'[22]

Fallon adds, '*Just behind the eyebrows and deep to the neocortex in the temporal and frontal lobes, is the extended amygdala. It is a key node in the brain circuit that mediates "animal instincts" and it contributes to making 2 per cent of the world's population psychopaths—and a few of the most versatile and talented of these become dictators.*'[23]

He elaborates further, '*What satisfies a normal person—such as reading a good book or watching the sunset—does nothing for someone with an underdeveloped amygdala. For some people, this means a greater tendency toward drug and alcohol addiction and severe painful withdrawal that gets progressively worse over time, leading to malignant dependent behaviours. For sadists, they become addicted to torture and killing; dictators get high on power, an insatiable drive that gets progressively worse, or malignant with time.*'[24][25]

Does it mean that anyone with such an amygdala can be a potential dictator?

It does not really work this way, but there have been experiments, which gave alarming results. The Stanford Prison Experiment was worryingly one such. The basic quest of that experiment was whether an ordinary, well-meaning person can turn into a repressive despot. Does power induce this effect?

> In the 1971 Stanford Prison Experiment...students were randomly assigned to be either 'prisoners' or 'guards' in a makeshift 'prison'. The guards became so abusive, and the prisoners so passive, that the experiment was shut down after less than a week.[26]

So, while it is not possible to stop every passerby and surgically probe his 'amygdala', as a broad categorization it will not be off the mark to say that egocentricity, deceit, manipulation and selfishness are the key traits of dictators. Yet, they can also be charming. The main reason for this is that their charm hides anti-social tendencies.

Another general observation about them is that the mask of authority unsettles the real face. But what happens when the hangers-on scatter and the autocrat is all alone in his office at the end of the day? What kind of man is he without his public mask?

- Is he an attentive spouse and parent?
- How secure does he feel about his power?
- Do his private thoughts differ from those he defends publicly?

Since most dictators are not socially amiable, there is only a rough sketch we can form of such a leader. It just about gives us a short answer, but the fact is that despite all the research the world over, we do not really know what drives them and, more importantly, whether their DNAs resemble each other sufficiently to form a pattern.

It can be said that in most cases a dictator's power places him in a dilemma. As ruthless as he was in its acquisition, he also becomes troubled by the question of its exercise.

Partly, therefore, dictators trust no one, particularly family, friends and the army. Even at the top, when they are the absolute master of the land, they are not calm within.

As Shakespeare wrote in *King Henry IV*, a boy manages to get restful sleep amid a rough sea, but despite living in luxury, sleep eludes the worried King:

Canst thou, O partial sleep, give thy repose
To the wet sea-boy in an hour so rude;
And in the calmest and most stillest night,
With all appliances and means to boot,
Deny it to a king? Then, happy low, lie down!
Uneasy lies the head that wears a crown.[27]

Alas, for the dictator, the science of psychology has yet to come up with a prescription for his unease.

FOLLOWING THE NAPOLEONIC MAXIM

The rise of a dictator could have been explained if it was a rare, one-off phenomenon. But dictatorship is not an exception; instead, force as a method of governance has been frequent.

It is also not the case that society has not resisted; it has occasionally tried to keep the powerful in check. But this struggle between the two is a delicate balance, needing constant vigilance. A slight let-up, a minor opening is enough for a dictator to slip through the crack and break free of society's checks. Then people, and their welfare, take a back seat.

When the world is distracted and the public is struggling for survival, a potential dictator sees a perfect opening to wiggle in. This often happens when a democracy is in decline, its economy is in stagnation, and corruption is at a high. When a democracy begins to slip down this slope, it is dismembered in four stages.

The slide begins when a demagogue is elected. People see in him a saviour who will rescue the country from the mess it is stuck in. Once he is comfortably ensconced in power, he begins to change the administration of the government by placing his favourites and the trusted in pole positions. In the third stage, he draws up new rules of governance. With this foundation in place, he begins to use these rules selectively against the opponents of the regime. By then, the ruler has acquired dictatorial powers and the rule of law translates to: *Everything done by my friends is lawful, for my enemies, the law*!

After this, the script is nearly always the same. Looking at the way they have performed in power, Napoleon must have been speaking for many dictators when he said, '*If you wish to be a success in the world, promise everything, deliver nothing.*'[28]

Most dictators scrupulously follow this Napoleonic maxim.

Sometimes dictators also maintain on governmental payroll an informally chosen court jester. His task is to convey to the boss sugar-coated opinion on every issue but a solution for none.

Unlike politicians, who have years of experience behind them, a dictator is not prepared for the job when he grabs power. He slips into the job, at the very top. On the way there, he does study the methods other dictators practise. But this is not sufficient because when someone is given absolute power, without any preparation it could go to his head. But even at his most irrational, a dictator knows what he is doing. He simply exploits to the full the possibilities for absolute power.

Invariably, every time a dictator rises, evil rises too. It has always been so, and it will continue to be this way because of the seductive myth that in times of crises and stress, people need a firm hand and a clear eye. Some say that in pluralistic societies an iron hand is the only way to keep peace between factions, ethnicities and religious groupings. But the actual experience is vastly different. Almost throughout the period a country is under a dictatorship, the same pattern of rule gets spooled one more time.

This time-tested script means that:

- history gets rewritten on an almost daily basis;
- truth is in perpetual flux; there is no news in truth and no truth in news;
- the constitutional and institutional framework is painstakingly put together as people's protection, but the dictator discards it with a scornful flourish; and
- it is a time for alternative facts where people are dispensable.

This, sadly, has been the pattern from the earliest times and their instinct is to be responsive to the emotion of the moment. In that fierce urgency of the present, a dictator ignores the inevitability of hubris. He forgets the universal truth that one day the sun will rise from the other windowpane. His unbridled ambition leads surely to frustration, but by then it is already too late for amends.

People, too, must equally be blamed. Time after time, they confuse a flesh-and-blood mortal for an icon. Instead, if they had been prudent and heeded Mahatma Gandhi's warning, the world might have been a more agreeable place to live in: '*It is not good for us to worship an individual. Only an ideal or a principle can be worshipped.*'[29]

7

CYROPAEDIA

It is common to find dictators wielding and using the stick hard, and being comfortable with the result. By their nature and due to their professional training, dictators lack the patience to tend to the population. Words like love, care and compassion are not in their dictionary.

However, not all is bad in the world of bad. Some who have ruled with a rod did so in the manner a parent is anxious for a child—that he should not stray. But this soft dictatorship is rare.

One of the earliest, and many say one of the greatest, benevolent dictators was Cyrus II of Persia (also known as Cyrus the Great). As proof, a replica of the Cyrus Cylinder is on display at the United Nations (UN) headquarters in New York. Written in Babylonian cuneiform around the time of Cyrus's conquest of the city, the cylinder chronicles his acts of mercy, especially his willingness to let conquered subjects retain their traditions. The cylinder is generally regarded as 'the first bill of human rights'.

A century after Cyrus's death, the Greek author Xenophon memorialized this ruler in his work *Cyropaedia*: '*He honored his subjects and cared for them as if they were his own children and they, on their part, revered Cyrus as a father.*'[1]

These words served as inspiration for Thomas Jefferson, one of America's founding fathers. He owned not one but two copies of *Cyropaedia*. Jefferson's inspiration from *Cyropaedia*, and America's enormous success ever since, can, in good measure, be ascribed to the path carved then by its founding fathers.

A similar quest for the right balance constantly engaged Mahatma Gandhi. He was wary of considerable powers being vested in the State. His focus was the welfare, liberty and the rights of the individual. For this, he argued, '*Real Swaraj will come, not by the acquisition of authority by a few, but by the acquisition of the capacity by all to resist authority when it is abused*.'[2]

This is an ideal that can be achieved in a truly functional democracy. It is the one that great constitutions aspire to when they begin solemnly with, '*We the people...*' But somewhere down the line, these words and their promise tend to get blurred because the strong ruler wishes to get things done his way.

Pandit Jawaharlal Nehru was conscious that in his hurry to accomplish tasks according to his preferences, he might become more dictatorial than benevolent towards people. Or, at least there was a risk he might be perceived that way. Ten years before Independence, in November 1937, an article titled 'The Rashtrapati' appeared in a Calcutta journal *The Modern Review*. It was written under the pseudonym Chanakya and it caused an immediate flutter. Because of the curiosity it generated, people were anxious to know the real name of the author. It didn't take them long to find out it was written by Nehru. The essay was reflective, a warning and an admonition to himself. It might also have been written to prepare people about what to expect.

> Jawaharlal cannot become a fascist. And yet he has all the makings of a dictator in him—a vast popularity, a strong will directed to a well-defined purpose, energy, pride, organisational capacity, ability, hardness, and, with all his love of the crowd, an intolerance of others and a certain contempt for the weak and the inefficient. His flashes of temper are well known and even when they are controlled, the curling of the lips betrays him. His over-mastering desire to get things done, to sweep away what he dislikes and build anew, will hardly brook for long the slow processes of democracy...We have a right to expect good work from him in the future. Let us not spoil that and spoil him by too much adulation and praise. His conceit is already formidable. It must be checked. We want no Caesars.[3]

The message Nehru probably wanted to convey was that people's adulation and a leader's conceit are a lethal combination. Together, they result in Caesars. It served as a good warning for him and an important message for people to heed.

There were some dictators who managed to successfully strike the right balance in governance. Peisistratus, the ruler of ancient Athens from 560 to 527 BC, was one such dictator. During his rule Athens flourished, becoming one of the most prosperous and beautiful cities in ancient times. Its fame rested on art, culture, literature and festivals. Peisistratus limited the power and privileges of the aristocracy and even took away their lands to give them to the poor. Little wonder, then, Aristotle spoke of his rule in these terms, '(The) *tyranny of Peisistratus had been the age of Cronus, or the golden age*.'[4]

BENEVOLENT DICTATOR: A CHIMERA?

It is the golden age that people wish for when a country begins its slide into chaos. At a juncture like this, Cicero's words begin to haunt: '[There is] *no nobler motive for entering public life then the resolution not to be ruled by wicked men.*'[5]

During such a dismal phase in a country's history, a democratic system appears like a luxury that cannot address the country's needs. The discussion among officials, businessmen and people generally ends up with a collective sigh against governmental inefficiency and systemic apathy. At this stage, the idea of having a leader with unfettered powers, who possesses a clear vision and is prepared to act swiftly and decisively, can be tempting. It sounds even more compelling when a country is trapped in an endless cycle of political crises.

Then, the Plato-like wish echoes all over again, '*What we need is a benevolent dictator.*'[6]

As evidence in favour, they cite the example of Lee Kuan Yew, prime minister of Singapore for 31 years, who corralled government corruption and thrust the city-state into the First World. There is also praise for Paul Kagame, who brought in a clean and efficient administration in Rwanda after a genocide. They complete the picture by admiration for China's efficiency to get things done. Some glowingly compare China's ability to quickly build 100 airport runways, while in the US they struggle to fill the cracks in their highways.

It is comparisons like these that make people wonder if the world America made after the Second World War, and then unmade, is entering its most treacherous phase. Will the post-War 'order' that served the world so well slowly degenerate into a law of the jungle where might is right? They also ask who can lead them safely out of this phase.

A thought that appeals then is this: is Plato's philosopher-king the ideal leader? Undoubtedly, there is longing for a leader who rules with care and guides the nation on to the right path. People feel such a leader knows what is in their best interests. Indeed, it should be so, but in reality this is a chimera. Howsoever attractive the concept of a benevolent dictator might sound on paper, it ends up as a disappointment in practice. In part, this is due to the unrealistically high expectations from him.

People hope the benevolent dictator will be able to fix everyone's every problem. But they forget he is only human; even with the best of intentions, he can only do so much. In most cases, the benevolent part of the dictatorship soon gives way to crony comfort and the arrogance of office. Besides, the concept of benevolent dictatorship is not a state of unadulterated bliss.

Take again the case of Lee Kuan, widely celebrated as a role model for a benevolent dictator. In this hero worship, it is forgotten that Lee was of the view that power could corrupt people, so they could not be trusted with it. For all practical purposes, he also eliminated political opposition to him. Many politicians were thus detained for two years without the right of appeal or trial. To ensure there was no criticism of his economic policies, Lee allowed only one political party, one newspaper, one trade union movement, and one language.[7] Therefore, despite the economic transformation of Singapore he is deservedly credited for, benevolence is a difficult balancing act in a dictatorship.

Long after Plato expressed his preference for the philosopher king, latter-day philosophers have made a course correction. Rather than ask '*who could best rule*?', they now ask '*what system prevents the worst rule*?' The vote invariably is in favour of democracy—a democracy where the will of *we the people* prevails.

Alas, this initial promise of rule by the people is soon betrayed. After all, masses can be uninformed, irrational, and prone to act in their self-interest rather than for the common good. Unchecked rule by the people can easily lead to illiberalism. Moreover, democracy's fundamental offering should be the right to life. This is precisely what people are denied when there is wretched poverty to live in.

We the people are then left wondering where they had misjudged. It is not just the people; even big powers sometimes get taken in by the promise of performance and quick decisions. For a long time, the US was of the view that it was easier to deal with a single point of reference in a developing country. Convinced of it, they promoted some of the coups there to install a dictator.

This quest for a benevolent, all-performing dictator has more often than not led to a bitter dead end. Yet, people have persisted in finding that perfection, hoping the next time they would find just such a leader. But they do so without a clear idea of what he should be. As in most other matters, Shakespeare put his literary finger on the basics of what could be the ideal combination of firmness with benevolence, '*It is excellent to have a giant's strength; but it is tyrannous to use it like a giant.*'[8]

Part 3: AFTER A PATTERN

8

FIELD GUIDE TO TYRANNY

Long before the American founding fathers, the founders of the Roman Republic placed checks and balances on the power of their leaders. Typically, though, the Romans then found a way to sidestep those checks and balances when strong leadership was needed. The Senate could vote to grant absolute power to one man, called a dictator, for a temporary period. The Roman dictator's power was absolute. He could rule by decree and even order executions without a trial.

The dictatorship was limited to six months. If a dictator refused to step down, he could be forcibly removed. But there were exceptions here, too.

Cornelius Sulla seized control of Rome in 82 BC, bypassing the Senate. Soon, he became a tyrant who was paranoid about his personal security. He was protected by 24 guards all the time. Each guard carried an axe bound by a bundle of rods called fasces, giving origin to the word 'fascism'. Sulla resigned at last, but only after thirty years of rule.

Sulla's case is an example of how a determined dictator seizes power and stays on for as long as he can. It is also a validation that no age in human history is immune from authoritarian rulers or from their determination to hang on to power. Nor is any country in the world exempt from the possibility that a dictator might soon be its overlord. Dictatorships have risen among prosperous, educated and cultured people who seemed safe from a dictatorship. Almost invariably, dictatorships are unexpected.

Germany was one such case.

In the late 19th century, it had one of the best educational systems in the world. It had early childhood education, the kindergarten. Secondary schools emphasized cultural training. Germans had developed modern research universities and its scientists were especially distinguished. How did such an advanced system for its age fall for a brute like Hitler? It shouldn't have, but for a lost war, a pervasive sense of national humiliation, and the punitive reparations imposed by the Allied powers which Germans were finding hard to pay. But for these national negatives, Hitler would have remained a nobody.

This is one example. But is it the textbook example other dictators follow? The short answer is there is no known 'one size fits all' guide for dictators to follow. There is no effective or known formula; each case is different and each dictator adopts the method best suited to the circumstance. As an example, the communistic spell was unique.

For much of the twentieth century, a number of countries were under communistic dictatorship. Overnight, people became propertyless paupers, anonymous individuals whose identity was subsumed by the label 'dictatorship of proletariat'. It gave them the illusion of belonging but the power and privileges belonged to the party elite.

Generally, however, dictators take over not so much due to the use of force or ideology, but because they are able to convince the public that they are competent. Once installed, the dictator quickly takes control of State propaganda, censoring independent media, co-opting the elite, and using tax agencies to suppress dissenters. Even incompetent dictators survive as long as economic shocks are not too large.

When a dictator gets or grabs power, his priority is to keep it. He does so in a predictably textbook fashion—as if there is a school for dictators, teaching them strategies to retain power after seizing it. Some elements in such a list include:

- The dictator must not be predictable.
- Dictator's rule should be firmed up through force and fear.
- Complete control of the media space is essential for the dictator to remain in power.
- Always keep people on their toes with sudden policy changes and imaginative follow-up.
- He must be omnipresent. Like God, he must observe you from everywhere.
- Anyone who attempts to develop a rival power base must be struck down.

If Benito Mussolini was alive, he would have been the natural choice as the Chancellor of such a school for dictators. Mussolini has often been dismissed as a buffoon, a small-time tyrant who ruled in the shadow of Hitler and Stalin. But that caricature of him is not a correct reading. In the world of twentieth-century dictators, Mussolini was a pioneer. He created fascism, a movement that would plunge most of Europe into darkness. From undermining judges to indoctrinating children, the methods he perfected during his stay in power were copied faithfully by many dictators of that period, and those who followed.

He was a pioneer of modern political theatre and master of propaganda. During his time as the supreme leader, Italy was a newspaper with Mussolini writing the front page every day. He knew a picture of him taking flying lessons was worth any number of carefully argued editorials. After his first propaganda radio broadcast in 1925, 40,000 free radios were distributed to elementary schools. By the onset of the Second World War, the subsidised sets numbered 800,000 and loudspeakers had been installed in town squares.[1]

His message was everywhere. An actor, stage manager, orator and self-publicist, Mussolini allowed his ideology to remain vague while spending more than half of his time curating his image. His image was omnipresent; it was even moulded into bars of soap so people couldn't avoid seeing him in the bathroom as well. Mussolini considered himself the greatest actor in Italy, so much so that he was jealous of Greta Garbo.[2]

The lights were kept burning all night in his office to convey to the nation the long hours he kept at work. The legend of his all-seeing eyes was intensified by Goth-style eye make-up in posters and newsreels. His 'personal' replies to 1,887,112 individual petitions were 'personal' to such an extent that they included prominently a publicity shot of Il Duce.

An early convert to the Mussolini school of total control was Hitler. By and large, he followed Mussolini's methods. Hitler also kept the lights on all night in his office and sold radios at prices lower than the production cost, to ensure a greater audience for his broadcasts. He deployed portable pillar radios to blare out party message at rallies. As with Mussolini, he overstated troop numbers, bussed in crowds, faked news, doctored photographs, and inflated supporter numbers. He too spent hours watching himself in the projection room and flooded the country with his image.

In an unguarded moment, Hitler claimed that he was 'Europe's greatest performer', meaning thereby greater than even Mussolini, who in turn claimed to be better than the best actors then![3]

It is not only the dictators who look to the examples of previous success of others to guide them. Business leaders too are known to seek inspiration from the masters of the absolute. Interestingly, and as a testimony to its wide appeal, it is not just dictators and some business leaders who turn to Machiavelli's *The Prince*, which has also been called the 'Mafia Bible' of gangsters. As a matter of fact, it remains a frequently referred-to book for a cutthroat approach to getting ahead. It has been called by some as the ultimate textbook for aspiring dictators, though others contend that there are regional and national tomes that do the job just as well. That may indeed be so; after all, Machiavelli was not the only acute observer of dictatorial methods in the world.

SMOKE AND MIRRORS

Why do people fear a dictator? Why is hatred so pervasive under a dictatorship? Why do dictators never run short of enemies? One short answer is that power, without prudence and restraint, degenerates into recklessness. This, in turn, gives rise to pessimism, suspicion and negativity in a repressed society.

Generally speaking, dictators have followed a largely similar path. A dictator employs processes by which communities are torn apart and individual humanity is systematically dismantled by the destruction of truth and logic. The resulting confusion and fear produce docile, atomised individuals whose ecstatic praise of the regime transforms large sections of society into liars. Banality warps everyday reality under dictatorship, sharpening the horrors with whimsical decisions, senseless waves of persecution, purges and wars.

Consequently, dictators who seize power through violence are by that circumstance inclined to maintain power through more violence. This, in turn, creates enemies who must be eliminated. After all, if a dictator can take power, others can too, raising the possibility of a stab in the back. Rivals, often just as ruthless, lie in wait for the dictator to slip his guard. In natural consequence, paranoia sets in as the dictator begins to see real and imaginary enemies everywhere.

As one result, there are some mutually contradictory messages. Dictators want people on their side as the source of their power, yet they devalue the rule of law and control the political discourse. They often present conflicting positions, so as to both attract and isolate the population and prevent any serious independent movement against the State.

With these conflicting pulls, how do dictators survive in power?

The general impression is through threats and brute force. Stalin, Hitler, Mao, Pol Pot, the Taliban and many others relied on mass terror. Military regimes from Franco's Spain to Pinochet's Chile also used violence to intimidate their opponents. Mobutu, Bokassa, Somoza and Duvalier too relied on gore.

More recently, a less carnivorous form of authoritarianism has emerged. This slight mellowing is effectively a window dressing to confuse the world and to avoid its intrusive interest. These days, dictators adopt a subtle form of persuasion; it is less physical than punishment but severe in effect. So they:

- simulate democracy and hold elections that they make sure to win;
- bribe, threaten and censor private press rather than abolish it;

- replace ideology with an amorphous resentment against an external power; and
- harass and humiliate political opponents, accusing them of fabricated crimes.

But the dictatorial slate is not filled entirely with their black deeds, and oppression of the population. There are some shades of grey and a few specks of white as well. Some of these leaders enjoy genuine popularity based on 'performance legitimacy', a perceived competence at securing prosperity and defending the nation against external or internal threats. State propaganda too helps boost the leader's ratings. In reality, however, there is a smoke and mirrors quality to the dictatorial rule, more promise than performance.

The question then is: how can a country prevent a dictator from rising and controlling its destinies? Charlie Chaplin's advice was that we should not despair, that in the end, the bad phase shall pass and once more people would breathe easy: *'The hate of men will pass, and dictators die, and the power they took from the people will return to the people. And so long as men die, liberty will never perish.'*[4]

HAILED BY THE WORLD

It is the hope of better days that sustains the world. Yet, at a realistic level, there is an obsession with the strongman. People tire routinely of the ponderous nature of democracy and its procedures. Soon, they begin to long for a firm hand, something that Aldous Huxley hinted about darkly:

> There will be, in the next generation or so, a pharmacological method of making people love their servitude, and producing dictatorship without tears, so to speak, producing a kind of painless concentration

> camp for entire societies, so that people will in fact have their liberties taken away from them, but will rather enjoy it...[5]

Was Huxley hinting at mass masochism? Was he conveying that a time would come when societies would long to be inflicted with pain, and actually clamour for suffering?

Perhaps he was warning of just such a pass, and such societies. After all, it is not just the average people who are enamoured of dictators. Some of the otherwise well-regarded world leaders, too, are prone to misjudgement. They might be doing so for a tactical reason, but how is the public to know? They take such praise of a dictator as an endorsement of him and his methods. Many dictators, therefore, manage to beguile the general public and in some cases, democratic leaders.

Winston Churchill once hailed Mussolini as '*the greatest lawgiver among living men*'.[6] American President Franklin Roosevelt was moved enough to praise Joseph Stalin as '*truly representative of the heart and soul of Russia*'.[7] Then there was Richard Nixon, who during his first trip to China, seemed excessively keen to win Mao's approval. He compared Mao Zedong and the communist leadership of China to George Washington and the other leaders of the American Revolution.[8] Nixon was equally blunt in his bias when he said of Nicolae Ceausescu, '*He may be a commie, but he's our commie!*'[9]

When foreign leaders give such extravagant endorsement to mass murderers, the message being conveyed to the citizens of that country is 'abandon all hope'. As subsequent events have proved, while praising a dictator may get you some immediate results, but in the long term this tactic is counterproductive. The tensions in America's relations with both Russia and China are proof of it.

Yet, such lessons of history are rarely heeded as the next dictator is approached. When Xi took over, many in the West hailed him initially as a Chinese Mikhail Gorbachev.[10] Some suggested enthusiastically that Xi would embrace radical reforms and democratize the political system. This turned out to be a fantasy. Instead, Xi has worked to establish his absolute power. He acts as 'chairman of everything'. Somewhat similar was the case when Donald Trump sought a new opening with North Korea. He gave discretion a go-by when he showered the full positive on North Korea's Kim. Trump was non-stop effervescent in his praise, *'(He) has got a great personality. He's a funny guy, he's very smart, he's a great negotiator. He loves his people, not that I'm surprised by that, but he loves his people.'*[11] With such a thumping endorsement, do the people of North Korea stand any chance of relief?

So how is a dictator able to mesmerize the otherwise politically savvy leaders of the democratic world? What is the subterfuge that a dictator employs?

Howsoever cruel he may be at home, a dictator wishes desperately to be accepted by the world outside as a capable leader. It is with this objective that an influencer is selected and is given carefully conducted views of the country. After he has had chats with cheerful locals, he is given quality time by the dictator himself. This script has seldom failed.

For instance, George Bernard Shaw was bowled over by Stalin's charm on a visit to Russia in 1931.[12] Thereafter, despite evidence to the contrary, he continued to regard Stalin as a hero right up to his death in 1950. He breathed his last under a portrait of Stalin.[13]

Dictators also turn on the charm to woo when it suits them. It is a pity that the otherwise discerning fall for the trap. For instance, Mao instructed that 'security, secrecy, warmth and the red carpet' be rolled out for American journalist

Edgar Snow.[14] Later, every sentence of Snow's 1937 book, *Red Star Over China*, was examined and, if necessary, amended by Mao.[15]

Politicians such as Barack Obama, Tony Blair and others of their ilk find it cunningly convenient to sweet-talk a dictator if it suits their immediate purpose. For instance, in 2001 Blair told the journalist Anna Politkovskaya, who was investigating Putin's war crimes in Chechnya, '*It's my job as prime minister to like Mr Putin.*'[16]

Sadly, these leaders forget that words beguile for long, that the endorsement they give quickly becomes a part of the historical record. It was a lesson that Edgar Snow too should have remembered as he wrote *Red Star Over China*.

Therefore, if the people of a country are complicit, directly or indirectly, in a dictator's rise to power, foreign leaders add to that original sin by signalling their approval. But why blame only the political leaders? Business tycoons are no less in pandering to a strongman. One such instance in 2023, of humiliating behaviour by America's wealthy, was lampooned in this fashion:

> Whatever the merits of this week's summit between President Biden and Chinese President Xi Jinping, there was no reason for U.S. business leaders to trip over themselves to get in on the action. Yet there they were Wednesday evening, kowtowing to Mr Xi at a dinner that delivered China a propaganda coup and the CEOs an embarrassment.
>
> The dinner, for which ticket prices ranged up to $40,000, sounds like some affair. Mr Xi received a standing ovation for taking the stage before he said a word. He garnered more applause—from an audience including Apple's Tim Cook to executives from Qualcomm and Boeing—for delivering such memorable platitudes as

> 'there is plenty of room for our cooperation' between the U.S. and China.[17]

When presidents, PMs and business magnates of the democratic world issue, so casually, the good character certificate to a dictator, can we really fault people for falling repeatedly into the dictatorial trap?

Still, since hope must be sustained, it is a fair question to ask: will the world ever be rid of dictators? John Steinbeck captured the cycles of the rise, fall and rise again of dictatorships in this chilling fashion:

> All the goodness and the heroisms will rise up again, then be cut down again and rise up. It isn't that the evil thing wins—it never will—but that it doesn't die.[18]

This, alas, is the way of the world. And therein lies the grim message—dictators will continue to rise.

9

DICTATORIAL WAYS

For his followers and admirers—and they can be legion so long as he is in power—a dictator replaces God. It has been so from the time myths were first spun. People's faith in a providential leader serves as a substitute for religion. Instead of icons, shrines to Lenin and Stalin sprang up in the traditional Red Corner in Russian houses.[1] Mao, when he was the supreme leader, asked wonderingly,

> *What is wrong with worship*?

Nothing, you might say.

The dictator, in turn, is acutely conscious of the fact that he must appear a cut above the rest. Gaddafi managed, almost always, to make a bold fashion statement no matter how humdrum the occasion. Sometimes he did so by adding a beret to his clothes or using a black mesh robe. He mixed Eastern and Western modes with flair and was not afraid of using some makeup. Gaddafi combined a penchant for ocular accessories with an Elton John-like eye for colour. He brought a certain pizzazz and imagination to the task because he understood politics is showbiz.

Putin too has a style, and he can carry it off well whether he is wearing a cowboy hat or riding bare-chested in the icy cold. Some fashion experts nod approvingly to say that he will be just right for the role of a villain in the next Bond movie, or as Bruce Willis' nemesis. Some others insist that with his icy blue eyes and Slavic cheekbones, he is handsome but in a cruel, thuggish manner. By common consensus, he looks sharp both in dark modernist suits and trim sweaters.

It is not just ordinary folk who look wonderingly at some of the more fashion-conscious dictators. Hollywood celebrities also watch their style. Cheryl Cole stunned audiences when she took to the stage to perform her first single 'Fight for this Love' clad in a Stalin-type military jacket, leather cap and trousers.[2] Victoria Beckham has been seen in Hitler-style wardrobe of a white coat and trilby hat.[3]

The message in all this is the care and time dictators spend in cultivating their image.

DICTATORIAL CHIC

Every brand needs a theme and an aesthetic. Dictators are also a brand, and, as we have seen, they spend serious time thinking about how they should dress and appear in public. Since the dictatorial chic is the announcement of their brand, let us also consider the buildings they live and work in.

The home and office they create is a place to inspire awe, harangue people, and settle scores. They are an architectural and artistic means of establishing the power of the occupant, of intimidating and impressing. Dictators find it difficult to understand why anyone would go for the scaled-back charm of the old-money houses. The whole point is that dictators' homes aren't for one's family, friends or private self.

If they are commissioning a new project, it is almost always hugely oversized. One of these was Mussolini's *Esposizione Universale di Roma* (EUR), planned as an international exposition to open in 1942. Due to the Second World War, the Esposizione was cancelled and the construction plans were halted. It was eventually completed ten years later. The 420-acre EUR is a marble behemoth which overwhelms you but remains confused about its utility. An odd, and for the most part uninspiring, array of half a dozen museums is housed in some of these buildings, where only the most determined venture.

Another such project was started in Romania in the 1980s by Ceausescu. A part of old Bucharest was demolished to make room for one of the largest government buildings in the world. They called it the People's Palace. Its massive dimension had nothing regal about its look, and, to date, a number of its outsized chambers lie vacant because functionally they are of little use.

Inside the building, most dictators seem to think along one standard line—'let me live surrounded by gold'. With all of the country's resources at his disposal, why not? Therefore, gold furniture, gold wall decorations, columns with gold capitals and gold taps are seen everywhere. Even Trump buildings are not exempt from this rule with a virtual blizzard of gold all over. The obvious reason for their fascination with gold is that it reflects opulence.

Besides gold, glass in all forms is the preferred choice of a dictator. Giant chandeliers with glass droplets and giant mirrors with gold in the frames cover as many walls as his fancy needs. Since the ground too must be bright, it is covered with shiny new marble—every square inch of the bathrooms, halls, bedrooms and tabletops is covered with marble polished to a mirror finish.

The dictatorial eye prefers the big size when it comes to choosing accessories. They are generally fond of macho beasts like lions and eagles, the stuff of legends and heraldry cast in precious metals, with jewelled eyes. There was, for instance Gaddafi's gilded metal eagle and the stuffed big cats in Josip Broz Tito's sitting room.

Beyond simply inspiring awe, there is a method in the dictator's desire to surround himself with the big and the monumental. He tries thereby to obliterate his poor past, the days of deprivation and suffering. The ostentation he surrounds himself with serves a double purpose. For the people, it creates an illusion of the otherworldly about him. And he himself begins to believe that the unreal proportions are the real him.

It is not just the buildings he lives or works in, or just his sartorial style; he digs deep into opulence when it concerns his spouse. An absolute dictator like Ceausescu did not pinch pennies when it came to his wife's demands. A ball-room sized hall was reserved exclusively for Elena Ceausescu's dresses. It was crammed full with wall-to-wall almirahs containing 500-odd coats and thousands of dresses for her. They were tailored at great expense to suit her peasant-like taste. After the revolution when people forced open the door, Elena's body odour spread about the room announcing to the world that she was the owner of that crass extravagance. The dresses are still on display there, as a reminder perhaps that money cannot buy style. When I went to see that collection, the first sensation that hit me was the odour. That mixture of her body smell and the stale air of a long-locked hall still lingers, issuing the grim warning that the past could become the future.

Regardless of the taste and style of the dictator, the people's destiny is sealed. The variation is in the padding. If a dictator is leftist by ideology, the attempt at radical reform causes famine and suffering to the population. A rightist dictator invariably leads his country to war. The consequences are damaging in both cases—popular suffering under the left-leaning dictator and shameful defeat for the country in the latter case.

WHERE ARE THE DISAPPEARED?

The intent behind this account is not merely to list or emphasise the extravagance of dictators. The bigger point in this exercise is to emphasise how they want to be seen. Their taste offers insights into their inner lives, their cultural reference points and how they relate to other people. While a dictator lives luxuriously surrounded by kitsch and ersatz, the ordinary people he deprives create their own world—a habitat reflecting their angst.

Take the case of Augusto Pinochet's military rule in Chile during the 1970s and 1980s. The arrest and subsequent disappearance of political opponents was a common feature of his rule. The anguished womenfolk of those who had disappeared expressed their pain by embroidering tapestries with groups of people. These colourful tapestries, called *arpilleras*, depicted scenes from their repressed lives. Some showed scenes of protest, or displayed dolls holding a banner that read, '*Where are the Disappeared*?' Some others showed scenes of torture. These anguished statements on tapestries allowed them to share their grief with others.

Did their pain reach the dictator in his marble palace? It never did. On the odd occasion that he looked their way in passing, the dictator's eyes glazed over.

The woes of Albanian women were no less during Enver Hoxha's long and absolute rule. The country was miserably poor, with hardly any industry to support employment. Consequently, men migrated to find jobs elsewhere in Europe. The womenfolk, who were left behind, often had to wait for years before seeing their sons, brothers or husbands again. Once, while in Albania, I heard a ditty popular during Hoxha's dictatorship. It describes heartrendingly the agony of these women,

> *Sometimes I wash my clothes with water,*
> *More often, I wash them with tears.*

But let's try and not view dictators through the relentless prism of negativity. At some level, they too are vulnerable, with their insecurities and their Achilles heel. Like everyone else, they also have desires and wants. Despite the heights they occupy, they too would have dreams. As Napoleon said,

> I was full of dreams. I saw myself founding a new religion, marching into Asia riding an elephant, a turban on my head and in my hands the new Koran I would have written to suit my needs.[4]

Viewed thus from the dictator's viewpoint, their needs and aspirations are no different from those of the less blessed people. It is their ways that are different.

10

TOO SALTY

Like the rest of us, dictators are also made of flesh and blood. They breathe the same air. By and large, they must have similar physical needs; they too need to eat to live.

Therefore, it is natural to ask: what is it the dictators eat that makes them different? Is it because of a certain type of food that they are so ruthless? Is there a particular meat or some special vegetable that makes them surly? Or is it the spice in their food that turns up their anger quotient? Since a majority of dictators came, and continue to come, from humble stock, it means their food tends to be anything but Cordon Bleu. So the type or quality of food is unlikely to be their priority.

Even if the blame for their evil acts cannot be attributed to any one type of food, some shades of its influence emerge. Some dictators become obsessed with the purity of what they eat, not because they are a gourmand or fond of eating enormous quantities, but because they worry constantly about plots against them. The possibility that an enemy might try to poison their food terrifies them.

Consequently, the fear of poisoning is a great concern for most dictators. When should they eat also becomes important, because their security must allow sufficient time to pass to see that the food taster has survived! It is only after that the dictator gets to eat his food. Hitler's security kept 15 food tasters for this purpose. If, 45 minutes after tasting the food, none of them dropped dead, only then would he eat that food.[1] The punctilious would turn up their nose at such an offering because the food would have lost its freshness during the wait.

But longevity of life rather than freshness of food is a dictator's greater priority. At any rate, he has serious matters of State on his plate, so he eats whatever is on offer. There are exceptions, of course, and a famous one is that of Roman dictator Lucullus who was known for hosting lavish dinners every day. Once, when he was dining alone, the chef served him a simple meal provoking the famous admonition, '*What? Do you not know that this evening Lucullus dines with Lucullus?*'[2]

YOU ARE WHAT YOU EAT

A lot also depends on the company a dictator keeps at his dinner table, who he eats with and how he eats. The entire process can affect his mood, his worldview, and his bowels. The stress and strains of office also take a toll on their digestive systems as no matter what the facade, and how much their acts may terrify the population, deep within they are insecure.

Hitler, Mao and Mussolini suffered from one type of stomach problem or the other. Hitler, in particular, suffered from chronic flatulence. He was so troubled by it that in desperation he allowed a quack, Dr Theodor Morell, to dose him with 28 different medicines, including one made from the extract of faeces of healthy young German soldiers.[3] On the other hand, the famously flatulent Gaddafi seemed to have been untroubled by this affliction. He unabashedly farted on![4]

Another surprise about Hitler was the type of food he ate. It is hard to imagine a man such as him could be a vegetarian. The reason for it was his belief that a meatless diet would relieve his flatulence and constipation. Towards the last stages of his life, he took only clear soup and mashed potatoes. Before he gave up meat because of gastrointestinal problems, Hitler was fond of eating the exotic dish *Petits Poussins à la Hambourg*. It is a preparation of a fledgling pigeon or squab stuffed with tongue, liver and pistachio nuts.[5]

All dictators are not simple or predictable in their taste. The food choice of Kim Jong-Il was varied and exotic. His favourite foods were shark-fin soup, salo, and dog-meat soup, which he believed gave him immunity and virility. He had some other idiosyncrasies. One of those maintains that he had a team of women to make sure every single grain of rice that was served to him was identical in size, shape, and colour. His preferred tipple was cognac, so much so that he was said to be one of Hennessy's biggest customers.[6]

All this is useful information, but it is not enough to be encyclopaedic. The reason for it is simple—most aides of a dictator do not know much about the personal life of a dictator. A chef is the only exception, and he is in the best position to reveal the food habits of the dictator he served. But chefs seldom open up. They remain afraid and reluctant to talk during the lifetime of dictators, and that sense of fear prevails even after a dictator has passed on. So, a combination of half-gossip and half-baked knowledge is all we get generally.

Some of it is wild guess based on the degree of cruelty of the dictator. For instance, a rumour in Cambodia maintained that Pol Pot liked to eat the heart of cobra. As his cook explained: *'I cooked cobra for Pol Pot...First, kill the cobra. Then cut off its head and hang it on a tree for the poison to dry in the sun, away from the children. Collect the snake blood in a cup and serve it with white wine. Chop the cobra into little pieces and mash it into a pulp with a handful of peanuts. Add boiling water, bitter leaf of the vine, the herb of the lemon grass and yellow ground ginger. Simmer for one hour. Serves one.*'[7]

There is a belief in some countries like China and Cambodia that cobra soup has aphrodisiac qualities, so it was vicariously tempting for people to believe that Pol Pot might be doing one better and eating the heart of the cobra.

But another rumour maintains that this earlier rumour was false. After he was removed, it emerged that Pol Pot did not like the sight of snakes. Like many other Cambodians, he ate chicken and fish. He had his preferences, of course. He didn't like just any other papaya salad; he liked it made with pieces of crab meat or some fish paté.[8] Whatever be the truth, people would like to believe his cook.

Mussolini preferred to eat his meals at home with his wife, Rachele, and their five children. But he was a stickler for order even at his daily meal. Everyone had to be seated and served at the table before his arrival. Mussolini rarely ate pasta or meat and called French food 'useless'. His favourite food was a salad made of raw garlic and olive oil, which he thought was good for his heart. His wife thought it made him smell of an odious garlic stink, so after dinner she retreated to a separate room. He also drank up to three quarts of milk a day to quell his stomach aches. Ironically, he tried to hide his milk habit from Hitler, fearing the Fuhrer would perceive this as 'unfascist'.[9]

Some of the otherwise severe dictators were simpletons in matters of food. Ceausescu was one of them. His favourite food when he dined at home was stew made with a whole chicken, including its feet and beak. When he was on a visit abroad, he insisted on his Romanian chefs bringing all his food on the trip. Once, when he was visiting Yugoslavia, his host Tito was shocked by Ceausescu's insistence on drinking raw vegetable juice through a straw at the formal banquet, where he avoided all solids.[10]

Ceausescu was essentially a quiet man of simple tastes. It was his wife Elena who was a terror with their domestic staff, punishing them with severe penalties for the smallest mistake like breaking a piece of china. Ceausescu, however, was courteous with his staff. If he got up for a midnight snack, he would not wake them up. Instead, he went down to the kitchen to make himself a sandwich.[11]

Some of the other dictators were not similarly considerate. Rather, there are examples of dictators who go to the other extreme. Once, when one of Idi Amin's sons had a severe stomach upset, Amin went to the kitchen, took out his pistol and pointed it towards the head of the first chef he saw. '*If the kid dies, I'm going to kill all of you*,' he shouted at him and the rest of the kitchen staff.[12]

However, such threats are best avoided even by a dictator, because a chef has a unique position in this matter. If he chooses to, he has the ability to poison the dictator. Or, at the very least, make an attempt to do so. Therefore, a chef's position is a delicate one based essentially on trust. Whether it is out of concern for personal safety, or proximity, it is not uncommon to find a dictator treating his personal staff well. Saddam Hussein gave expensive gifts like gold watches to his chef. But if he didn't like the food, he would impose a fine on the chef and make him pay it in Iraqi dinars for the ingredients used in the cooking process.[13]

As an aside, it should be mentioned that besides the chef, a dictator is also vulnerable to the decision of the food taster. An indication of what a food taster goes through was provided by one such long after Hitler's death. Margot Woelk was among the fifteen young women employed to taste his food. She recalled, '*The food was delicious, only the best vegetables, asparagus, bell peppers, everything you can imagine. And always with a side of rice or pasta. But this constant fear—we knew of all those poisoning rumors and could never enjoy the food. Every day we feared it was going to be our last meal.*'[14]

With most dictators, as with a large number of ordinary people, what one ate as a child remains the food of contentment. Tito was happiest eating a slice of warm pig fat. Portugal's dictator António de Oliveira Salazar loved to eat sardines. It reminded him of his impoverished childhood when he had to share a single sardine with a sibling.[15]

In some providential ways, ours is a small world and there can be unintended connections that establish a link of sorts between dictators. For example, Putin's grandfather, Spiridon Putin, worked as a chef for both Lenin and Stalin.[16]

In his younger days as a Bolshevik revolutionary, Stalin took a liking to the prized Russian nelma freshwater fish. Sometimes he cooked too—making shashlik was one of his specialties. He was a foodie and occasionally hosted all-night banquets that served Georgian sweet wines, pickled cheese and savoury meats. These large get-togethers at his dacha were usually a buffet with home-cooked bread, beverages, starters, salads, soups and hot dishes. The staff would serve the food and leave the room. Stalin and his guests would then help themselves with everything they wanted to have, without any servants. Such dinners could last for six hours or longer.[17] Often, he used these all-night bacchanalias with a purpose: '*Getting his guests drunk and listening to what they had to say in a state of extreme intoxication was an old trick of Stalin's...*'[18]

Even though it was widely believed that Napoleon died of poisoning, a recent autopsy reveals he might have died from stomach cancer.[19] Experts attribute it to his diet which probably included salt-preserved foods, roast meats and a few fresh fruits and vegetables, all of which were Napoleon's standard fare during long military campaigns.

But Napoleon ate only if he was hungry when on campaign. His preferred meal was a simple fare consisting of beef, beans and white bread, washed down with cheap Chambertin wine. He feasted on roast chicken when it was available. However, his austere food habits might have had something to do with the rigours of military campaigns. After he was exiled, he did indulge in rich foods, which contributed to his weight gain.[20]

In contrast, Saddam was a foodie and he relished eating good stuff as if to make up for the deprivation he suffered in his childhood. Some of his staples were sides of lamb and beef with the fat trimmed off, fresh shrimps, live lobster and olives from the Golan Heights. He particularly liked traditional Bedouin dishes. While a glass of Mateus Rosé sometimes accompanied his main meals, camel's milk with bread and honey was his usual breakfast. He was partial to the Old Parr whisky and Quality Street sweets.[21]

Since very little is known to people about the type of food dictators eat, the talk about their food habits often takes a gossipy turn. There were, for instance, persistent rumours during his lifetime that Idi Amin ate his military rivals. But once when asked if he was a cannibal, he replied, '*I don't like human flesh; it's too salty for me.*'[22]

In fact, his favourite food was roast goat, cassava and millet bread, and he would eat as many as 40 oranges a day, because of their claim to be 'nature's Viagra'. It is a matter of speculation whether that enormous daily consumption stood up to its claim, but this practice did earn Idi Amin the nickname Mr Jaffa.[23]

None of the dictators I have listed above displayed a particular affinity for food in the way that some people crave designer clothes as a means to make a fashion statement, and assert their place in society. They ate what was suggested to them as good for their health or in continuation of their largely simple childhood offerings. It is also true that cares of office hardly leave most dictators the time to plan the next meal carefully. Yet, like everyone else, they too must eat. As Luciano Pavarotti said, '*One of the very nicest things about life is the way we must regularly stop whatever it is we are doing and devote our attention to eating.*'[24]

11

TIGER'S TEETH

Why do dictators, or many of them, behave bizarrely? Do they do it consciously as a put-on act, an instrument of their unpredictability? Is it a way to instil even more fear in people as Caligula, the original bad man among dictators, said, '*I don't care if they respect me, so long as they fear me.*'[1]

For understandable reasons, no one has thought it wise to analyse a dictator's extraordinary behaviour during his lifetime. On the other hand, memory plays tricks when people try to recall his actions posthumously. Moreover, the recollection of events that transpired is always contested.

Still, very broadly, it could be said a part of the blame must be put on the dictator's hangers-on, who applaud every act of his. Each time they praise him and pander to his ego, it encourages him to believe that besides being all-powerful in the country, he is the ocean of all knowledge in the world. Consequently, even though a dictator knows exactly what he is doing, he simply exploits to the full the possibility of absolute power and self-indulgence.

Since no one dares to show him the mirror, it is easy to imagine how power can go to a dictator's head. Add to it the fact that most dictators catapult themselves into this position without a political background or a previous spell at governance.

For instance, psychologists would say Caligula's young age was to blame for his weird behaviour; after all, he was just 24 when he assumed power. But to call him mentally unstable because of his eccentricities would not be correct. In fact, Caligula possessed a clear understanding of his actions. He was simply manipulating, as per his whims, the possibilities of unbridled authority.

There were many manifestations of his erratic behaviour. A prominent one was about ordering his troops to gather sea shells during a military campaign against Britain. An equally bizarre account concerned his horses. Caligula loved race horses to the extent that he lavished his favourite horse with a house and a battalion of slaves to massage, bathe and feed him. This horse was served wine only in golden goblets. As if that was not enough, Caligula also made his horse a senator.[2]

There was much more that was weird about him. He declared himself a god, committed incest with three of his sisters, and had sections of the crowd at the games thrown to the lions.[3]

ERRATIC FLOURISHES

It isn't just the inexperienced, or the young, among dictators who are given to strange behaviour. Some of the awe-inspiring figures in recent history have had really strange habits. Mao's peculiarities were one such. He didn't brush his teeth, insisting the tea he swished around his mouth would do the trick. In support of this practice, he cited an example from the animal world, '*A tiger never brushes his teeth. Why are a tiger's teeth so sharp*?'[4]

Despite all his power, Mao did not have the constitution

of a tiger. As a result, his teeth were covered in thick plaque. It seemed as if they were coated with green paint and his gums were so badly infected, they oozed pus.[5]

Mussolini was another one with a complicated view of food. He was convinced that eating raw garlic was medically most useful. This despite suffering a painful stomach ulcer, and bad, garlic-laced breath! Even so, many women found him irresistible.[6]

Both Mao and Mussolini were well-known international figures. So their actions invited great intrusive interest. But there were others, lesser known, yet equally bizarre in their behaviour. Tucked away in another part of the world, next to India, is Myanmar (earlier called Burma). It has largely remained out of the public view, in part because this suited its rulers. One of its longer-lasting dictators was General U. Ne Win, who ruled Burma for 26 years until he was overthrown in 1988. A megalomaniac with lavish tastes for gambling, golf and women, he was prone to violent rages like throwing an ashtray at his wife's throat, or assaulting an underling he believed was flirting with his wife. He used to bathe in the blood of dolphins which he thought would keep him young.[7]

Devoted to numerology, astrology and 'yadaya' (a form of Burmese ritual magic), Ne Win's decisions were guided almost as much by soothsayers as by his advisors. When an astrologer warned him of an assassination attempt, Ne Win stood in front of a mirror and shot at his image with a revolver to ward off the evil.[8]

In another bizarre case, he was taken in by the recommendations of an astrologer that nine was an auspicious number for him. Accordingly, in 1987, Ne Win ordered the removal of 100 kyat banknotes from circulation. These were replaced by notes of 45 and 90 kyat denominations—both divisible by nine and both being numerals that added to nine. The result was immediate and devastating. The Burmese economy was shattered and people lost their life's savings. Only the black marketeers prospered.[9] This was the proverbial last straw for people and, at last, they took to the streets. In 1988, these mass protests forced Ne Win to resign.

Like Myanmar, there exists a nearly forgotten country in Europe. In miserably poor Albania, Enver Hoxha lasted in power for 41 long years, from 1944 to 1985. His was a murderous regime of paranoia and absurdity. Hoxha was so paranoid of an invasion that he ordered the construction of over 750,000 bunkers, making an average of 5.7 bunkers for every square kilometre of Albania, or one for every fifth Albanian (Albania's population was 3.3 million). His obsession with bunkers led him to build them all along the Adriatic coast, in farmlands and on mountain tops. These bunkers were meant to shelter citizens against attacks by Albania's enemies which, according to Hoxha, ranged from Italy to Yugoslavia, the Soviet Union and the US.[10]

He was peculiar in other respects as well. For instance, he refused to have his face printed on banknotes lest witchcraft be used against him. He was so paranoid about an assassin getting to him that a body double was found for him. An Albanian man who bore a resemblance to him was taken away from his village; after a series of plastic surgeries, he began to resemble Hoxha. The team of surgeons that performed this transformation to perfection was driven off a cliff into the Adriatic Sea.[11]

The double was taught how to walk and talk like Hoxha, eating the same food and reading the same books. He was made to open factories and give speeches in Hoxha's place. He was even taught how to die properly for the cameras in case he was shot.[12]

Equally weird was Saparmurat Niyazov, the burly dictator of Turkmenistan. To ensure his immortality, in Turkmenistan at least, he ordered the months of the year to be renamed, with January re-dubbed Turkmenbashi in honour of his own official title. But becoming a calendar fixture wasn't enough. So, in his quest for permanence, he had a fifty-foot-tall gold-plated statue of himself placed in the centre of his miserably poor capital. This constantly revolving statue always faced the sun, so that a golden glow radiated all the time from his replica. To educate people about his thoughts, he wrote a book called *Ruhnama* (Book of the Soul). The dense contents of this book had to be memorized by people in order to be granted a driving license.[13]

Niyazov banned opera and ballet because he considered them 'unnecessary', and eventually, he outlawed the playing of all recorded music on television or at public events.[14]

Among his erratic flourishes were a national holiday in honour of melons, an ice palace in the capital, and a lake in the middle of a desert. He was fond of horses, so a $20 million leisure centre for horses was built, equipped with a swimming pool, air conditioning and medical facilities.[15]

If he was solicitous of equine welfare, he had an altogether different idea of what was good for his people. Niyazov dismissed 15,000 public health workers and closed all hospitals outside Ashgabat to encourage people of the countryside to come to the capital. In 2006, one-third of all Turkmenistan's elderly had their pensions cancelled. They were also ordered to pay back the previous two years' payments.[16]

Around that time, Zaire's dictator Mobutu Sese Seko kept the people of his mineral-rich country in poverty, but exploited that wealth for personal extravagance. One of his palaces had its domes covered with gold, and he had conveyer belts installed in the dining area to bring champagne and exotic food for his guests. He was weirdly whimsical in his decisions. In one such instance, he had his foreign minister fired, then tortured and imprisoned, only to have him released and appointed prime minister.[17]

In the not-too-distant past, there was Francois Duvalier in Haiti. A voodoo physician, he was extremely superstitious and so ordered the killing of all the black dogs in his nation. He believed he was guarded by voodoo spirits on the 22nd of every month. He claimed to have placed a voodoo curse on US President John F Kennedy, and said Kennedy's assassination on 22 November 1963 was caused by his powers.[18]

In Europe, in communist Romania, Ceausescu was not just superstitious; he was weirdly so. He was convinced certain things brought him good luck. Every time he had to do something terribly important, he would keep a cobbler's nail in his coat pocket. It was the same nail he had carried to the Communist Party meeting that elected him the supreme leader. His elevation came as a big surprise even to him, because he had leapfrogged to the position over more senior and capable leaders. Ever since that day, he took to carrying that nail as a good-luck charm. The nail was preserved carefully in Ceausescu's bedroom.[19]

A donkey was another of his good-luck charms. He would walk with the animal every evening in his villa's garden. His household staff used to wonder at the level of intimacy between the two. Every few steps, Ceausescu would whisper something into his ears, and the animal would turn his head towards him to nod in agreement. At least, that is what Ceausescu thought.[20]

But Ceausescu wasn't the only one with this peculiar habit. In antiquity, emperors used to keep a donkey as a good-luck charm. They would personally walk the donkey to keep it in good humour. But there was something even more special about Ceausescu's donkey. His animal used to wear a cross in communist Romania.

LIKE SORE THUMBS

People used to dismissively remark that Ceausescu's peasant-like faith in a donkey was due to the lack of education. His reading was limited to picture books. Even these he leafed through only occasionally, flipping over the pages disinterestedly. In fact, book covers interested him more: their silver or gold-coloured hardcovers invariably made a profound impression on him. The over-decorated, ornate and rich look appealed to him. It helped him forget his poor past.

That's why the bigger and the brighter appealed to him. All furniture items and the interiors of his house had a Baroque look. The People's Palace he built in Bucharest was to be the biggest in the world. Eventually, it turned out to be the second largest, second only to the Pentagon. His office in it was second in size only to the one Hitler built for himself. [21]

Except for that streak of megalomania, there was nothing that distinguished Ceausescu from an ordinary man on the street. His taste in films was also simple. He would repeatedly watch cowboy movies and propaganda documentaries about him.

His biggest drawback was his self-pitying approach to life. Despite all his good luck, he was not a happy man. Gloom overwhelmed him constantly and as a small-town person, this feeling was accentuated further in a big city. Romania's all-powerful dictator, Nicolae Ceausescu, felt very lonely in self-centred Bucharest.

Then there was Kim Jong-II in North Korea. The stories about his odd behaviour leaked out in driblets from the forbidding iron curtain with which he had enveloped the country. Some were deliberately let out to perpetuate the myth of his greatness. According to official accounts, a double rainbow and a bright star appeared in the sky when he was born, and when he died, a giant lake of ice cracked in half.[22]

Take also the case of Brazil's former President Jair Bolsonaro. Brazil is otherwise a country on the go. It is blessed with considerable natural resources and its population is diverse, with pools of talent. Yet, Bolsonaro continued to whimsically rule this reasonably modern State, as this passage reveals: '*He attended Brazil's most famous military school as an adolescent. There, he learned about the National Security Ideology...This anti-communist ideology preaches that Brazil and South America will be unsafe unless all the left ideas and people are eliminated, physically if possible. Bolsonaro was "frozen" in this period, and he has never learned anything new.*'[23]

It is not just in their country that dictators are given to the whimsical turn. When dictators attend international gatherings, they stick out like sore thumbs among other leaders. Their vocabulary is vastly different from that of the modern and liberal world. Yet, they are tolerated because of the position they hold, and because of the importance of their country to the outside world. Gaddafi was famous for his eccentricities, yet bemused world leaders fawned on him because of Libya's oil wealth. The Taliban in Afghanistan were cruel in the extreme, but they controlled the global tap of terror. So even as Afghanistan was considered a pariah State, world powers secretly held out a hand to the Taliban to keep them and their forces of evil under some restraint.

Some dictators, while keeping their own population on a tight leash, provided comic relief abroad. Idi Amin was one such. He sent love letters to Queen Elizabeth II of England, asking her to marry him and make him the King of Scotland.[24]

However, it will be unfair to blame only individual

dictators for outlandish behaviour. Some other forms of governments have also made bizarre rules. Communist China, for instance, has banned Buddhist monks in Tibet from reincarnating without the government's permission! According to a statement issued by the State Administration for Religious Affairs in 2007, the law which strictly stipulates the procedures by which one is to reincarnate is 'an important move to institutionalize management of reincarnation.'[25] Since rebirth is a supernatural phenomenon, some wits have wondered whether the Chinese State has sent a copy of its *firman* to the higher forces for compliance.

Sadly, all this while people suffer. When dictators last as long as Ne Win did in Burma, or Hoxha in Albania, entire generations grow up in an unreal atmosphere. The effect on development in these countries is acutely negative; for all practical purposes, they are a virtual discard of the world as long as the dictatorial spell lasts. All through their rule, people long for any sign that holds out the promise of better days, of a time when they don't think they have fallen off the global map. In Albania, for instance, the day after Hoxha died, the very first signboard that appeared in its capital Tirana was that of Coca-Cola. For Albanians, its effervescence represented their freedom.[26]

'VERY SPECIAL PEOPLE'

The question that bothers people is this: what drives these powerful men to irrational behaviour? Are they driven by a hidden and sometimes irrational fear? It will not be correct to pin it all to a standard formula. But, broadly put, they indicate a pattern:

> They see themselves as 'very special' people, deserving of admiration and, consequently, have difficulty

> empathizing with the feelings and needs of others... Not only do dictators commonly show a 'pervasive pattern of grandiosity', they also tend to behave with a vindictiveness often observed in narcissistic personality disorder.[27]

By its dictionary meaning, narcissism denotes a person who is self-absorbed and overwhelmed by self-interest. Such individuals possess an exaggerated sense of their importance and tend to be preoccupied with their achievements and abilities. They feel entitled to the admiration of others. Over the course of their rule, they become steadily more preoccupied with fantasies of unlimited success and power. To them, the thought about others and their good is incidental to the grand project of personal legacy.

Is such a person capable of being generous to others? Can he rationally think of the public good? A former German Chancellor Helmut Schmidt had been blunt in declaring, '*Politics without a conscience tends towards criminality.*' [28]

This invariably means opponents are seen as obstacles to the dictator's vision. To counter them, a favoured course dictators follow is to retaliate in cold blood; they try to punish those that stand up in opposition to them or their policies.

Vindictiveness apart, there are other explanations. One is his essential inability to govern. A dictator disciplines, so the expectation is that dictatorship will bring in order. But it does not always work this way because power needs the presence of chaos as a source of legitimacy. Since power and chaos feed each other, power grows from the act of bringing order to chaos.

There are risks to this strategy, and the time comes when a dictator cannot control the forces of chaos. This is when he risks being devoured by the demons he has pampered.

With their self-centred nature, lack of empathy, and

absence of guilt or remorse, the most malignant of dictators commit unspeakable atrocities. Given such a negative combination, is it any surprise that their behaviour should be extraordinary?

12

COLONIZERS AS TYRANTS

Before the partition of India in 1947, a big change in 'map making' happened in 1919.

After World War I, a small group of Western leaders had the power to decide and alter the destinies of faraway people. Many of the new borders they carved out for countries in Africa and Asia were whimsical lines that divided people without much relevance to their traditions, culture, geography or history.

The map makers were a pair of British and French officers. The new boundaries they sliced out were of their former colonies, and it was done without compassion or care. This heartlessness was for the inanimate territory, but even so, it reflected their contempt for the people. Had it been otherwise, global dictionaries would not have had terms like 'slaves' and 'indentured labour'.

The British, the French, the Spanish and the colonialists from Portugal had a largely similar contempt for the people they ruled. The variation was in the language, the difference largely in the scale of ridicule they reserved for their subjects. The common factor was their conviction that the people who served them were a lesser breed.

That feeling of contempt persists. Otherwise, the EU's

foreign policy chief Josep Borrell would not have made the bizarre claim that: '*Europe is a garden...Most of the rest of the world is a jungle, and the jungle could invade the garden.*'[1]

Deep in their hearts, racism continues to pump the former colonialist's blood. It is rare for people in Europe to learn about colonial history unless they specialise in it at university. Across the channel in the UK, the empire evokes a vague sense of nostalgia for the average British conservative. The campaign for Brexit, with its slogan 'take back control', was based on an amorphous vision of a return to the times when Britannia ruled the waves.

A French account of Napoleon's iron rule in the Caribbean is another case in point:

> '*Napoleon was a military pragmatist,*' says Prof. Malick Ghachem, a historian with France's Foundation for the Memory of Slavery. '*For him, as for many others, having a massive slave empire in the Caribbean was good for the greater glory of France and the French economy.*'[2]

Did Napoleon and others like him ever take a pause to think that Caribbeans, Asians, Africans and South Americans also had human rights?

Clearly, that minor matter never troubled them.

The former colonies are equally to be blamed for not having learnt from the history of their misery. There has not been a studied effort to research and bring out the facts and narrate history from the point of view of the suppressed. There have been episodic efforts in books like *The Wretched of the Earth* and *Roots*. But these are far too few to capture the global imagination and to prevail over the conventional wisdom saturated by the colonial mind.

In contrast, the extensive narration of Nazi atrocities during the Holocaust via books, films, TV shows and educational systems has ensured the world rightly never forgets. The same can't be said for the genocidal acts inflicted on the colonies by Europeans. The reason is that the British, French and even Americans who long benefitted from slavery would be the villains in any such narrative. It is a lot easier for them to just ignore the matter. Even when an account is written as history, it is done by the victors and their descendants from their point of view. These narrations portray the colonial masters as forces for good.

There is no scope for interrogation in this prejudiced look at the past. To illustrate this point, let me take the case of Christopher Columbus. The historical accounts uniformly portray him as a great explorer who first reached America. This picture of him sailing across the uncharted waters remains imprinted in people's minds as the example to follow for daring and adventure. But this carefully crafted sketch hides the ugly reality of a rapacious colonial.

> Christopher Columbus...was a greedy and vindictive tyrant...As governor and viceroy...in what is now the Caribbean country of Dominican Republic, punishments included cutting off people's ears and noses, parading women naked through the streets and selling them into slavery.[3]

Columbus was doing what countless others were later practising on behalf of their countries, for colonial empires and for commercial profit. Sadly, this desire for absolute control over land, people and trade was never limited to tyrants or dictators. States, too, desired over-lordship on other countries. But the sheer scale of imperial repression has never been fully laid out.

Ironically, though, one gets the perverse Western view of a colony and its people in Joseph Conrad's novella, *Heart of Darkness*. In it, a seaman named Marlow sees a tribe of Africans gather on the shore of the Congo River where his steamer is travelling. He says, '*We are accustomed to look upon the shackled form of a conquered monster, but there—there you could look at a thing monstrous and free.*'

Later in the book, he compares the African 'savage' who serves as a fireman on his ship to '*a dog in a parody of breeches and a feather hat walking on his hind legs.*'[4]

Accounts like this should be enough to classify the colonials as monsters in the category of history's worst tyrants, dictators and autocrats. This should have been etched in history books, but unfortunately the attempt has not been successfully made.

Occasionally, some leaders from the former colonies are visceral at international fora, but having let off their steam they rest till the next shot at rhetoric.

Sadly therefore, deep in their hearts, people remain singed. For example, the almost continuous colonial rule in India and piecemeal foreign domination in China meant that two rich, glorious civilizations were brought to their knees, their lands lost, and their people forced to endure suffering throughout.

This national trauma continues to inform their reaction to the forced past.

CONTEMPT FOR A LESSER BREED

The sun, it was proudly claimed, never sets on the British empire. They should have added that some of the worst crimes against humanity were conducted by the British under that scorching sun, in broad daylight. For instance, Britain systematically sucked the life-giving juice out of India as these excerpts bear witness:

> ...extreme poverty in India increased under British rule, from 23 per cent in 1810 to more than 50 per cent in the mid-20th century. Real wages declined during the British colonial period, reaching a nadir in the 19th century, while famines became more frequent and more deadly. Far from benefitting the Indian people, colonialism was a human tragedy with few parallels in recorded history.[5]

Even more brutal was the toll in human terms:

> ...somewhere in the vicinity of 100 million people died prematurely at the height of British colonialism. This is among the largest policy-induced mortality crises in human history. It is larger than the combined number of deaths that occurred during all famines in the Soviet Union, Maoist China, North Korea, Pol Pot's Cambodia, and Mengistu's Ethiopia.[6]

But nothing illustrates the level of their depravity more than this description given by British officer Lieutenant George Cracklow in his letter written after the First War of Independence in 1857. He describes gleefully what happened to captured Indian rebels:

> The prisoners were marched up to the guns... and lashed to the muzzles,' he wrote. 'The guns exploded...I could hardly see for the smoke for about 2 seconds when down came something with a thud about 5 yards from me. This was the head and neck of one of the men...On each side of the guns, about 10 yards, lay the arms torn out at the shoulders.[7]

Yet, India did not carry its historical grudges to a vengeful extreme. On a practical note, it chose to shun retribution. It opted to forget the sorry chapters of its colonial past and the unnecessary amputation imposed on it.

V.S. Naipaul, never a gentle wielder of pen, described this attitude somewhat mockingly in his book *The Area of Darkness*:

> No other country was more fitted to welcome a conqueror; no other conqueror was more welcome than the British. While dominating India they expressed their contempt for it, and projected England; and Indians were forced into a nationalism which in the beginning was like a mimicry of the British.

Like India, most former colonies took the pacifist view and chose not to remember their colonial pain. In doing so, these former colonies took pride in their ability to accommodate their conquerors. This hesitation to put the colonial dictator to account is partly explained by the fact that most former colonies remain weak; they are in no position to put their former masters in the dock, or shame them.

While the colonials got away unscathed, the wounded colonized kept seeking salve. But the partitions of states and wars between them caught their populations in a meat grinder. Having lived together peaceably for generations, these multiple ethnicities got caught overnight in the cataclysm of history, transforming into each other's murderers. India's partition bore its bloody burden.

This tendency to easily forget and forgive is now being questioned, albeit meekly, episodically and gradually. There is a new consciousness that they must remember what they went through.

In some cases, the soft emotion of nostalgia started to turn over time into the hard conviction of fundamentalism. Consequently, some of the postcolonial states produced parodies of nationalism.

Another, though unrelated, phenomenon was the response

of intellectuals. For many intellectuals, to be postcolonial was to share a sense of historical kinship with others who had suffered under the lash of colonialism. The writers among them accurately, if dyspeptically, depicted the spaces in which was staged the drama of their untidy national identity.

But everyone does not forgive and forget. There are exceptions to the rule and China's is a prominent example. The textbooks in its schools remind children of the troubled past when foreigners had colonized them. For masses of Chinese people, modern history begins with the first Opium War of 1840, when Britain defeated the Qing Empire. This launched a century of 'humiliation' that ended in 1949 only after the victory by communists. The idea is to instil in their nascent minds the lesson that history must not be allowed to repeat itself.

But actual history is more nuanced than the narratives created by nations to serve their political goals. Otherwise, the resulting bias prejudices both sides. In his essay 'Shooting an Elephant', George Orwell describes the split personality of a colonial agent. The protagonist of the essay, a white colonial policeman in Burma, ponders about this duality:

> With one part of my mind I thought of the British Raj as an unbreakable tyranny...with another part I thought that the greatest joy in the world would be to drive a bayonet into a Buddhist priest's guts.[8]

This was the mindset that drove the colonial Hitlers of this world to crimes against humanity. It is this contempt for a lesser breed that some armies reserve for civilians. It is misadventures of this kind that have bred dictators in today's lesser countries.

But the colonizers were not done yet. They continued to exercise control indirectly even after they left. For this, it was convenient for the departing colonial to have a single point of reference in the colonies they had freed. Dictatorships were the result, and a subtle form of colonialism continued through arms sales and loaded trade deals.

Then, in a sudden spurt of humanitarian impulse, the world thought of coming to the rescue of the oppressed people around the world. The UN had then coined an evocative term for it: '*responsibility to protect*'.[9]

It became a fashionable point of discussion in think tanks and at the UN. The Western powers, in particular, were fond of flaunting the term because it opened up for them a fresh opportunity to exercise proxy colonialism. Therefore, the West interpreted the 'responsibility' part of this coinage as their sanction to intervene in the internal affairs of other countries. In most cases, however, this intervention ended in failure, leading to a greater mess. In some cases, it led to a new dictatorship. After a short while, and after repeated failures, the Western world had to slink back into its corner, having achieved little with its thinly disguised colonial-style crusade.

But this may just be a temporary retreat. The West has a way of coming up with new forms of domination, because exploitation is the foundation of their riches. However, the developing and the previously colonized world, too, must bear the blame. As Barack Obama put it, '*The worst thing that colonialism did was to cloud our view of our past.*'[10]

We are yet to clear that mental fog.

Part 4: THEY TOO HAVE A HEART

13

SOFT CORE

It is hard to imagine that there may be a sentimental, soft or intellectual side to men of violence. Yet, it is a fact that a delicate and sensitive art form like poetry appeals to many authoritarian leaders. Some have even fancied themselves as poets.

One of the earliest such pretenders was Nero. He donned a stage costume and sang of the capture of Troy, while Rome burned to the ground. A Roman historian Suetonius quotes Nero as being greatly delighted with the beauty of the flames.[1] There were many such contradictions in him and his misdeeds continued all through his reign. Ultimately, the Roman Senate gathered the courage to declare him a public enemy.

When the end seemed inevitable, Nero decided to take his life. Since he lacked the courage to do it himself, he ordered a freedman to cut him with a sword. But right till the last moment, he continued to fancy himself as a great artist. So great was his conviction that before the freedman plunged his sword into him, Nero cried out, '*Oh, what an artist dies in me!*'[2]

In direct contrast was Karl Marx, a genuinely great man of letters. He wasn't a dictator himself, but the creator of an '-ism' that became authoritarian in practice. Unlike Nero, this was his parting shot, '*Go on! Get Out! Last words are for fools who haven't said enough!*'[3]

Iran's Ayatollah Khomeini was another man who moulded a nation after his fashion. It might seem hard to believe, but Khomeini was a poet too. His devotees may be keen to read his verses allegorically, but others might regard them very differently:

> I have become imprisoned, O beloved, by the mole
> on your lip!
> I saw your ailing eyes and became ill through love...
> Open the door of the tavern and let us go there day
> and night,
> For I am sick and tired of the mosque and seminary.[4]

Dictators are not content with just writing poetry or singing songs. They also like to be seen by others as keeping good company and possessing cultivated tastes. Addressing his country in 2004, Ayatollah Ali Khomeini said, '*In my opinion Victor Hugo's* Les Misérables *is the best novel that has been written in history...*Les Misérables *is a book of sociology, a book of history, a book of criticism, a divine book, a book of love and feeling.*'[5]

TOWARDS LITERARY IMMORTALITY

Many dictators are obsessed by the desire for immortality. Some have a fascination for writing and a secret wish that a part of their legacy must be as intellectuals. Just as the dictator wants his words to become action, he also wants his essence to be preserved in his words. Accordingly, the book is his means of achieving immortality. In this, they wish to emulate God. When God says something, it happens. '*Let there be light*,' He said, and '*there was light.*'

Like God, authoritarian leaders aspire to this union of word and action.

As the dictator does not trust others to truly reflect his greatness, so he writes his history himself. In this respect, they follow Winston Churchill who said, '*History will be kind to me for I intend to write it.*'

At the other extreme, some like Saddam Hussein have sought divine help to ensure their legacy. On his 60th birthday, Saddam commissioned a Quran to be written using 27 litres of his own blood.[6]

However, neither intent nor an appeal to the divine is enough. Even employing a ghost writer does not guarantee a good read. From Mussolini to Mao, dictators have written atrocious books. These are revered as sacred texts while their authors are alive, only to vanish almost as soon as their regimes fall. Hitler wrote two volumes of *Mein Kampf*, including a Braille edition and a luxury 'wedding edition' for newlyweds.[7] The Führer seems to have suffered self-doubt regarding the quality of his work because he also admitted, '*Ich bin kein Schriftsteller*' ('I am not a writer').[8]

Saddam wrote romance novels under the pen name S. Hussein. One of the books written by him was titled *Zabiba and the King*.[9] It was a sexually charged autobiographical novel set in ancient Iraq. In its strange plot, female bears are tender lovers who seek to please the herdsmen they desire by stuffing them with nuts, cheese and raisins.[10]

Stalin tinkered with poetry but depended on a ghost writer for his literary immortality. Mao made *The Little Red Book* compulsory reading. But the concept of what should be compulsory reading sometimes varies. For instance, Xi Jinping's *Thought*, a compact booklet, is now mandatory reading for Chinese students.[11]

In a similar vein, Haiti's dictator Duvalier once remarked

that 'when one is a leader, one must have a doctrine'. So he wrote *Essential Works* and demanded that everyone in the country should learn at least three-quarters of it by heart.[12] It was a tough diktat to follow because 90 per cent of the population was illiterate. But statistics are mere numbers for a dictator, to be used and discarded as convenient. Therefore, regardless of how many people read more than a page of his book, Duvalier was awarded the title of 'Grand Master of Haitian Thought' by a Haitian organization. Haiti's State radio then elevated him to the level of Plato, St Augustine and Rudyard Kipling![13]

Mao went a step further and considered himself a combination of philosopher, sage and poet. To be fair to him, he did have literary gifts and coined some striking catchphrases, such as 'A revolution is not a dinner party,' 'Imperialism is a paper tiger,' and 'Political power grows out of the barrel of a gun.'[14]

Overall, though, Mao had a love-hate relationship with books, and there were two distinct phases in his life related to this. In the 1920s, Mao ran a bookshop and publishing house in Changsha which he named the *Cultural Society of Books*.[15] It was in this phase that he started to call himself a communist. Yet, around forty years later, the same Mao was responsible for the mass-scale burning of books during the Cultural Revolution.[16]

Hitler, an avid book reader personally, was another dictator who presided over the burning of books. In the 1930s, the Chief Propagandist for the Nazi party Joseph Goebbels organized large bonfires of books in Berlin. Millions of books by Jewish writers were burnt even as Hitler was exterminating millions of Jewish people.[17] Anticipating perhaps just such a pass in the affairs of men, the Jewish poet Heinrich Heine wrote in 1822, '*Where they burn books, they will, in the end, burn human beings too.*'[18]

Still, and as was the case with many of them, dictators like to be seen on every printed paper in the country. In part, this must be due to an obsession with their image: the population must see him, and him alone, all the time. Even after the massive defeat of the German army in Stalingrad in 1943, when everything including paper was rationed, four tonnes of paper a month were earmarked for Hitler's official photographer. The pictures of the Führer were considered of strategic importance for the country.

Mao did things on an even grander scale. Seven factories were built in Shanghai to print Mao's portraits, posters and *The Little Red Book*.[19]

Ironically, the worst dictators tend to be the most enthusiastic readers and writers. Hitler died with more than sixteen thousand books in his private libraries.[20] Stalin wrote a book that was printed in the tens of millions, though this is easy to do when you are the publisher, own all the bookstores, and edit all the book reviews.[21] Mussolini co-authored three plays while ruling Italy, and was the honorary president of the International Mark Twain Society.[22]

In some cases, the literary gift comes with their genes. Italians do not have to make much effort to excel in art; they are naturally gifted. After all, Italy is the country that produced some of the greatest art in the world during the Renaissance. There must be something special in the soil of the country and its people's DNA that this tradition has continued almost uninterrupted from ancient days up to now. The form may vary, but the substance of great imagination is a constant. From Marcus Aurelius onwards, there have been philosopher kings and advisors like Machiavelli.

Unlike Aurelius, who was truly a great writer, Mussolini was not a significant writer, but he published more than fourteen volumes in and out of office, including a bodice-ripper, *The Cardinal's Mistress.*[23] Mussolini would recite a canto by Dante every morning. He was also a passionate violinist.[24] And to remind foreign dignitaries of his interest in literature, Mussolini left the works of eminent poets ostentatiously open on his desk when he was expecting a visit.

Then there are some dictators with democratic pretentions, like Pakistan's former Prime Minister Zulfikar Ali Bhutto, who believed that reading the works of Hitler and Mussolini would do him good in practical politics. Once, a few years before he became the Prime Minister, Bhutto invited Pakistan's then President Yahya Khan to dine at his Clifton home in Karachi. When they had their drinks in their hands, Yahya's attention drifted briefly towards the bookshelves: '*Yahya* (Khan) *stood in* (Zulfiqar) *Bhutto's opulent reading room, looking up at the shelves. His eye caught a beautifully embossed silver book displayed smack in the center. Puzzled, Yahya read the title:* Mein Kampf.

'*"Aha! I see you are admiring my collection. That one is my absolute favorite, aside from the Mussolini's to the right, just over there," Bhutto said.*'[25]

But all dictators do not pretend; some have been genuinely interested in literature. Their reading list may not have been large but they understood and, in a few cases, followed what they were reading. Fidel Castro, for instance, was a great admirer of Ernest Hemingway. He met Hemingway twice and kept a signed photo of 'Papa' on his desk. In his autobiography, Castro revealed that he enjoyed reading Hemingway's monologues where his characters talk to themselves.[26] Castro may not have taken his cue from them, but he was known to ramble for hours in his speeches.

WHEN TYRANNY MEETS ART

Some dictators had other interests as well. General Francisco Franco was fond of painting landscapes.[27] It is a different matter that the end product of his labour had just about a passing resemblance to the scene he thought he had painted.

A number of others had no pretentions of any sort insofar as the finer things in life were concerned. Idi Amin was one such. He loved slapstick comedy and was a great fan of children's cartoons, especially *Tom and Jerry*.[28]

Unlike the crass Idi Amin, Hitler's case is an example of the artist denied. As a young man, he painted and sold postcards showing city scenes from Austria. They were mostly serene and tranquil illustrations of architecture and city life. They were reasonably good; looking at them, one could hardly guess that the artist would later become a heartless monster. But it is difficult to guess what destiny has in store for a person. Hitler had been rejected twice by Austria's Academy of Fine Arts for one of its courses.[29] Had he been selected, he may not have migrated to Germany.

CAGED BIRD

Dictators might write books, they may also be seen reading books, but do they respect writers? Or are they wary of them?

One example of this love-hate syndrome was Stalin. In 1932, he cheerfully summoned forty of the leading writers of the Soviet Union to dinner. There, he exhorted them with language one might expect from a faculty dean making a case for literature:

> Our tanks are worthless if the souls who must steer them are made of clay...And that is why I raise my glass to you, writers, to the engineers of the human soul.[30]

Of the writers attending that dinner, Stalin had eleven murdered before the end of the decade.[31]

Stalin's contradictory conduct may or may not point towards a split personality. But this behaviour was not unique only to him. A well-known Latin American writer, Mario Vargas Llosa was used to seeing dictators take over with a sickening regularity. With that considerable experience he said, '*Dictators are afraid of literature.*'[32]

Llosa may have been generalising, but there is an element of accuracy to his assertion that dictators are not overly fond of writers. In fact, they often tend to be wary of them because ideas and opinion, by their multiple shades and their many interpretations, are a warning sign for an absolute ruler. To him, writers are magicians with words. Their narrative imagining new worlds is a challenge to the one the dictator has established.

So, does the written word disturb a dictator? Anecdotal evidence tells us that criticism bothers them because despite their pretention as writers, dictators worry that the written word can be a destabilising force against their regime. Therefore, they view with suspicion fiction as a literary genre. After all, a novel can duplicate the actions of a dictator who has clawed his way to the top by playing on the prejudices of people and by delivering overblown promises to them.

Among the many examples of fiction imitating reality are the fictional characters including Berzelius 'Buzz' Windrip in *It Can't Happen Here by Sinclair Lewis;* Willie Stark in Robert Penn Warren's *All the King's Men*; the imitation of the Dominican dictator Rafael Trujillo in *The Feast of the Goat* by Vargas Llosa; and Napoleon in George Orwell's *Animal Farm*. Gabriel Garcia Marquez had famously sketched a dictator's paranoid mind in *The General in His Labyrinth*. More recently, Lord Voldemort in the *Harry Potter* books has an important message about people who support crazy leaders.

The debate about a dictator's desire for immortality, and a writer's need to tell the truth as his heart and mind perceive it, is age-old. Essentially, it is a contest between might and right. It is also a contest of wills because howsoever strong a dictator's arm, the written word somehow manages to float free. It overwhelms, then, the dictator's efforts to write his own version of history. But till then, till history delivers its verdict, there is a period of struggle. Rumi may have had this constant tussle in view when he advised, '*Raise your words, not your voice. It is rain that grows flowers, not thunder.*'

Reflecting on this broad theme in October 1963, President Kennedy brilliantly articulated his deep dedication to the arts and to the need to celebrate the role of the artist in society. He said this in Amherst College at an event honouring poet Robert Frost:

> When power leads man towards arrogance, poetry reminds him of his limitations. When power narrows the areas of man's concern, poetry reminds him of the richness and diversity of his existence. When power corrupts, poetry cleanses. For art establishes the basic human truth which must serve as the touchstone of our judgment.

Kennedy wasn't finished yet. He had more to say:

> The artist...becomes the last champion of the individual mind and sensibility against an intrusive society and an officious state... In pursuing his perceptions of reality, he must often sail against the currents of his time. This is not a popular role...If art is to nourish the roots of our culture, society must set the artist free to follow his vision wherever it takes him...the highest duty of

> the writer, the composer, the artist is to remain true to himself and to let the chips fall where they may...[33]

This was lofty vision by a celebrated leader. Alas, in effect, it was only a wistful wish.

In sharp contrast, a lesser man, an ersatz leader like Imran Khan celebrated when the Taliban toppled democracy in Afghanistan in 2021. His weirdly worded message to Afghans was, '*When you adopt someone's culture...you end up becoming a slave to it.*'[34]

Alas, it is small minds like Imran's that lead our world today. They can scarce relate to Kennedy's soaring vision. On a practical note, however, Kennedy's dream is tinged with idealism. The reality is that the two are forever in conflict: the dictator's desire to chain the writer and the latter's struggle to break the shackles. In this tussle, a dictator's deeds are a fertile field for a writer's imagination.

However, if it were possible, what is the least a dictator should do?

They would do well by not writing at all. Emperor Augustus set a good example for them when he said, '*Have I played the part well? Then applaud as I exit.*'

Sadly, dictators think otherwise. For some of them, nothing in life—for good or bad—is ever accomplished except through language. No mass atrocity has ever been initiated unless through the medium of rhetoric. It is by clever manipulation of words that they sway the people.

They are, therefore, acutely conscious of the fact that words can be used to breach their fortress; that language can rewire people's brains and that literature can be dangerous. They know that in the slippery game of power nothing is 'just words'.

Since self-pity, insecurity and envy are at the core of many of their own writings, what should be acknowledged is the charged and dangerous power of words. While the tyrant uses these skills for malignant power, the writer, using the same tools, resists. This is the core of tyrants' animus towards writers: that they use words and narrative for the construction of new worlds.

And therein lies the conflict, because speaking truth to power is a crucial role of the writer and the poet. That's why pithy and powerful poetry is popular at protests. It is commanding enough to gather crowds in a city square and compact enough to demand attention on social media.

Poet Maya Angelou brings this out through the symbolism of a caged bird:

> The caged bird sings
> with a fearful trill
> of things unknown
> but longed for still
> and his tune is heard
> on the distant hill
> for the caged bird
> sings of freedom.[35]

14

CHARISMA

Some call 'charisma' a divine gift, while others term it a special power possessed naturally by a few. There are still others who, on a more realistic note, assert charisma is beyond accountability. Whatever it is, and whichever way they influence people, the sway of a charismatic leader is mesmeric.

As with many other usages, this term, too, traces its roots to the Greek *charismais* (*khárisma*), which means 'favour freely given' or 'gift of grace'.[1]

It was a most suitable application considering its initial results. The centuries between 800 BCE and 300 BCE were a period of immense development of philosophical and religious concepts. Charismatic figures like Jeremiah, Gautam Buddha, Mahavira, Lao Tzu and Confucius, besides Socrates, wielded remarkable influence during this period. They were effective principally because of their charisma, and their ideas transformed entire societies.

Subsequent generations saw other leaders with immense charisma. George Washington, Giuseppe Garibaldi, Abraham Lincoln, Vladimir Lenin, Mahatma Gandhi and Winston Churchill mesmerized people with this special gift. Take also the case of Napoleon for the effect charisma can have. An adversary once remarked that Napoleon's presence on the battleground 'was worth forty thousand men'![2]

So long as their magic lasts, the charismatic persons hold you in their spell. This holds true for a dictator, a liberal, a business leader and an actor as well. Take the case of Bill Clinton in his prime. When he spoke, he made you feel as if you were the only person in the world. This is the essence. A charismatic person makes you laugh, makes you feel heard and feel special.

But charisma is a tricky label to categorize people with because, unlike *karma*, charisma does not come in good and bad packages. It is what you make of it. President Kennedy oozed it, but so did Hitler. However, if we leave aside for a moment the semantics of good and bad, we will find some features that are common to charismatic leaders:

- They have a strong passion that triggers powerful emotions in those around them. Even in anger, they make people feel happy to join a cause.
- They use metaphors extensively to simplify their message and make it easily comprehensible.
- They communicate in emotionally charged ways, using both positive and negative emotions to engage the audience.
- They show obvious pleasure in experiences, and actively encourage others to partake in this same experience.
- They are good storytellers; and for this, they frequently use voice as also body gestures.

In addition, charismatic leaders believe destiny has specially chosen them. Napoleon often spoke of destiny. Garibaldi believed destiny had chosen him for victory; this belief, in turn, inspired his followers.

Beyond all this, what matters ultimately is the effect

charisma produces. As Peter Drucker, writer, management consultant and professor, said, '*The three most charismatic leaders of the 20th century inflicted more suffering on the human race than almost any trio in history: Hitler, Stalin, and Mao. What matters is not the leader's charisma. What matters is the leader's mission.*'[3]

Yet, as the case of the three above shows, people do not seem to have been troubled by the evil in their mission. Despite knowing that he will be bad for them, and for society, people are drawn to the charismatic leader. In 1932, British psychoanalyst Roger Money-Kyrle briefly visited Berlin. There he had the occasion to hear both Joseph Goebbels and Hitler address a vast crowd of fawning Germans. The impression he gathered, then, of the hold an authoritarian leader exercises over masses is valid for other such leaders as well. Giving his opinion in an article titled 'The Psychology of Propaganda' (1940), he noted:

> The speeches themselves were not particularly impressive. But the crowd was unforgettable. The people seemed gradually to lose their individuality and to become fused into a not very intelligent but immensely powerful monster...[that was] under the complete control of the figure on the rostrum [who] evoked or changed its passions as easily as if they had been notes of some gigantic organ.[4]

Listening to Goebbels and Hitler led Money-Kyrle to the idea that for propaganda to work, such a leader must draw out a sense of helplessness in the audience, and then offer them a magical solution:

- identify a minority or group of outsiders as perpetrators of people's suffering, and
- and offer a cure.

As Money-Kyrle writes further in his article:

> Self-pity and hatred were not enough. It was also necessary to drive out fear...So the speakers turned from vituperation to self-praise. From small beginnings, the Party had grown invincible. Each listener felt a part of its omnipotence within himself. He was transported into a new psychosis. The induced melancholia passed into paranoia, and the paranoia into megalomania.[5]

SENT FROM GOD

Basically, there are three ways a charismatic leader influences others: force, reason, or charm. Of these three, force and reason are rational (even when we are 'forced' to do something, we obey for a good reason); charm is not. Charm, like love, is blind; it is based on emotional manipulation and, as such, has the ability to bias our views and trump any rational assessment. When charismatic leaders run out of charm, they turn to force.

The irony is that often charismatic leaders become enraptured by their own rhetoric and start believing in it. Even those who are otherwise staunch democrats remain deluded long after their followers have realised otherwise. For instance, Tony Blair continues to think the invasion of Iraq was a moral triumph.[6]

All this explains the leader and his motivation as well as the behaviour of the people who share, vehemently, the leader's ideological belief. But there is still the rest, the vast majority of the ordinary, who lose all sense of proportion when they hear a charismatic leader. Why do these otherwise middle-of-the-road individuals lose their sense of balance? Generally, such people are charmed by others only when they share their core beliefs. The same applies to their faith in a leader. In other words, the same set of people would not find someone charismatic if his vision did not align with theirs. As Laurence Rees writes in *The Dark Charisma of Adolf Hitler*:

> ...German children were taught that Hitler was 'sent from God' and was their 'faith' and 'light'...Hitler was seen less as a normal politician and more as a prophet touched by the divine.[7]

Hitler was a unique example of imposed mass adulation. But the broad principle holds true for others as well, as in the case of Pakistani leader and former PM Imran Khan. By all accounts, he is not intellectually gifted. He is known to be self-centred, selfish, manipulative and a man of many flaws. Yet, none of these diminish his appeal; rather, sex scandals about him seem to add to his aura and the frequent reports about corruption or his maladministration are dismissed by his followers as motivated propaganda. What matters to them are his lofty promises to transform Pakistan and his appeal as a handsome sports star.

A charismatic leader is seen as omniscient, omnipotent and always benevolent. His words define the horizons of reality. He must always be praised and appeased, and never challenged. Thus, to the mesmerized people, those who oppose the charismatic leader are in league with the forces of evil.

On a note of caution, it must be added that leaders in the conventional sense are not the only charismatic figures in public life. Terror heads can also have a mesmeric hold on people, as was the case with Osama bin Laden. For that matter, sports stars like Pele and, at the other extreme, a mafia boss such as Al Capone can capture people's imagination long after they are gone.

EPHEMERAL HAPPINESS

Generally, it is political leaders, even those not naturally gifted with charisma, who seek and cultivate a charismatic persona. Somewhat differently, an astute and naturally gifted charismatic leader realises that charisma alone is not enough. It certainly wins people's attention. But that's just the beginning. Once a leader has the audience's attention, he must have something to tell them. He must spin magic with his promises.

The more charismatic leaders take considerable care to script their public appearances. It is only when there are moments of unscripted crisis that a leader's character and mettle get tested. But politics is not a game, and the unfortunate result of charisma in politics is that it distracts and destructs.

Yet, almost every dictator convinces himself that he is the best always, in any situation, and on every issue. To maintain that superior image, he makes all important decisions and comes up with all ideas. He is reluctant to delegate, unable to share the spotlight, and slow to praise—all of which are signs of bad leaders.

Consequently, even after the initial honeymoon period, the charismatic leader continues to crave high approval ratings. It is another matter that this pursuit distracts him from actual goals. But it is not just the leader who keeps a constant eye on his approval ratings; his followers also become addicted to the leader's charisma, reinforcing displays of populism and perceiving unpopular decisions as deal-breakers. The result is a reciprocal dependence that encourages both sides to distort reality in order to prolong their 'high'.

Reality, when it finally dawns, is sobering because charismatic dictators provide a vision of the world that does not yet exist.

Eventually, the inability to perform according to that vision is the reason a dictator begins to lose his shine. The starting point of this slide is when he considers criticism as disobedience.

Once things start to go wrong and the economy begins to falter, his supporters start to distance themselves. His erstwhile followers feel betrayed when they suspect that they might not get the expected payoff. Then they react with opposition, anger and hate.

When the dictator's power begins to crumble, his charisma starts to fade and people come out of their trance. Was this really the man, they wonder, who had kept them enraptured? The same person now begins to sound ordinary, just like any other street-smart operator.

If that is the case, it will be fair to conclude that charisma is a cosmetic add-on. Its effect is anaesthetic and lasts only as long as the dosage endures. Once that wears off, reality begins to hurt. As post-war Germany's first Chancellor Konrad Adenauer admitted to Henry Kissinger,

> The Germans were a deeply troubled and conflicted people...not only because of their Nazi past but also, in a deeper sense, because of an absence of sense of proportion...[8]

In a different age, and in another context, Nietzsche had pondered over such an issue. He viewed the matter differently and his conclusion was philosophically stoic: '*To live is to suffer, to survive is to find some meaning in the suffering*.'[9]

Such forbearance may not always be easy to live with for an entire society. Still, combining Adenauer's lament with Nietzsche's practical note, I prefer to conclude with this rider for societies under a spell: '*Happiness lasts as long as charisma holds*.'

15

DICTATOR'S WIFE

Socrates is said to have counselled a young man in this manner: *'My advice to you is get married: if you find a good wife you'll be happy; if not, you'll become a philosopher.'*[1]

It is not on record whether he had a view on marriage and its influence on a man's dictatorial turn. For that matter, there isn't much evidence about a major philosopher talking about a dictator's wife.

However, conventional wisdom maintains that a good-looking, stylish woman married to a pudgy dictator is a familiar feature of many of the world's authoritarian regimes. Soong Mei-ling, the wife of China's Generalissimo Chiang Kai-shek, was one such glamorous spouse. Mei-ling's husband presided over China during a tumultuous period in the country's history. He took over just before World War II, to soon find himself in the midst of a huge civil war and the struggle to keep communists from seizing power. To maintain control, Chiang Kai-shek committed horrible atrocities leading to a million deaths.

But his well-educated wife Mei-ling worked to mitigate people's suffering through her social work. She established orphanages for the children of people killed in the Chinese

Civil War. These orphanages, built on a thousand-acre site in Nanjing, had well-appointed facilities with playgrounds and swimming pools.[2]

Mei-ling, though, was an exception. Apparent similar exceptions turn out to be a put-on show, as was the case with Jean-Claude ('Baby Doc') Duvalier's wife. In 1980, American-educated, stylish Michèle Duvalier married Jean-Claude Duvalier, dictator of Haiti, one of the world's poorest and most corrupt countries. She also set up hospitals and orphanages. Apparently, she seemed determined to pull her people out of their poverty. Or so she claimed.

The publicity surrounding her work was such that even Mother Teresa got taken in. She visited Haiti in 1981 and praised Michèle Duvalier, saying, '*I have never seen the poor people being so familiar with their head of state as they were with her. It was a beautiful lesson to me.*'[3] Mother Teresa added she could tell that the First Lady really cared and was '*someone who feels, who knows, who wishes to demonstrate her love not only with words but also with concrete and tangible actions.*'[4]

This high praise did not stop Michèle from spending millions on things that had nothing to do with 'demonstrating her love' for the Haitian poor. In 1985, while Haiti faced bankruptcy, she flew to Paris and spent $1 million in a week on her shopping. Having run out of money, she asked for another million from the governor of the Central Bank. And she got it.[5]

British-born Asma al-Assad, wife of Bashar al-Assad of Syria, is another glamorous first lady. In March 2011, *Vogue* ran an article on Asma that praised her stylishness, grace and enthusiasm for modern ideas. The article also enthused, Asma was '*glamorous, young, and very chic—the freshest and most magnetic of first ladies.*' It emerged later this article was part of a campaign by the public relations firm Brown Lloyd

James for 'handling and improving the public image of the (Assad) regime.'[6]

POWER WITH PURPOSE

Fancy clothes and charitable works aren't just a casual occurrence: the dictator's spouse is an important part of maintaining power. But there is a limit to what she can do with pretty dresses and sophisticated PR. The glamorous spouse can, at best, help reinforce a despot's personality cult. But it is one of the many means to that end and some day it, along with the rest, comes crashing down, as all artificial constructs do.

Some spouses begin moaning the moment power slips out of the dictator's hands. In a satirical opera, 'The Dictator's Wife', the glamorous yet tormented wife of a once-powerful dictator moans that now she has to answer for the terrible atrocities committed by her husband. Meanwhile, in the opera, as the country falls apart, the once all-powerful dictator has taken to cowering in the bathroom.

Most spouses, however, have it good. The thought that they may not retain power forever does not cross their minds.

Imelda Marcos, the wife of Ferdinand Marcos, a former dictator of Philippines, once ordered a plane to do a U-turn in mid-air because she had forgotten to buy some cheese in Rome.[7] Her flashy lifestyle ended in 1986 when her husband was overthrown by a popular, army-backed uprising. The family fled to Hawaii taking hundreds of belongings with them, including 24 gold bricks and 413 jewellery items. But in their hurry to flee, they had to leave behind Imelda's enormous shoe collection at the presidential palace.[8]

Dictators routinely lavish luxuries on their wives. But all this pampering does not make them generous and caring towards others. In most cases, they are seen to be self-centred and self-indulgent. The generosity of a dictator's wife may, at best, extend to her side of the family. It rarely ever includes acts of kindness towards the dictator's family. Take the case of Elena Ceausescu. Nicolae's brothers could not enter the house uninvited. This restriction applied even to Ceausescu's second child. In fact, their son and daughter-in-law were only allowed to come up to the door and leave their child there. The security guard would then take the child into Elena's room and, at a predetermined time, the parents could come back to take their child.[9]

Her behaviour towards Nicolae's father was worse still.

Ceausescu's father Andruta was a kind old man. Sometimes, when he visited Bucharest, he would go to a pub for a drink. There, he would meet his old acquaintances. Occasionally, one of them would say: tell your son to get us a gas cylinder, or something of that sort. Andruta would faithfully pass on the request to Nicolae. 'Why don't you get him a cylinder,' he would urge.[10]

This used to irritate Elena, because she felt he was meeting people of lower strata, the undesirables. So, one day she ordered that the pub he used to go to be razed to the ground. It was a cruel way to convey a message to her father-in-law, but it was effective. Thereafter, no more requests came via the old man.[11]

Once, some people from Ceausescu's staff were driving with Andruta to his village in Scorniceşti. When they were well out of Bucharest, Andruta told the driver, '*Popescule, stop at the next pub. I want to have a drink. Normally when I visit them in Bucharest, that witch empties out all my pockets. She sends me back without a single lei. But today I managed to hide 25 lei inside my waistband. Here, you see, he said touching the waistband and taking out the currency note.*'[12]

If a dictator is indulgent towards his wife, and panders to her every wish, it does not mean he is caring towards women in general. In fact, the list of autocratic leaders includes many sexists.

Napoléon decriminalized the murder of unfaithful wives. Mussolini claimed that women 'never created anything'. In recent times, Xi Jinping has silenced women who accused powerful men of sexual assault, and excluded women from the Politburo's Standing Committee.[13] In Afghanistan, one of the first acts by the Taliban in government was to bar women's access to education and representation in public office.

These rules, and their restrictions, do not apply to the dictator's wife. No one can show her a restraining finger as long as her husband is the absolute leader. But the loathing of the people for her comes out in the open the moment the dictator loses power. The case of the former Tunisian leader Ben Ali's wife Leila Trabelsi is an example. Described as the woman who sparked the Arab Spring, Trabelsi liked to be called Madame La Presidente and inspired dread in people. As a book by her former butler mentions, '*...she would ritually sacrifice chameleons to supposedly cast spells over her husband... she punished one cook by plunging his hands into boiling oil.*'[14]

When people rose up in revolt against Ben Ali's regime, Trabelsi was a prominent figure of their hate. Eventually, when they fled the country, she took with her one-and-a-half tons of gold that she had stolen from the Central Bank of Tunisia. '*Hang them all, but first bring back our gold,*' was the mob's reaction as they ransacked her palatial villas.[15]

In some cases, the wives of dictators find their world of comfort splintering the moment the halo of power deserts them. A life of luxury is not always guaranteed then. Post-divorce, Sarah Kyolaba Amin, the Ugandan dictator's fifth wife, made ends meet working as a lingerie model in Germany before moving to the UK. Mussolini's wife fared just a little better. While Il Duce's mistress Claretta Petacci was executed by Italian partisans, Rachele Guidi Mussolini survived the war and spent the rest of her life running a little pasta restaurant in her home village of Predappio.[16]

As for people, the awakening usually happens after the dictator has been deposed. It is not unusual for the once-fawning public to discover that their dictator's wife was actually a Lady Macbeth. Her outward show of feeling for people and their welfare was just that—a carefully choreographed show. And her charity work was a public distraction against the brutal realities of the dictator's rule. Ultimately, these spouses inspire varying degrees of hatred because of the fortunes they have looted and their expensive wardrobes.

Let me give the final word in the matter to a satirist. P.G. Wodehouse may have been irreverent as usual, but this quote by him sums up the issue in the manner typical of him: '*You can't be a successful dictator and design women's underwear. One or the other. Not both.*'

But to be fair, the dictator's wife should also have the chance to share her final thoughts. Then, in the manner of Marie Antoinette, she might say this: '*I was a queen, and you took away my crown; a wife, and you killed my husband; a mother, and you deprived me of my children. My blood alone remains: take it, but do not make me suffer long.*'[17]

Part 5: REIGN AND RUIN

16

MESMERIZE WITH WORDS

The process of decision-making in authoritarian regimes has for long intrigued foreign observers. Such curiosity is natural among people living in democracies because there the leader cannot change laws on a whim. The law first needs to be debated and passed by the Parliament. This is not the case with a dictator. He keeps people guessing about his next move. He changes laws simply by issuing an order or steamrolling its passage through a pliant Parliament. Winston Churchill may have had this constant state of tension in mind when he described Soviet policymaking as '*a riddle wrapped in a mystery inside an enigma.*'[1]

By and large, the same description could well apply to the authoritarian regimes of all types, both past and present.

At best, we can superficially guess an authoritarian's ways. But much else remains unknown and unknowable. For instance, it is impossible to tell how objective he is in his estimate of international politics. Outsiders, on their part, do not know for sure how much influence the security services have on him.

However, it can be said with a fair degree of confidence that to survive, a dictator must remain a step ahead of others. It is true that as with every other aspect of human life, authoritarian methods too have periodically undergone change. But the substance of their iron rule remains the same. On that there is no compromise. Occasionally, though, the strongmen have adapted to changed circumstances and adopted new methods of control. This does not imply they have given up the old wicked ways. It means they have added new ways of control to their repertoire.

Besides repression, there is a constant that defines almost every dictator's basic method. We can broadly term it as the ability to mesmerize with words, the promise of a new dawn being his hallmark. A dictator is invariably an accomplished demagogue.

The term 'demagogue' is as old as democracy. It, too, traces its origin in ancient Athens combining *demos* ('the people') and *agogos* ('leader'). Despite its anodyne etymology, it took on a negative connotation almost immediately. Thus, the demagogue was a leader who led by bullying and by converting his charisma into influence. He was a populist who appealed, in particular, to the lower classes. As Aristotle said, '*Revolutions in democracies are generally caused by the intemperance of demagogues...*'[2]

What Aristotle declared then continues to be valid many millennia later. But Victorian novelist Anthony Trollope differs with this assertion. In his 1855 novel *The Warden*, he demurred he wasn't sure where lay the red line of distinction between a regular politician and one who could be classified a demagogue:

> Now I will not say that the archdeacon is strictly correct in stigmatizing John Bold as a demagogue, for I hardly know how extreme must be a man's opinions before he can be justly so called.[3]

So, instead of getting entangled in dialectics, let us try to understand it better based on recent global events. It was difficult to imagine a thriving and vibrant democracy like the US would allow itself to be led by a lout like Donald Trump. Yet, that is exactly what happened. As evidence of how immune societies can be to common sense, a full seventy million Americans voted in 2020 to try and get him re-elected. Trump, with his pounding fist, his cheeky baseball cap and his late-night Twitter insults, represented an uneasy compromise in America's democratic experiment. He was the living proof of the maxim that democracy was a device that ensured we would be governed no better than we deserved.

Leaders like him often enjoy genuine popularity based on a perceived competence at securing prosperity and defending the nation against external or internal threats. However, there are exceptions. Salazar was neither a demagogue nor exuberantly ostentatious as some of his ilk. Still, he held absolute power for forty years. He could do so by muzzling the press and keeping the economy reasonably stable, though a majority of people remained poor and illiterate.

There is a shift, in recent times, in the style of governance as well. Hitler and Stalin sought to fundamentally reshape citizens' world views by imposing comprehensive ideologies. Present-day autocrats do not have new ideologies to offer. They are more surgical: they aim only to convince citizens of their competence to govern.

Earlier, totalitarian dictators often employed propaganda to encourage personal sacrifices for the 'common good'. Their current-day successors seek to manipulate citizens into supporting the regime for selfish reasons.

More worryingly, still new forms of dictatorships could emerge. For instance, the use of lumpens was considered essential in the past. They used to do as they were directed and paid or motivated to. Once the assigned mission was completed, they melted into the background. But what will happen when:

- Lumpens form the *terra firma* of the autocrat's party?
- Artificial intelligence (AI) exceeds human intelligence and escapes human control?
- Fake news generated by the authoritarian leader's command acquires a life of its own?
- A State wishes to manipulate another country's elections through fake news?

Some of this is already happening. China, for instance, is exporting its model of digital authoritarianism. It has supplied surveillance or censorship equipment to Ethiopia, Iran, Malaysia, Pakistan, Russia, Zambia and Zimbabwe.[4] The big issue with this Chinese largesse is that a capability of this nature could be put to transnational use to influence populations beyond borders and spread fake news that incites.

BAD MOON RISING

In future, a dictator could possibly use people-control methods in three areas: the physical, the informational and the cognitive. Over time, the importance of the cognitive domain will increase, eventually becoming the pivotal point in opinion control. With the development of AI, neuroscience and digital applications such as social media, it will be possible for a dictator to influence people's brains to affect human cognition directly.

Indeed, AI might, for all practical purposes, take over the day-to-day running of the government. Elon Musk warns of just such a possibility and its consequences: '*...when there's an evil dictator, that human is going to die. But for an AI,* *there would be no death. It would live forever. And then you'd have an immortal dictator from which we can never escape.*'[5]

This is not merely a rhetorical flourish from a man working successfully on the frontiers of technology. What Musk warns about could happen, and it may be sooner than we realize.

It does not mean that a people will one day elect a robot as their leader. What it means is that a stage will come when, as is already so in many industrial shop floors, human action becomes practically redundant.

Bureaucrats, and their copious notes, may no longer be needed by the formally elected PM. Instead, he will come to rely more and more on pre-analysed AI options. Such a menu of policy choices will give options limited to A, B or C. All the leader has to do is pick one. This will be convenient for the leader for it avoids the endless and sometimes fruitless debates of a committee. Over time, and as the leader's reliance on AI-given wisdom grows, the solutions presented to him will become a virtual command. There will be only one option that can be exercised. Then, AI becomes the virtual dictator—the 'immortal dictator' Elon Musk warns about.

Let me dwell a bit on the scale of new technology and the hold it has on people. This is important because of the enormous platform it offers. Animation is one of the largest sub-niches in the entertainment world. In 2022, it was estimated to be worth $391 billion.[6] To put that in perspective, the worldwide movie industry was worth $33.9 billion in 2023.[7]

With so much money and with over 100 million regular users, such a platform is a potential captive market for a dictator-inspired new ideology. And it will yield quick results.

Let me provide further explanation from a comparative standpoint. In the past, books and their printed words gave people the time to absorb, reflect and remember the message. They also had the option to accept or reject what they had read, since they had the luxury of time to contemplate, to chew over what they had read.

But ours is an impatient age with limited attention span. Now visual is the message and it overwhelms the user with its intensity and instantness. An application such as animation does not give time for reflection. It compels acceptance on its terms. For a dictator, this is an ideal situation.

Let me take this a step further. How might such dependence work at a leadership level? If gaming applications numb a society into going by whatever they hear and see on the screen, these applications' more sophisticated versions could take over the entire decision-making process of countries.

A research-based large language model takes in a question, forms a probability for all of the words in its vocabulary, and then chooses one of them as the likely next word. It does that again and again and again, until it stops. So, it doesn't have facts per se. It merely knows what word should come next. Put another way, it does not try to write sentences that are true. But it does try to write sentences that are plausible. These applications are being used by engineers, architects, lawyers and others despite the risks associated with the limitations of a machine jumbling words. Yet, it is convenient.

In future, this ease could tempt the leadership to go in for ChatGPT-type applications. These might be convenient, providing quick answers and more than one choice. But who will take the responsibility if the decisions leaders take on this basis are flawed? The chances are that while these AI aides will provide ready answers and facilitate quick decisions, the limitations of this system could be mind-numbing and the consequences crushing.

Despite yielding to and being overwhelmed by AI, the spirit of dictatorship will not change. Roman emperors used to get the face of their predecessors, from the neck upwards, chopped off from statues. They would then have the face replaced by their own copy. It was a quick and economical way of announcing that a new leader had arrived. This urge by the dictator to rub out the name and achievements of the predecessor and to emboss his name forever on the imagined new successes of the country will persist, as it has from the earliest times. Just as the will to dominate and deceive people has existed from before the recallable past, so too has the dictator's need to device new ways to entice and mesmerize people.

But the wheels of change do not turn only at his bidding. People too are constantly engaged in this game of catch-up. If a dictator in future chooses to use AI deviantly, there will be some vigilant citizens who will find a counter to it. In this manner, yet another chapter in the age-old cat-and-mouse game between the dictator and people will begin.

Though this time, there will be a third party in the game.

AI will be the new, sometimes unpredictable, occasionally even uncontrollable, spoiler—not itself the dictator, but in his control. Yet, the world watches helplessly AI's march. It also notes ominously that a bad moon is rising in the world. But instead of worrying about it, and doing something, people have opted to keep their eyes shut.

17

SPIN DOCTORS

Once, a tyrant could wave a hand and a band of soldiers would dispatch the dissidents instantly.

This killed the body but did not destroy the mind. It is the power of thought that worries the most powerful of dictators. Left unchecked, a single anti-regime spark could soon become a forest fire. It is to prevent this negative thought from finding space that rulers are anxious to know the pulse of people.

In earlier times, some rulers went in disguise at night to the market to listen to the bazaar gossip and gauge public opinion regarding their regime. Now, dictators do not venture out because of security reasons. So, public relations (PR) agencies step in. First, as a barometer of public opinion, and second, to mould public opinion.

It might sound bizarre but in 1933, Hitler hired a major NYC PR firm, Carl Byoir & Associates, to portray Nazi Germany in a positive light to an American audience. The agency was paid $6,000 per month.[1] Even if the agency succeeded initially, the US joined the allies in the war against the Axis powers led by Germany. Still, that setback did not take away much from Hitler's conviction: '*Make the lie big. Keep it simple. Keep saying it, and eventually they will believe it.*'[2]

While Byoir & Associates worked for Hitler, there were others like Edward Bernays (Sigmund Freud's nephew) who listened to their conscience. Bernays, considered the father of PR, refused to work for Germany. He was concerned how his work might be used by the Nazi propaganda chief Joseph Goebbels.[3]

In the times before PR agencies were formally established, dictators depended on their own ingenuity and the support of their sympathisers among artists and the media to spread the word in their favour. This effort started even before they turned dictatorial. Napoleon was a pioneer at self-promotion. The habit of fantastic exaggeration, of imagining things as they should be, not as they actually were, began quite early in his military career.

In 1796, during the Battle of Lodi at a small town outside Milan, Napoleon stormed a bridge held by the Austrian Army. Most other generals would have waited for the enemy's retreat, which seemed imminent. But Napoleon saw in it an opportunity for easy glory. It was a small military gain, but Napoleon inflated its importance in his report by claiming to have defeated an army that was twice as large. This liberty with truth was the norm with him; he regularly exaggerated victories and played down setbacks. In tune with that he said, '*The truth is not so important as what people think to be true.*'[4]

True to character, he transformed that minor, unnecessary victory at Lodi into a major act of military significance. Within four years of this battle, Napoleon had built up a compelling myth of himself as a hero and a saviour. Artists and writers added to it with poems, plays, songs and newspaper articles. Swayed by this deluge, Napoleon became for people the great preserver of French liberty.[5]

DESIRE TO DOMINATE

Controlling the narrative is the preferred way with dictators and autocrats even now. They go about it methodically, as described by writer Milan Kundera:

> The first step in liquidating a people...is to erase its memory. Destroy its books, its culture, its history. Then have somebody write new books, manufacture a new culture, invent a new history. Before long the nation will begin to forget what it is and what it was. The world around it will forget even faster.[6]

But the dictator cannot do this all by himself. Like Napoleon, he needs an accommodating media to spread the message.

Some in the media get taken in by the charisma of the dictator, others fall in line because their media empire could suffer otherwise, and still others become the victims of their own propaganda—they start believing it. This happened to the most powerful media moguls of the UK and the US before the Second World War.

In the years leading up to the Second World War, there were '*...six most powerful media moguls in the United Kingdom and the United States, whose newspapers together reached a majority of their countries' readers every day. All dismissed the fascist threat and called for appeasement, and some unashamedly embraced fascism, anti-Semitism, and xenophobia. Moreover, they spread a polemic, sensationalistic, and personalist style of news writing that often crossed the line into outright untruth—a power in which they revelled.*'[7]

Times have changed, but the dictator's desire to dominate the national narrative remains the same. And invariably the media responds in the same way because its monetary stakes in survival have increased. Moreover, the concentration of media in the hands of a few capitalists makes it even more convenient for a dictator, or even a democrat, to use pressure and persuasion. Once again, the cases of the US and the UK are illustrative:

> In 2017, Bernie Sanders wrote of how Comcast, News Corp, Disney, Viacom, Time Warner and CBS—just six companies—owned 90 per cent of the media in the country. *Forbes* wrote in 2016 that 15 billionaires owned all major national newspapers, including *The New York Times*, *The Wall Street Journal* and *The Washington Post*. In 2015, 71 per cent of the UK national newspaper market was dominated by three companies: News UK, Daily Mail Group and Reach. By 2019, their market share had grown to 83 per cent, and by 2021, to 90 per cent...[8]

With so much at stake, can the media truly reflect the mood of the people?

THE ART OF PERCEPTION MANAGEMENT

In our new age, running a dictatorship is no longer what it was earlier cracked up to be.

The concept of human rights, the equality of human beings, and limitations to the power of the State have greatly complicated the act of taking human lives. Therefore, the dictator needs a greater variety of tools at his disposal. PR agencies then step in to provide that additional support.

How do the PR firms help against these odds?

They come up with an alternative narrative that the client wishes to promote. In this task, the first step is to find out what people are saying about the client. Major PR firms maintain 'mass surveillance systems' that track everything from social media to the mainstream press. If their client is sledged in X's 280 characters, chances are they will find it. Besides countering it by fake inserts, the PR firm creates favourable blogs and websites and pushes out a stream of 'good news' press releases.[9] The aim is to bury the bad news under a pile of propaganda.

Basically, the task involves suppressing information and preventing people from reading bad things about the client. For this, they might manipulate online spaces to make finding critical content difficult, if not impossible. It is done by driving the critical content down the rankings of the search engine. After all, very few have the desire or the patience to click beyond the first page of results. Knowing this, the PR firm creates new, positive content that fools the search engines into pushing the 'dummy' content above the negative, thereby hiding the articles and comments they do not want people to read. Moreover, the addictive appeal of fake news lies in its simplicity. It offers the believer the satisfying sense of having special, privileged access to the 'manufactured' truth.[10]

This reach over social media is one of the many reasons why PR companies have entered the picture in an increasingly significant manner. Some of the bloodiest regimes in the world have hired PR firms to defend their activities. At times, even the otherwise open societies and democracies have hired PR firms to create a fog of illusion.

This was done successfully in the build-up to the 1991 Persian Gulf War. A PR firm Hill & Knowlton put out the story that Iraqi soldiers were throwing Kuwaiti children out of hospital incubators. Later *Covert Action Quarterly* (Spring 1993) discovered that Hill & Knowlton were paid $11 million to conduct an entire campaign by the 'Citizens for a Free Kuwait'.[11]

President Putin is an accomplished influencer himself. But even he found it useful to hire a top Western PR company,

Ketchum, to lobby for the Kremlin's interests in the West.[12]

The latest case in this respect is the war in Ukraine. It befuddles people to the extent that it is hard to distinguish between fact and fiction. As one experienced commentator put it: '*A measure of this "historic success" is the war in Ukraine, news of which is mostly not news, but a one-sided litany of jingoism, distortion, omission. I have reported a number of wars and have never known such blanket propaganda.*'[13]

As the instances cited above show, disinformation is not restricted by national boundaries. Even worse, the global reach of social media and its intense use by people means two things. One, people tend to consume information without filtering it. Two, easily digestible fake news spreads rapidly, almost like a wildfire. A result of this is the use countries like China, Russia and the US have put it to. The US is an illustrative case: '*The United States dominates the Western world's media. All but one of the top ten media companies are based in North America. The internet and social media—Google, Twitter, Facebook—are mostly American owned and controlled...the United States has overthrown or attempted to overthrow more than 50 governments, mostly democracies. It has interfered in democratic elections in 30 countries. It has dropped bombs on the people of 30 countries, most of them poor and defenceless. It has attempted to murder the leaders of 50 countries. It has fought to suppress liberation movements in 20 countries.*'[14]

But why do governments feel the need to hire professional firms? After all, they have their own spokespersons and well-staffed ministries of information, which could do the job just as easily. The short answer is no, they cannot. They lack the reach and would fail the credibility test. As governments worry about their image, they need outside, and seemingly neutral, help.

Accordingly, governments that regularly violate human rights, stamp down on protests or lock up journalists invest heavily in public relations. They do this not just because they want to look good to the outside world; they are also motivated by practical considerations. A poor image can harm the prospects of trade and investment into their country. Moreover, countries can face sanctions and those already under sanctions would want to have these lifted.

It is not just governments; major companies, too, seek the assistance of PR firms when they encounter challenging situations. Chinese telecom giant Huawei paid the Democratic party's power broker Tony Podesta $1 million over a six-month period to lobby the Biden White House on its behalf after it was blacklisted by the US.[15]

To help tide over questions being asked of it after the global financial crisis of 2008, multinational giant American International Group retained PR agency Burson-Marsteller. It was only one among a list of such crisis-ridden organizations that sought help from Burson. The reason Burson gets these calls is because it has a robust, well-recognized crisis management practice. Its list is long enough for it to be said, '*When Evil needs public relations, Evil has Burson-Marsteller on speed-dial.*'[16]

Interestingly, even warfare, as Napoleon proved so effectively, can do with some media help. In fact, wars are not just for generals and troops; it is a complete conflict in which public opinion matters a great deal. Terrorists, too, spend considerable time to mould public opinion. Al-Qaeda, in particular, used technology to manipulate people's perception. It was so effective that Osama bin Laden was one of the most recognized figures of the twentieth century. At the height of the war on terror, he received more media coverage than his opponent, President George W. Bush! As a former

US defence Secretary Robert Gates once wondered, '*How has one man (Osama Bin Laden) in a cave managed to out-communicate the world's greatest communications society*?'[17]

What surprises experts is the fact that people repeatedly fall for fake news. It is not just ordinary folk, even the media-savvy get taken in. A recent example of this was an established TV anchor in India who was lured out of her job by the promise of a non-existent professorship at Harvard. It is because this fakery is so effective that leading governments of the world, and dictatorships, have tried to sell such bubbles as the real thing. Mind control is the ultimate objective of these efforts and the PR firms involved in these exercises call it perception management.

Invariably, the public falls for it.

'PUBLIC HAS NO RIGHT TO KNOW'

In the game of 'reputation laundering', London has emerged as the city with the most PR firms.[18]

It is the place to go to when dictators, and sometimes even democracies, are looking to give their image a scrub. Unlike the gullible public, they get what is promised to them because the reputation of the PR firms depends on their ability to deliver. The reach and sophistication of London's PR industry also helps. Equally importantly, this exercise requires discretion. London provides that assurance of confidentiality. This secrecy is not available in the US, as lobbying firms in the US working for foreign governments are required to register their activities under the Foreign Agents Registration Act (FARA). There is no equivalent for it in the UK.

There are more surprises in the PR business. Yesterday's seekers of help become today's givers of it, at a price, of course.

Take the case of Tony Blair. Once he was known for being upright. But that was when he was a working politician. Since then, his values have accommodated a new ethos. Leaked documents show the fees of over £5 million annually charged by Tony Blair Associates (TBA), a company he set up. The company demanded $2.65 million from Kazakhstan to provide 'political advice'—$2.55 million to help Nazarbayev uphold the rule of law, and a further $1.1 million to run Kazakhstan's civil service academy.[19] Its efforts seem to have provided only temporary relief to Nazarbayev, because he was made to quit following a popular revolt against his government.

Why do companies like TBA attempt to pull the wool over people's eyes? It is an act of deception, pure and simple. Even more lamentable is the fact that it is not just the dictator, the bad man, who is involved. The entire eco system of society, especially its elite, has a role in it. Worse still is the fact that it is often a trans-border exercise involving politicians, think tanks, opinion writers, newspapers and PR firms of major democratic states who are all participants in it!

Engaged in this fakery, they disregard the fact that the choices they make show truly who they are.

But making choices may not be that difficult for individuals who believe they are invincible at the peak of their career. This was the case with a number of politicians and high-profile journalists associated with a lobbyist in what became known in India as Radiagate. One journalist admitted as much: '*I look at some of the conversations, and I do feel I should have been more alert*'...'*I should have been more sceptical. I should have known better.*'[20]

But all media people do not have a post-event call of conscience. Some are actually proud of what they do, as was the case with some of the biggest and best-known media barons of the UK and the US:

> In the United Kingdom, Lord Beaverbrook, who boasted that he ran newspapers 'purely for the purpose of making propaganda', called for isolation and appeasement. Lord Rothermere, who founded several British tabloids, praised Nazi Germany and fascist Italy as the 'best run' countries in Europe, while secretly writing Hitler to encourage him to invade more countries. In the United States, William Randolph Hearst whitewashed Hitler's actions...[21]

Then there is the question about the morality of this exercise. Are PR firms correct in taking up such clients and advancing their cause? On this, the professional code of conduct of PR firms is quite clear: '*We are faithful to those we represent, while honouring our obligation to serve the public interest.*'[22]

Do PR firms truly adhere to this sentiment, or is it just empty talk? From a technical or legal perspective, it is possible for a PR firm to represent any client. But it is also the moral responsibility of the firm to quit the moment it realises the job on hand is not about truth and it fails the test of public interest.

However, this is not how it turns out in practice. It never has and it never will. It is what the lobbying business in the US is largely about—providing access and pushing the line the client pays for. This, in sum, is what they get hugely paid for. Morality and values can wait for another time.

In a report published by Brussels-based think tank Corporate Europe Observatory, Ivo Ilic Gabara of the PR firm BGR Gabara says, '*Mother Teresa doesn't need our services. She isn't going to come to us as a client. It's always the difficult issues. If someone is willing to spend money on media relations, it's because they have a problem.*[23]

Then there is also the case of Peter Bingle, former chairperson of Bell Pottinger Public Affairs, who was questioned by a committee of British MPs. They asked him,

> 'You've worked for mass murderers, racists, people who've oppressed their own people... Doesn't the public have a right to know who your clients are?'

Bingle looked right back at them and replied with a straight face:

> 'The public has no right to know.'[24]

Despite Bingle's brazen stab at democracy, the committee of the British MPs was not able to change the working and the methods of London's PR firms.

Let me now relate a practical example.

During an interview with WNYC Studios, Harper's Contributing Editor Ken Silverstein disclosed that, in 2007, he went undercover to investigate two PR firms that tried to help dictators win friends and influence people. His cover was that he was working on behalf of Turkmenistan. The gist of what he said reveals the mechanics of their working:

> They (PR firms) were falling all over themselves to win the contract...because it was such a horrible dictatorship, they were saying that they'd have to charge me more. In fact one of the lobbying firms I approached wanted to charge 5 million dollars over three years, they said... we'd actually have to charge you more if something bad happened...
>
> So they love these clients. The dirtier, the better. It's much more lucrative...APCO specifically said they would write and place op-eds in American newspapers. And what they do is, that a staffer at APCO would write it. Then they'd go out and recruit an academic or somebody at a think tank to put their name on it. And then they would go place it in an American newspaper,

> so it would look like some independent, thinking human being, as opposed to a paid flack for a dictatorship. And they said that would be very simple.[25]

It must be 'very simple', otherwise they would not be in business. Not just simple, they would have to be effective as well, or else governments would stop employing them because dictators, countries and private corporations in crises need help in projecting their view when things are at their worst. Crisis experts are essential then; they know how to spread the right word.

But there is nothing quite like many of today's strongmen who are themselves the 'masters of spin'. They work hard at faking democracy. Strongmen like Vladimir Putin, Recep Tayyip Erdogan, and Viktor Orbán are known to distort information.[26] They simulate democratic procedures to spin the news. But there is a condition to it. Spin dictators tend to be popular when their economies are doing well. Since economic booms do not last forever, spin dictators need to build and preserve support, especially in bad times.

To do that, they co-opt PR firms. These, in turn, manipulate the media and use it to project an image of the strongman as a skilled, benevolent and democratic leader. When the facts are good, they take credit for it; when the facts are bad, they have the media obscure them. The media slanders and discredits any possible alternative party or leader, so the incumbent looks good by comparison. So long as that works, the dictator is popular.

However, they, and the PR firms they employ, forget that media can only provide hype.

It can work on the margins, it can make a noise for this issue or that, but it cannot make black into white forever. Lacking any other means of a genuine feedback, dictators forget that media is an amplifier at best. It is not the sound.

The sound is on the ground, the sound is the people.

But where is the time to think and rationalize what is good and what is better when a person is riding the wave. The constant effort, then, of a dictator is how to package failure as success. Ancient Rome's historian Tacitus described it thus,

> ...when in their wake nothing remains but a desert, they call that peace.

18

CRUEL DICTATOR

When nearly all the warriors of the *Mahabharata* are lying dead, when their blood has soaked the earth, Yudhishthir, the Pandava King, decides that he no longer wants the throne of Hastinapura.

What is the point of ruling, he says, when you have got there only through deceit and death?

> *Aatmanamaatmana ahatvaa*
> *kimdharmaphalamaapnumah*
> *Dhigastukshaatramachaaramdhigastubalamaurasam*
> *Dhigastvamarsamyenemaamaapadamgamitaavayam*
>
> (Since we slaughtered our own, what good can possibly come from ruling?
> Damn the ways of kings! Damn the might that makes it right!
> Damn the turmoil that brought us to this disaster!)[1]

Like Yudhishthir, there have been other kings who cared for the call of their conscience.

But dictators do not suffer from self-doubt. Had it been otherwise, they would not have made a grab for power. In fact, an unwritten code of dictators is their conviction that they are smarter than everyone else. This invariably leads them to the slippery slope. Ideally, therefore, they need to learn the art of self-critique. It would help if the dictator gave an aide the authority to whisper every morning into his ears, '*you are only human.*'

Sadly, very few have done so in recorded history. Ibn Sina being one of the few:

> The barbarity of the early Muslim invaders in India shocked even the Arab and Persian intellectuals. Sheikh Bu Ali Sina (Ibn Sina), a respected physician and biologist, refused to come to India with Mahmud, whose plunder and loot, he felt, was destroying Indian science.[2]

Ibn Sina did well to dare and say no. As a conscientious objector, he must have wondered how art and science could prosper in the midst of a world of clashing swords, burning towns and plundered temples. In refusing to accompany Mahmud Ghazni on one of his raid-and-plunder trips to India, he was conveying a deeper disapproval, questioning why one must be so rapacious.

Since Ghazni was not the only tyrant in history, it is only natural to ask: whose hands have been the most bloodied in history?

This question has engaged people through the ages and their response has varied from Stalin to Mao. Others such as Taimur Lang and Genghis Khan should also be in the reckoning, but the count of their victims is not exact. Moreover, they did not stay in a place long enough to wipe out an entire population. They entered a city like a whirlwind, blowing away everything and everyone that came their way. Having conquered and looted, they left for the next destination. It was only after they left, and the dust of their fury had settled, that the survivors could count their losses.

Usually, the number of killed was in high thousands and only rarely in hundreds of thousands.

Whatever the number, the world has for long suffered the aberrant behaviour of cruel rulers. A fourteenth century ruler of the Delhi sultanate, Firuz Shah Tughlaq is remembered largely for whimsical decisions like shifting his capital from Delhi. But *Tarikh-i Firoz Shahi*, a historical record of his rule, notes some acts of cruelty as well. One of these concerns an expedition to the state of Odisha in 1360. Anticipating that once the soldiers reached there would be mass killings, nearly 100,000 men and their wives and children took refuge on an island not far from the coast. Alas, they were not safe even there. The Sultan's soldiers massacred the men and took the women and children as slaves. When Tughlaq died, these and other slaves under his service were executed to be piled high in a large heap.[3]

The Turk Enver Pasha was another mass murderer. When his army suffered a humiliating defeat at the Battle of Sarikamish (1914–15), Pasha's response was to take bloody revenge. He ordered the large-scale destruction of Armenia, accusing it as the cause of his army's defeat. The term 'genocide' was used then to describe the slaughter of 1.5 million Armenians out of a population of 2.5 million.[4]

The killing machine became systematic and was on a mass scale in the twentieth century. Hitler, Stalin and Mao were the pioneers, each with his own special way of extermination. But unlike Hitler, the atrocities by Stalin did not receive the critical attention they deserved. By the beginning of the 1930s, Stalin had already executed nearly a million Soviet citizens. A few million more died due to forced labour, deportation, famine and torture by Stalin's security forces. In some cases, a quota was established for the number to be arrested and for the number to be executed.[5] If we go by the official count, at least 3 million were executed during Stalin's reign. Some more recent, and independent, estimates put the number at 15 million to 20 million. Despite this large scale of cruelty, *Time* magazine put Stalin on its cover 11 times.[6] And to date, Russian public opinion polls rank him near the top of the greatest leaders of Russian history.

Yet, even this does not make him the cruellest dictator in history.

The biggest, or rather the worst, mass murderer in history was Mao Zedong, who began to lead China when it was regarded as the 'sick man of Asia'.[7] Mao introduced the Great Leap Forward (1958–61) policy in order to catch up economically with the West in 10 years. To pursue this dream Mao wanted to build a steel mill in every commune, for steel to him was the currency of economic power. In the drive to produce steel, food production dropped steeply, even as demand for food in urban China went up, resulting in a famine that was the main cause in the death of nearly 45 million people in three years.[8]

The story did not end with this huge human loss. Following the disastrous failure of the Great Leap Forward, Mao put his experiment on hold. However, after fixing the food deficit, Mao returned to the theme of national reconstruction and Chinese glory. The Cultural Revolution was Mao's next big pursuit. Its basic purpose was to create a new man who would give up everything for the larger cause of building the Chinese nation. Those who resisted lost their lives. About 1.6 million Chinese died within the first three years of the Cultural Revolution.[9] Yet the Chinese people do not hold it against him.

In a different continent, in Africa, Idi Amin, Uganda's brutal leader during the 1970s, claimed he kept the decapitated heads of his political enemies in his freezer.[10] During his eight years at the top, at least 80,000 were killed: almost 27 executions a day. His victims included bankers, intellectuals, journalists, cabinet ministers and a former prime minister.[11]

If Idi Amin was brazen in his brutality, Albania's dictator Enver Hoxha was clinical. He bumped off much of the intelligentsia to the extent that, by the time of his death, virtually no one in the Politburo could boast of more than a high school education. One of the most dangerous positions to hold during Hoxha's reign was that of the Interior Minister; he killed almost every one of them. Old school friends and high school crushes were also purged. The person who had given Hoxha his scholarship to study in France was executed, as was the friend who let him live rent-free in his Paris apartment. Scientists and intellectuals were his targets; anything foreign was denounced as a danger. Hoxha jailed painters for liking Picasso, writers were banned for having read Sartre, and musicians were banished to re-education camps for playing Mozart.[12]

The government controlled the list of names that could be given to newborn children. There were only about 40 to choose from. In 1967, Hoxha turned Albania into the world's first atheist State and closed down all churches and mosques.[13] He also banned beards because they could remind people of Islam and Orthodox Christianity. He was spiteful and petty to the extent that when Mother Teresa's mother was dying in Albania, she was not allowed to come and pay her a farewell visit.[14]

It is not just dictators and tyrants who are brutal; history is littered with tales of cruel kings. One name remains impaled in memory both because of his extraordinarily cruel practices and because Bram Stoker fictionalized him as the blood-sucking Dracula. Stoker's inspiration for the book *Dracula* was a 15th century prince, Vlad Tepes, or Vlad the Impaler, who lived and ruled in the Romanian province of Walachia.[15]

An estimate maintains that during his rule about 80,000 were killed, of which about 20,000 were impaled.[16] Among the more remarked events was an occasion when a group of Turkish envoys had an audience with Vlad in 1459. This group refused to remove their turbans in his presence, citing a religious custom. Commending them on their religious devotion, Vlad commanded that their hats should forever remain on their heads. His soldiers then nailed the turbans to the skulls of Turkish envoys.[17]

Vlad's victories over the invading Ottomans were celebrated throughout Transylvania and the rest of Europe. On one occasion, nearly 20,000 Turkish soldiers were impaled and hung in a row of stakes along the route from the sea that the invading Turkish armies usually took. Since fierce winds were common in the region, they produced eerie whistling sounds as they passed through by the skulls of the impaled. The sight and the sounds were so repulsive that the next invading Turkish army retreated in fright.[18]

It isn't only individuals who can be dictatorial. Some institutions and commercial enterprises, too, try to forcibly impose their will on others. The British East India Company is an extreme example of tyranny when it had an entire country in its grip. A researcher maintains there was an 'untold holocaust' which caused the deaths of almost 10 million Indians over a 10-year period beginning in 1857. According to the British Labour Force archives, one British official of the time recorded:

> the undisputed display of British power (was) necessary during those terrible and wretched days—millions of wretches seemed to have died.[19]

It wasn't only the nameless British official who celebrated

the massacre of Indians. The otherwise much-lauded writer Charles Dickens was also shockingly intemperate in his comment:

> I wish I were commander-in-chief in India...I should proclaim to them that I considered my holding that appointment by the leave of God, to mean that I should do my utmost to exterminate the race.[20]

In our times, a leading global investment bank is believed to have secretly controlled the world. The magazine *Rolling Stone* once accused it of having '*engineered every major market manipulation since the Great Depression,*' adding that it was '*a great vampire squid wrapped around the face of humanity...*'[21]

Mercenaries are another class that have existed, with the State's approval if not connivance, from the earliest times. They commit atrocities, but it is a convenient extra-judicial body whose crimes are not a blot on the State's name. Then there are security forces and intelligence wings of governments that have the sanction to apply the roughest methods known to man. Water boarding and electric shocks are only the minor ones among them.

HISTORY OF CYCLICAL HORROR

When massacres happen, we who survive moan in retrospect. But the cruel hand, the cause of it all, gets away with it. During a dictator's lifetime no one, not even the most vocal activist, will dare raise a voice in protest. Besides the fear of consequences, this can also be cynically explained in Stalin's words, '*One death is a tragedy, a million deaths a statistic.*'[22]

As if in response to the advances in, and the acceptance of, modern international criminal law, the world created international courts and tribunals, including an International

Criminal Court. This faith in accountability never produced the results hoped for. It did not stop Yahya Khan, Pol Pot, Milosevic or the Taliban from committing mass atrocities. Still, there was for some time the hope that these institutions would be effective. That faith is wavering today. Rather, it is steadily giving way to the age of strongmen.

Instead of looking to international institutions as a restraining influence, the hope now is that the dictator or the authoritarian leader will restrain his hand because social media spreads beyond borders and beyond his reach. But even there, the dictator has found ways of manipulating social media. As the Greek philosopher Democritus said long ago, '*Many, while performing the foulest deeds, use the fairest words.*'[23]

So, the question that rankles is: why should there be adulation of dictators despite the horrors they inflict on people? Is it because the successors were not good enough, or were they even more terrible to people and ruinous for the country? There are other questions as well:

- Why are dictators remembered centuries after they had committed unspeakable crimes against humanity?
- Why do people remember with awe an Attila the Hun or a Genghis Khan? Why does Hitler's *Mein Kampf* still find thousands of buyers in India?[24]

The clues as to why it happens are few and half-hearted, even as questions continue to fester. Is it a case of collective self-harm? Or is it that a tyrant keeps us paralysed to no reaction long after he has gone? Fear indeed is the common factor dictators use for their rule, and the fear of their deeds lingers long after them.

There are also reactions that range from 'never again' to the vehemence of belief that the dictator was good for the country. A prime case in the context of the latter point is Mao, a horrible dictator who showed no mercy and never expressed any regret over it. Yet his legacy trails you in China. Mao's face can be seen on Chinese money. Long queues begin to form every morning at Tiananmen Square to visit the mausoleum of Mao Zedong. Visitors pass solemnly by his embalmed body. There is a larger-than-life portrait of Mao right near the entrance to the Forbidden City. There is just no escaping Mao, he is everywhere.

Mao, like some other dictators, is an exception. Generally, however, it is the evil in a dictator that is recalled. For example, Robert Clive who established East India Company's rule in India is remembered as a most hated man. After his death, Samuel Johnson wrote Clive '*had acquired his fortune by such crimes that his consciousness of them impelled him to cut his own throat.*'[25] Reflecting upon Clive's loot of India, Horace Walpole wrote, '*We have murdered, deposed, plundered and usurped...*'[26]

It follows, then, that this question should be asked: why hasn't England thought it necessary to return the loot and apologize for Clive's atrocities? Aren't succeeding generations in Britain complicit by keeping the plundered fortune?

Sometimes, though, a dictator's family members decide to atone for his sins. Adolf Hitler didn't have any children. But there were five members of his bloodline who had descended from Hitler's father's first marriage. They vowed never to have children so that Hitler's legacy could end with them.[27]

On the other hand, there are cases where the dictator's family does not escape his cruel hand. The Mughal king Aurangzeb poisoned his father, Emperor Shah Jahan, and ordered the beheading of his elder brother, Dara Shikoh.

Let me, however, give the last word on the subject to Charles Dickens, who wrote this about King Henry VIII:

'The plain truth is, that he was a most intolerable ruffian, a disgrace to human nature, and a blot of blood and grease upon the History of England.'[28]

Like Henry VIII, many other dictators have polluted the face of this fair earth. Sadly for the masses, new dictators keep rising from among us. And dictators, almost without exception, are cruel. The history of our world, therefore, is the history of brutality, murder, mass extinction, cyclical horror, and every form of venality.

There have been moments of relief, but they were all too brief.

19

COUP

A coup no longer commands the level of international attention it once did.

Its frequency and the extensive media coverage a coup used to receive must have saturated people's curiosity. However, when it began, the camera coverage of a coup was a novelty in the nineties. The first televised revolution of the world was in December 1989 when masses of angry Romanians forced their dictator Nicolae Ceausescu to flee. Their frenzy and their eventual liberation from dictatorship was extensively transmitted live by camera.

A decade later in 1999, pictures of soldiers climbing over the walls of a TV station to announce a coup by General Pervez Musharraf also made dramatic news internationally the next morning. In contrast, the subsequent coups in Thailand and Myanmar were noted and frowned upon by other leaders in their capitals, but hardly caused the storm of lasting disapproval. The world had moved on.

In some cases, 'silent' coups have taken place without firing a bullet and before the world had the time to sit up in alarm and say 'not again'. Worse still, the world seems to have forgotten the horrors it had to go through because of Hitler. And despite spontaneous outrage at the illegal takeover in Afghanistan by the Taliban, the global news cycle soon shifted to cover the next 'breaking news'.

There is a change in coup mechanics as well. Once, staging a coup meant bringing out tanks into streets or launching a massive popular revolt to topple a government. This was largely the case in the 20th century. Now, would-be dictators don't take risks. They take over the system and topple the government from within. Autocrats from Recep Tayyip Erdogan in Turkey, Daniel Ortega in Nicaragua, and Nicolas Maduro in Venezuela, to Vladimir Putin in Russia chose this process. They manipulated democratic norms, wearing them down to a thin shell that contained only the wrecked remains of democracy.

Soon, this democratically elected leader becomes indistinguishable from a dictator. By the time most people realize what has happened, it is usually too late. By then, the leader is already in full control of a false narrative, yet enormously popular. A government of, for, and by the people becomes all about protecting the rule of one individual.

The world, however, sits up in alarm and makes a noise about democracy only when Western economic interests are threatened. But as the firmness of coup-makers in Niger and Gabon has recently shown, there is very little, beyond issuing threatening statements, that countries like France can do. The world has become wise to the fact that such theatrics are a camouflage for the loss of lucrative mining contracts that the French have stitched up with the corrupt democratic regimes of these countries.

NEW MODELS OF COUP-MAKING

Clearly, coups are not as uncommon as we might assume. In fact, these figures should surprise us with their frequency:

'280 autocratic regimes took power between 1945 and 2010...45 per cent of authoritarian regimes in this period were the result of coups.'[1]

To break it down further into actual successes, nearly eighty countries have had a successful coup since World War II. Thailand has the dubious distinction of being the country with the most coups in the world. It has had thirteen successful and nine unsuccessful coups in the last century.[2] Ghana too has not done badly on this dubious score. It has had 10 coups, or attempts at a coup, between 1967 and 1981.[3] Bolivia and Syria each have had eight coups in the past seven decades, while Argentina has had seven. Coups are more frequent in Central and South America, Africa and, to a lesser extent, the Middle East and Southeast Asia.[4]

Let's take a closer look at Africa, especially its Sahel region. The coup d'état in Niger in July 2023 marked the sixth successful change of government in two years in this region. The Niger coup also meant that the entire landmass from Sudan in the east to Burkina Faso in the west, a distance of over 5,600 km, is now under military rule, making it the longest military-ruled corridor in the world.[5]

There was a 'new model of coup-making' in the recent coups in Sahel. These were led by young military officers, were less violent, and in most cases enjoyed considerable public support. Except in Sudan, most other coup leaders were 34–41 years old. Another significant feature common to these recent coups was that they were mostly bloodless.[6]

Nearly 80 per cent of the population in sub-Saharan Africa now lives in countries whose regimes are classified as 'electoral autocracies', that is, countries where elections cannot be described as free and fair. The picture is not vastly different in the rest of the continent. Forty-five of the 54 states in Africa have experienced at least one coup attempt since 1950!

Surprisingly, it doesn't always take many conspirators to carry out a coup. Wits in Pakistan have termed the 111th Infantry Brigade, or Triple-1 Brigade, as the 'coup Brigade' for its involvement in almost all military takeovers there.[7] In Libya, in 1969, Muammar Gaddafi staged a coup with the help of a small group of soldiers and 48 rounds of ammunition. Like Gaddafi's, many coups are set in motion due to the grievances of military officers. In some cases, it is because they have been denied promotion or put to disadvantage because of their ethnicity.

So, if there were to be a coaching class for future coup-makers, what would form the essentials of that course—the basic dos and don'ts a coup-maker should follow? Though every situation may differ, still the following might form the basics of such a course:

- Broadly speaking, a coup cannot succeed unless it has popular support (a military coup falls in a different category). Or, at least, the plotters should be sure the general population will not defend the old order. It is, therefore, of utmost importance that the coup is planned with the greatest secrecy. Not a whiff of it should reach friends or colleagues, who hold the pro-government view.
- The speed of execution is of essence. A coup should be executed with such speed that it soon becomes a *fait accompli*.
- Coup-makers should quickly seize control of and dominate the State's transport and communications networks: roads, rail links, ports, airports, television, telephones and the media.
- They should also immediately neutralize the existing leadership. Its top echelons must be arrested to deliver a shock effect.

- The spectacle of a leader fleeing a country and seeking asylum indicates the coup's success.

LIVE, AND DIE BY THE SWORD

The list above is for classical coups, where the civilian government is replaced by force. But can a coup happen against a coup-maker? Yes, because coups and coup-makers do not come with a lifetime warranty. Around a third of autocracies end up with a coup against them; close to a fourth are brought down in an election.[8] The mismanagement of economy often leads to the fall of dictators. The Soviet Union stands out as a spectacular example of how economic decay, elite misperceptions of reform and its consequences, and the withdrawal of international support can result in a decisive collapse of government. In the case of the Soviet Union, it resulted in the disintegration of the State itself.

Though at first sight it seems improbable there can be a 'coup' against a dictator, it isn't really a contradiction in terms. There can be coups, counter-coups and counter-counter-coups. One such series happened to Justinian II, an early Byzantine emperor.

Justinian II ascended the Byzantine throne in AD 685 at the young age of 16. All went well initially and the young emperor scored early victories against the Arabs and Slavs. But by AD 695, he had alienated both the military and the civilian population of the Empire. One of his generals, Leontios, took advantage of this discontent and staged a successful coup. After first being paraded in chains throughout Constantinople, Justinian's nose was slit before he was sent off to exile.

In exile, over the next ten years he gathered an army. Finally, in AD 705, aided by the Bulgarians and now wearing a prosthetic nose made of gold, Justinian loaded his army into ships to sail back to his homeland.[9]

During the journey, a giant storm struck his fleet. One of his aides beseeched Justinian: '*If you promise God you will be magnanimous, and not seek revenge on your enemies when returned to the throne, we may all be spared.*'

To this Justinian retorted: '*If I spare a single one of them, may God drown me here*!'[10]

He survived the storm, took back the throne, and beheaded his enemies.

But the coups did not end here. His mutilation and years of exile had not softened him. Instead, he embraced tyranny even more.

In AD 710, Justinian II turned his vengeance towards Cherson, the Crimean city where he was first exiled. A Byzantine fleet sacked the city, with Justinian II personally roasting seven of its greatest nobles by tying them to spits over fires.[11]

Sacking one of the Empire's own cities was the breaking point for the Byzantine army and they rebelled under the general Philippicus Bardanes. When the Emperor sent a fleet to quash the rebellion, they defected to the rebels and immediately sailed back to Constantinople. Justinian II initially escaped capture and fled towards Damascus, but this time his luck ran out. He was captured by Philippicus' forces on 4 November 711 and executed to ensure that there would be no third chance for the 'Slit-Nosed' to return to power.[12]

This and many other cases of coup validate the old saying '*those who live by the sword die by the sword.*'[13]

This is one of the main reasons why dictators tend to be on their guard from the time they seize power. They give the outward appearance of invincibility but deep within they remain insecure.

Generally, a dictator faces three types of challenges to

his regime—from his senior aides, especially those from the military, the threat of foreign intervention directly or indirectly, and a genuine popular uprising.

As a rule, a dictator discourages power struggle within the ruling elite, keeps potential rivals on a tight leash, and crushes any attempt to form a subversive coalition. He anticipates and tries to eliminate these threats by manufacturing an image of invincibility. For example, a dictator mobilizes crowds to participate in ritualistic ceremonies, obtain huge turnout at the polls, and win rigged elections with large margins.

A strong military is an ever-present danger to its creator. If the elite of a country decide to form a strong military, they have to live with the hazard their action can cause because a strong military may not always work as their agent. By the nature of their training, their capability, and the mass of strongman power available to them, the army has the monopoly on the means of violence in a society.

Because of his dependence on the army, the dictator needs to keep it in good spirits. Therefore, the cost of using repression in non-democratic regimes is high. He does so by what can broadly be termed 'fiscal appeasement', by paying 'efficiency wages' to soldiers or making social or policy concessions to the military to minimize resentment among them.

In contrast, democratic regimes are bound by bureaucratic norms, and the need to keep balance in society. If a concession or a pay rise is given to army, similar benefits will have to be given to the civilian side of government. Since the overall finances of the State have to be kept in view, a political leader cannot order such concessions by a wave of his hand. Consequently, a political leader is most vulnerable when he is not strong enough to reform the military and cannot commit to making concessions to it. But a dictator can be arbitrary, pro-army, and more nimble in making such a decision.

Sometimes, the threat to a dictator's stability takes the form of an uprising. Though infrequent, it is a major threat when mass unrest does happen.

It is, therefore, important to understand how much a dictator's survival at the top is threatened by protests, and what determines an authoritarian regime's capacity to resist disruption in the streets?

Usually, a dictator is sanguine that the threat to his regime will not come from a mass movement because his intelligence network would get wind of it at the initial stages. After all, mass uprisings are rarely spontaneous; to succeed they need careful planning and organisation, which always runs the risk of being found out by the dictator's agents. The first sign is enough for the dictator to put the conspirators in jail and crush the uprising.

In any case, most citizens are loyal to the dictator out of fear. They are conscious that as individuals they are powerless to stand up and oppose him. In fact, they are anxious to signal their loyalty to the dictator, but in private the same individual's views may be vastly different. The few who hope to get favours from the regime may strongly endorse it. For the rest, it could range from detesting the regime to being indifferent, yet resentful. This latent feeling, and suppressed rage, ensures that public sentiment can swiftly turn against a dictatorship. A determined opposition can then cascade into an overwhelming movement of dissent.

THAT RARE DARE

Dissent against the dictator, however, is not a 'given' to all people. For instance, we in India are a study in contrast. We submitted to the yoke; some collaborated with the masters.

For almost a thousand years, conquerors from foreign parts kept marching into India to take control. Yet, we remained somnolent. People rarely rose up to take a stand. We might have behaved this way for the longest period, but we were not the only ones. Our example of resigned acceptance was also the case with some other populations of the world.

Why is it that certain people rise up in revolt while others opt to submit in fatalistic acceptance?

Étienne de La Boétie has addressed this issue in his bluntly titled work, *The Discourse on Voluntary Servitude*:

> Resolve to serve no more and you are at once freed. I do not ask that you place hands upon the tyrant to topple him over, but simply that you support him no longer; then you will behold him, like a great Colossus whose pedestal has been pulled away, fall of his own weight and break in pieces.[14]

This is indeed what many races do. Afghans, for instance, are an example of it. Though they have suffered enormously in the process, yet through centuries they have resisted the occupier. People in the Eastern Bloc continued to suffer communist dictatorship for seven decades, but they remained sullen all through. Eventually, they rose in protest to break free of their chains.

History also records many instances where an individual has taken the first bold step. That rare dare, risky as it is, can turn into a mass revolt. The Romanian revolution of 1989 offers one such example.

László Tökés was a priest in the town of Timisoara facing eviction from his church apartment. His crimes, in the regime's book, were two. First, he was of Hungarian descent. This minority was not looked upon kindly by the majority Romanians. Second, he was preaching against the Ceausescu regime's policy of restructuring towns and villages. In order to punish him, Timisoara authorities ordered him to vacate the apartment allotted to him. When he refused to follow that order, it became a cause célèbre.[15]

By early December 1989, it was not only his parishioners who were standing guard to protect his flat, even ethnic Romanians joined the growing crowd. Together, they formed a protective ring around the property by linking their hands. Despite strict censorship of the media, the news of this dare quickly travelled throughout Romania. Within days, protests against the Ceausescu regime proliferated. Finally, it was the anger of the crowd in Bucharest that forced the Ceausescu couple to flee the capital in a helicopter.[16]

The revolt in Romania followed the old-fashioned pattern of organising people by word of mouth. But that carries the risk of being found out in a regime where people suspect each other, where the best friend and your close relative may be informers of the regime.

A more recent instance of a single spark becoming a raging fire of revolt was the series of successful Arab revolutions. It started in Tunisia in December 2010. Resentment against the Ben Ali regime had been simmering for some time. The peasants were sullen because the government was not doing enough to subsidize them; students were apprehensive of their job prospects in a faltering economy where the unemployment rate was 22 per cent and the general population was unhappy because of rising prices.[17] In this background, stories of high living and corruption by Ben Ali's family and his cabal inflamed passions.

Finally, it was not a call for democracy which triggered the uprising but a call for employment. On 17 December, a fruit and vegetable seller Mohamed Bouazizi, working as a street vendor in the city of Sidi Bouzid, set himself on fire after the police roughed him up and seized his cart. A recording of it went viral on social media. This was the spark people were waiting for. The protests and riots started from the interior of the country and spread quickly to the capital, Tunis. By early January 2011, the revolution had reached the point of no return, forcing Ben Ali to abdicate.[18]

The Tunisian revolution, variously called the Bread Revolution and the Jasmine Revolution, was the inspiration for the Arab Spring that followed in the Arab world.[19] It also had an interesting sequel. The Tunisian National Dialogue Quartet (a group of four civil society organizations that steered the country through the revolution towards democracy) was awarded the 2015 Nobel Peace Prize for '*its decisive contribution to the building of a pluralistic democracy in Tunisia in the wake of the Jasmine Revolution of 2011.*'[20]

These two revolutions—the Romanian and the Tunisian—were success stories. They were also proof that when a dictator was past his prime, and the resentment against his regime was widespread, the risks multiplied for him.

STUMPED BY IPHONE

However, if a dictator is agile and quick to react, he can beat the odds even when a powerful revolt against him is well underway.

This was the case in Turkey.

In July 2016, a faction of the Turkish army attempted a coup against President Erdogan. It was planned well and initially executed with success but was defeated tactically by an iPhone.

In the initial stages of the coup, the rebels occupied a major TV station and used its facilities to broadcast and create an impression that they had succeeded. However, they made a major mistake by not detaining Erdogan and immobilising him. He was quick to react and used the iPhone of one his aides to counter the putschist claims of a successful coup. He was thus also able to organize civilian resistance effectively against the rebels. Angry crowds surrounded their tanks and all major opposition parties denounced them.

A big mistake by the leaders of the coup was to assume that a single claim on TV was enough to give them victory. This is not so in a modern country, with numerous TV, radio, social media and internet channels. The Turkish authorities were quick to saturate the media with counter-assurances and by dismissing the rebellion as already defeated.

The cost of this failed attempt was high for the rebels, in human terms. Nearly 300 of them were killed and over 2,000 were wounded. After the coup, around 32,000 people were jailed. Criminal investigations were undertaken against 70,000. Among them were soldiers, policemen, judges, prosecutors, journalists, teachers, academics, bureaucrats and others.[21] It was a coup that could have succeeded but the price of failure turned out to be high.

Whether there is a military coup or a silent coup, where the elected leader himself accumulates dictatorial powers, the result has never been good—neither for the leader, nor for the people. So, is there a way a country can become dictator-proof and prevent a coup? There is only a slim chance that this can happen, and a country remains undisturbed in democratic bliss. Still, one possible way could be by installing a corruption-free and competent democratic leadership.

Since that may not always be possible, let me view the issue from another angle: what are the factors that lead to a coup?

This list is relatively easy to make because the world has a vast experience of coups in all their variety.

A muddled and meddlesome democratic process is sure to lead to a coup. Then there are other factors like a restive army, or general grumbling about the inefficient, even incompetent, political leadership. If a weak leadership panics and co-opts the army into running the country, then a military takeover is just a short step away. Yet another reason for a coup against the elected government is the weakening of the media and the judiciary.

It might seem convenient for the moment to chip away at their ability to question, but ultimately this becomes an exercise in self-deception. The weakened institutions cannot stop a usurper. Ideally, therefore, a working constitution and an efficient government are the best preventives against a coup. This is the perfect solution.

But it is our limitation that we are not perfect.

COUP-PROOFING

The ideal of perfection is seldom achieved in a democracy because we are not led by Gods. Our leaders are frail, made of flesh and blood, and their temptations are many. If democracies falter, autocracies do no better.

Invariably, autocracies succumb to what could be called the 'dictator trap'. The strategies they use to stay in power tend to trigger their downfall. Rather than being long-term planners, many make catastrophic short-term errors. Most dictators begin on a wrong note by crushing dissent and jailing opponents. It creates a culture of fear useful in establishing and maintaining control. But that culture of fear comes at a cost. The dictator starts living in a vacuum, far removed from the reality on ground where sullenness is brewing into revulsion.

Mere hatred is not enough because revolutions against

dictatorship are often frustrated by those they seek to overthrow. But the energy created by an unsuccessful revolutionary protest can trigger a process that builds momentum over weeks, months and years. When the dictator senses people's unease, he maintains a façade of calm. However, deep within, the dictator is afraid. This uneasy state of affairs between an autocrat and the people was described by Thomas Jefferson in this way:

> When government fears the people, there is liberty. When the people fear the government, there is tyranny.[22]

Can this gap be bridged? History tells us that has never been the case. The evidence of ages is that a dictator keeps accumulating power and authority to give him an aura of omnipotence. Such passion for power contains within it the seeds of hatred. Moreover, the fear that his good days may be getting over keeps a dictator on guard and wary of the plots against him. As a result, even the closest aide is not above suspicion.

Egypt's dictator President Hosni Mubarak made sure none of his senior officers was popular enough or smart enough to stage a coup. Field Marshal Mohamed Abd al-Halim Abu Ghazala, the defence minister, was his only rival. He had helped save the Mubarak regime by bringing in tanks when new military recruits rioted in 1986. But Mubarak dismissed him in 1989. In contrast, Field Marshal Mohamed Hussein Tantawi, who then took over as defence minister, was seemingly so obsequious that he was called 'Mubarak's poodle'. Yet, it was Tantawi who forced Mubarak out.[23]

Somewhat similar was the case in Pakistan. Prime Minister Zulfikar Ali Bhutto promoted General Zia-ul-Haq as army chief, superseding many other senior and more capable generals. Bhutto did so because he felt secure with a servile

Zia. Yet, it was he who staged a coup against Bhutto and later had him executed.

Though it is no insurance of their stay in power, such coup-proofing is typically a tactic of dictators. But it is also used in democracies. However, a coup need not always be physical in nature. Indira Gandhi felt that she was the victim of a judicial coup when her election was declared invalid by a High Court judgement. To counter it and to remain in power, she told a stunned nation in 1975, '*The President has proclaimed Emergency. There is nothing to panic about.*'[24] Her terse announcement over the All India Radio (AIR) marked the beginning of a 21-month period in India's history often described as one of the country's 'darkest hours'.

This is one example, but there are a variety of other options leaders can choose from as a 'coup-proofing' measure. These work in one of the two ways—they either aim to address grievances that may motivate coups, or aim to make coup attempts more difficult to carry out. A common strategy involves counterbalancing the military with other security forces, such as presidential guards, militarized police and militia independent from military control.

Many, if not most, democracies have at least one militarized police or another security force capable of counterbalancing the military. For instance, the relatively fragmented system of military and police power in the US was also designed, in some measure, to help prevent the military from becoming powerful enough to intervene in politics.[25] Similarly, in post-Independence India, leaders were acutely conscious of the risk of a coup. One aim of the expansion of the Central Reserve Police Force and other paramilitary forces in the 1960s was to contain the military's influence. By it the military was relieved of internal security tasks that would have brought it into domestic politics. After the assassination of PM Indira Gandhi, a new security force, the Special Protection Group (SPG), was created to protect the PM. One of the many reasons was that it should act as an immediate physical foil for the PM in case there was an attempt at a coup.[26]

It is equally true that in their methods of control, dictators are taking advantage of new technology for comprehensive surveillance of the population. As new methods and techniques evolve in this cat-and-mouse pursuit, human ingenuity will find newer ways of unseating the strongman and, conversely, the dictator will look for ever more effective methods of coup-proofing.

However, none of these measures are absolute. They give only partial protection. Ultimately it is sound policies, seen to be so by people, that offer maximum protection. But a dictator lacks the patience to put his ideas through the filter of bureaucracy. Hence, he takes many rash decisions.

It is the people who pay a price for these impulsive decisions, but by then, the authoritarian leader's attention has shifted to newer fancies. People, too, forget their recent sufferings and watch enraptured as the dictator unfolds for them yet another illusion. This cycle goes on endlessly because authoritarianism is second nature to all forms of life. Axiomatically, therefore, it exists as the oldest form of government.

Today, the world is at a stage where decreasing faith in democracy is driving the dominance of autocracy. Sadly therefore, democratic recession is underway in many countries. Even more worryingly, there is talk of democratic 'backsliding' on a global scale. A result of this almost constant state of tension is that the passage of life in a dictatorship is always cloudier than in a democracy.

POWER GRAB AND ITS CONSEQUENCES

Overall, and on their part, dictators are constantly on their guard. Their outward bravado is a put-on act, otherwise the possibility of a plot against them is their constant concern. Generally, therefore, they follow the following broad pattern to retain and maintain their hold on power:

- Capture elite support and, when necessary, demonize them too.
- Money, vast amounts of it, is essential even for autocrats to retain their hold on power. This is one of the reasons why they cultivate and support some oligarchs; just a few, not too many.
- The autocrat finds it convenient to rage against the country's past; finding fault with its history becomes a kind of neurosis for him.
- Most autocratic leaders exploit the fault-lines within complex societies to solidify their support. This they do through appeals to populism and nationalism. An often-used tactic is to promote fears about migrants and refugees. In some countries, religious nationalism has helped maintain an autocrat's power.
- By their very nature, authoritarian governments make laws and policies without seeking the opinion or consent of people.
- They control citizens' efforts to hold government accountable and repress dissent.
- They put restrictions on the funding of opposition parties by internal and external sources. They also place other bureaucratic limitations to silence dissenters.
- Authoritarian leaders strengthen their hold on power by simultaneously weakening the governmental

institutions that provide checks and balances. The usual technique is to extend executive power and cramp the ability of Parliament and the judiciary to question. The key is to use legal means to enhance and extend their hold on power.

- Since political parties have the organizational base to encourage a mass movement against the regime, it is a priority for the dictator to cripple the opposition. This they do by damaging the opposition parties, while not completely destroying them.

Among the many methods they use are those of infiltrating parties, co-opting their members and using scare tactics. The older and once often-used methods of vote-rigging and vote-buying as a path to power are no longer in the essential playbook of a potential dictator. The new tactics include hampering media access, gerrymandering, changing election and voter eligibility rules, and placing their favourites on the electoral commission.

Thus empowered, a dictator forgets that:

- At its moral centre, society is confronted by what remains an unspeakable truth: authoritarianism is reprehensible.
- Tyrannical longevity is the exception, not the rule.
- The more onerous the rule of an autocrat, the more the risk of his overthrow.
- People are essentially plural. And, as a wit once said, nothing succeeds like a successor.

The dictator should also remember that in the long term, only popular rule is sustainable. No amount of coup-proofing can save him from the denouement. Otherwise, the consequences for the dictator are as the Roman historian Suetonius wrote, '*The terror inspired by Caligula's reign could be judged by the sequel.*'[27] Romans were so terrified of Caligula that it was not enough to assassinate him. They wanted to *see* him dead.

Part 6: IN THE LONG RUN

20

ILL WINDS

A society's challenge is not the rise of and settling in of an authoritarian. This is now an established fact. The question that has puzzled successive generations is this: why does it happen? Why do people repeatedly get taken in and choose a despicable Trump over a relatively reliable Hillary?

Throughout the second half of the 20th century, dictators were a Third World phenomenon, tolerated in the West by being a convenient single-point reference for decisions favouring them. The countries behind the Iron Curtain were, almost in their entirety, ruled by strongmen. But they, and the condition of their people, did not bother the free world except to use them as a stick to shame them in human rights fora. But this millennium is different. Dictatorship has gained wide acceptance. It is no longer on the wrong side of a global argument between freedom and control. As the poet Dante Alighieri wrote in *Inferno*, '*all hope abandon* ye who enter here.'[1]

The big worry of our age is that with all the knowledge of the world available at a click, we still submit to a maverick despite knowing that an authoritarian's rule is arbitrary. It is a rule full of nasty surprises, where one of the key features is the absence of any reliable legal or political structure, and one where the citizen never knows when the knock on the door might come.

Few puzzles in political philosophy are more daunting than the problem of one-man rule over multitudes:

- Why does it happen over and over again?
- Why in the current stage of human development, when nature and science no longer hold many secrets, people are unable to spot and stop a strongman before he grabs power?

These questions are age-old, and there have been multiple attempts in history to explain them. But none of them provides a complete answer that fits all situations. One reason for this semi-failure is that human nature is complex and neither the ruler nor the ruled are alike everywhere and in all circumstances. Therefore, the answer we seek may be a combination of many factors:

- Is it because secretly we wish to be dominated?
- Is it because the capacity of the State matters more to people than the type of regime or its oppressive nature?
- Is it our principal concern that the machine called the State must run efficiently?
- Is it that the ends justify whatever be the means? Are people convinced that if the State is to perform optimally, it must maintain discipline? Is this why people feel only a strong hand can ensure it?

The absolute ruler on his part feels that total control is necessary for governance. As Shakespeare maintains in his play Richard II, '*We were not born to sue, but to command.*'[2]

But even in command, must a leader be a butcher? Is ruthlessness essential?

Unfortunately, this is the general case. It is human experience that the greatest political catastrophes occur at the intersection of ambition and desperation. A dictator's world is driven by both and, invariably, he makes controversy his currency.

From earliest times, those who ruled by force rose by adopting different methods. Sometimes, they supplemented the political means of obtaining power with a touch of drama. Once, Peisistratus of Athens went to a public function accompanied by a woman dressed as a goddess. The intention behind this elaborate charade was to suggest there was divine sanction for his rule.

Since then, the style may have changed but the substance of deception remains largely the same. And people continue to be deceived.

Consequently, absolute power is neither new nor variable. Its prevalence, whether now or in ancient times, has depended on physical superiority. In his celebrated work *The Republic*, Plato wrote about this phenomenon. '*The people have always some champion whom they set over them and nurse into greatness...This and no other is the root from which a tyrant springs; when he first appears above ground he is a protector.*'[3]

Plato's prescription has stood the test of time.

Centuries later, Dr B.R. Ambedkar put in a cautionary note on the extent of a people's gratefulness to a leader. In his final speech to the Constituent Assembly on 25 November 1949, he said:

> There is nothing wrong in being grateful to great men who have rendered life-long services to the country. But there are limits to gratefulness...[4]

That is the red line, a necessary reminder every time people begin to go overboard in their praise for a new leader. But emotions usually run unbridled and people tend to get carried away because an authoritarian leader's rhetoric is a carefully constructed emotive cocktail. Therein lies the rub. Adulation turns his head and feelings of grandeur overwhelm the new leader. He starts to believe he is the chosen one people needed.

PEOPLE ARE COMPLICIT

A dictator does not rise in a vacuum. He needs support for that initial ascent. Accordingly, a question that must be asked, but is not asked often enough and researched deeply enough, is: what is the role of a people in the rise of a dictator or a tyrant? Why do they aid a leader who disdains and discards people at will and has all the makings of an autocrat?

Is it because deep down every one of us is a control freak to some extent? After all, people are known to wish 'if only I could rule the world!'

Or, conversely, do they acquiesce out of fear?

The obvious answer is the fear of consequences—who will dare to be the first to raise the hand of defiance? In the rare case an attempt has been made, vested interests have stepped in. These 'interests' are part of the establishment, who one day hope to seize power just as the dictator did. It is in their interest a precedent is not established. So, dictator after dictator continues to oppress in the confidence that he would not have to account for his actions.

Khalil Gibran gives the stamp of his approval to this phenomenon. A free and proud people, he says, cannot be subjugated. '*And if it is a despot you would dethrone, see first that his throne erected within you is destroyed. For how can a tyrant rule the free and the proud, but for a tyranny in their own freedom and a shame in their own pride?*'

Since fear restrains people, the unchecked dictator rules

as fancy strikes him. Like a hedge-fund manager, he takes big risks because he is not playing with his own money. As he is not answerable to anyone in the State, he is willing to subject the country, and the wider world, to more risk. If and when he wins, it is because of luck, not brilliance.

Still, the dictator alone is not to be blamed because tyranny is as much facilitated by the evil of the leader as the indifference of citizens. The average, well-intentioned German who lived in Nazi Germany was paralysed with inaction, partly due to the fear of standing alone against the regime.

But there certainly are exceptions to this sense of fear. Gandhi and Nelson Mandela stood up against tyranny. In 1989, at Beijing's Tiananmen Square, a lone protester stood in front of a line of army tanks. It became one of the iconic photographs of the last century, symbolizing dare. There have been others too but, by and large, self-preservation overrides heroism.

Whichever term we might use for such inaction, this mass stasis is just the crack the dictator needs for stepping in and staying on. Thereafter, for their self-perception as well as international reputation, dictatorships require the acclamation and participation of large numbers of citizens. Consequently, people are condemned to faking enthusiasm for their oppressor. Adulation and constant endorsement are the dictator's oxygen. In the absence of free and fair elections, it is also their political legitimation. Therefore, unlike the ancient despotism, modern dictatorships tend to rely considerably on the involvement of masses. Naturally then, a streak common to most modern dictators is the ability to create an illusion of mass support while turning the population into a nation of terrorized prisoners.

YOUR SOCIETY IS DOOMED

However, a dictatorship is not the doctor's prescription for a society's ills. It cannot be because its arbitrary nature seldom leads to measured, balanced decisions. The result is ad hocism and favouritism. In such a scheme of governance, a few favourites prosper but society suffers. As author Ayn Rand wrote in *Atlas Shrugged*:

> When you see that money is flowing to those who deal, not in goods, but in favors—When you see that men get richer by graft and by pull than by work, and your laws don't protect you against them, but protect them against you—When you see corruption being rewarded and honesty becoming a self-sacrifice—You may know that your society is doomed.[5]

This sense of doom seems overwhelming as the present millennium progresses.

Our times are tough, and increasingly we will find ourselves looking for answers to questions of life and death. Will we survive the waves of pandemics and climate change? The global picture gets even more disheartening when people feel there is hardly a visionary leader in sight, that the world is being led by men of little wisdom. In such times, the desire for a capable guide, a mesmerizing leader, who boldly leaps across multiple disciplines to provide simple, confident answers, tying it all together, is understandable. Invariably, his solutions are not realistic.

Typically, dictators and the societies under them follow this broad pattern:

- Autocrats propose answers to complicated national issues that are simple, seductive and ultimately very wrong.

- They are good at targeting socially and economically vulnerable people. Autocrats exploit the rage and frustration of this section of the population through the psychological process of 'identification with the aggressor'.
- Adversity is not the only aspect that encourages extreme measures. The failure of political leadership is yet another temptation for the strongman to step in and take over. Ambition is also a strong motivation.
- Autocrats not only lie to others as a matter of course but also lie to themselves.
- Truth becomes relative when information threatens to overwhelm wisdom.
- Once an autocrat gains power, he disrupts and defeats checks and balances.
- In an autocrat's polarized world, productive disagreement is a rare occurrence.
- The normal set of politicians do not have the language to disrupt the reality-concealing rhetoric of autocrats.

■

Anglo-Irish philosopher Edmund Burke had put it pithily when he said, *'The greater the power, the more dangerous the abuse.'*

Not surprisingly, a dictator seldom follows the straight line. This impunity, the confidence he is the unquestioned and unquestionable supreme leader, is in large part because of the feeling that no one will dare raise an enquiring eyebrow. As George Orwell put it, *'During times of universal deceit, telling the truth becomes a revolutionary act.'*[6]

For instance, in 1940, Mao promised the Chinese people a multi-party system, democratic freedoms and protection of private property. Within two years, he reversed the policy with the Rectification Campaign, seizing anything privately owned, including independent thought. Mao's Communist Party, like the Bolsheviks, the Fascists and the Nazis, was held together not so much by a programme or a platform, but by a chosen leader. These arbitrary turns are in practice again in China where Xi is the supreme leader of everything. Businesses and the media have ever-narrower space to function in China because of the abrupt limits set by him.

Xi's case is yet another proof that when a dictator is in power, the only things which stand between people and the dictator are wakefulness of reason and restrictions imposed by law. The carefully nurtured structure of 'institutions' in democracies is that great wall which protects people. Once that gets attacked by the dictator, this last safety net crumbles.

Still, all iron fists are not clumsy economists. Many Asian strongmen have reigned over tiger economies. But they are exceptions to the general experience that a dictator takes a nation's economy into a desperate dive. Myanmar and Zimbabwe were two such cases. In Myanmar, the military's erratic policies sometimes caused prices to rise threefold. There were periods of such deprivation that many parents went without food to feed their children. In Zimbabwe, hyperinflation under President Robert Mugabe left the currency just as valuable as the paper it was printed on. People were reduced to poaching wildlife, from hippos to squirrels, simply to survive.[7]

A list of such dictatorial mis-actions can be fairly comprehensive, for their blunders are not limited to poor economics. For instance, unlike many dictators, Napoleon was exceptionally brilliant, but he also had a capacity for catastrophic errors. De Gaulle thought of Napoleon as a rare genius that only appears once in a millennium, but also blamed him for squandering French power and prestige: '*He left France smaller than he found her.*'[8] As with France after Napoleon, a dictatorial rule generally leaves the country in a sorry state.

Still, the dictator's people tend to overlook the enormous burden of proof against him. Instead, they tend to latch on to a single positive stroke as the sign of genius. Hitler's shrewdness in asserting that Stalin would trust him not to invade Russia, or that France was not prepared to fight, was enough to convince his followers of his genius.

Like Hitler, a dictator pushes the society into darker realms where optimism becomes a form of faith. Curiously, an authoritarian still remains a symbol of a nation's emotional conflicts, a blank slate on which people can project their prejudices, hopes and fears.

Essentially, people have an ambivalent relationship with dictators and dictatorship. They welcome its promise of strength, but dread its brutal practice. Therefore, in a curiously masochistic way, the story of absolutism has not yellowed with time.

Many other things, too, have not changed over time. There's a high degree of megalomania in dictators who refuse to surrender power. Their absolute power, it seems, not only corrupts; it can also confuse them. A common thread among them is a fundamental miscalculation that their end stares them in the face. For months, rebels encouraged Gaddafi to leave. But he showed no interest in fleeing, till the day the rebels stormed into his compound in Tripoli. By then it was too late. Likewise, Hitler did not talk in terms of his own lifetime. He talked in terms of 'the next thousand years'.[9]

Eventually, however, disillusionment creeps in like late afternoon shadows. Inevitably, then, like Hitler, Gaddafi, Ceausescu and many others, the dictator gets overthrown.

After him, the torture chambers are the first to be opened.

The electrical cables and bloodstains splattered there testify to his crimes. Sometimes, the torturers keep meticulous records, taking pictures up to and including the subject's gruesome death. As light shines into those fetid cells, emotional cleansing begins.[10]

This ritual is essential to warn people of what could happen again.

Yet, the cycle never ends. Sadly, therefore, after all the '-isms' are dead and buried, when the government remains just as an illusion, even then dictatorship will prevail. Democracy may get ushered in another time, but it is invariably a temporary shelter for societies, only to be flattened by the winds of a strong hand.

Alas, ill winds do not cease.

This is the truth of all ages; the ones long gone by, those within our memory and of our own age. It will also be the truth of our tomorrows.

21

A CASE FOR DEMOCRACY

In about 380 BC, Plato asked, '*Does not tyranny spring from democracy*?'[1]

History has repeatedly proved Plato right because democracy has often squiggled to let a dictator slip in. Once he grabs power, the future begins to look dark for that state.

This act of grabbing power by a strongman is neither innocent nor an escapist's relief. It has never been attractive or likable in its effect. Instead, it is a phase of cruelty, fear, exploitation, even slaughter. Therefore, though there is enough evidence in support of Plato's assertion that tyranny springs from democracy, it will be fair to add the rider it is not the fault of the democratic system when dictators inveigle themselves into power.

As against Plato's pessimistic observation, Cicero provided hope and an alternative. He advocated a middle path, an amalgamation of the best in each system:

> Of the three forms of government, monarchy, aristocracy, and the people, the best is a mixture of all three for each one taken on its own can lead to disaster. Kings can be capricious, aristocrats, self-interested, and an unbridled multitude enjoying unwanted power more terrifying than a conflagration or a raging sea.[2]

Cicero here issues a cautionary note that it is not the theory of governance in a system but its practice that makes the crucial difference. Since Cicero is advocating balance in governance, let me assume he is hinting at something approximating democracy.

To carry on along his line of thinking, let me delve for a bit into the foundations of democracy. As a start, let me begin with the concept of liberalism.

At its core, the liberal assumption is that man is a rational being, not evil by nature. It prioritizes the protection of individual rights, including freedom of thought, religion and lifestyle. In essence, liberalism concerns the limit of power. It is a citizen's lifeline against mass opinion and abuses of government power.

It is these essentials that led to democracy. Yet, and this is the ironic twist, democracy is also about the accumulation of power and its use. As a result, the tension between liberalism and democracy is about the extent of governmental authority. For this reason, many eighteenth- and nineteenth-century liberals saw in democracy a force that could undermine liberty.

Because democracy is a double-edged sword of liberty/tyranny, it is necessary to restrain the powers and the reach of governments. That is best done through a Constitution that limits the actions of majorities, whether directly or indirectly, through their elected representatives.

Once constitutional safeguards are in place, and in fair practice, a country is well on its path to sound democracy. Then, a government formed by the vote of a population is considered a hard-won right for people. These are the basic building blocks of a democracy, further intertwined with freedom of speech, an independent press, and the right of people for peaceful assembly for political and cultural reasons. Such a freely elected government represents the people's hope that it will protect citizens from arbitrary and unrestrained power. This is how it should ideally be.

DESTINED TO PERISH

It does not always play out this way. An appeal to democracy can be a smokescreen for majoritarian tyranny.

Take, for instance, the case of Donald Trump. In four years of his presidency, he managed to pull down America from the lofty perch of the greatest democracy in the world. In his last days in office, he exceeded himself by virtually leading an insurrection against his own office! But why blame the democratic system for the events of those few days when American democracy was precariously poised on the brink? It is the people who must be blamed for electing a self-absorbed person like Trump as their President.

That he was monumentally unfit to be the President of America was evident even before his political campaign began. As far back as 1990, a *Vanity Fair* report quoted Trump's ex-wife, Ivana, assaying that her husband kept a book of Hitler's speeches in a cabinet near his bed.[3] Others allege that Trump's phrase 'Make America Great Again' resembles Hitler's slogan 'Make Germany Great Again.' Yet, he was elected President.

Since this man guided America's destiny for four long years and influenced the world in many ways, can America still claim to be the greatest democracy in every respect? The fact is that Trump's four years has left America a flawed and divided democracy. That, plus an increasing global trend favouring authoritarian leaders, raises a question like never before in living memory: is democracy losing the battle?

Admittedly, this is neither a new concern nor a new

debate. It has engaged thinkers long enough for us to ask: how far is the world today from the ideal envisioned by the seventeenth-century Enlightenment philosopher John Locke? He had said all humans were endowed with 'natural rights' and that government existed to protect those rights. If it did not, people had the right to overthrow it.[4]

Alexander Hamilton, founding father of America, added to this line of argument. He elaborated on what he felt were the '*sacred rights of mankind*'. He said they were not to be found among '*parchments or musty records*' but were '*written, as with a sunbeam...by the hand of the divinity itself.*' They could never be '*erased or obscured by mortal power.*'[5]

Essentially, both Locke and Hamilton were alluding to the Constitution as a guarantee of people's rights. The idea may not have been formalized by then, but the seed was sown. A sound, well-thought-out Constitution and the separation of powers between the executive, legislature and judiciary were and have been the perfect foil against the authoritarian hand. This is essentially what the two were also advocating.

Alas, the world has changed enormously since then. So has people's value system. An American actor and director Orson Welles aptly reflected this shift:

> In Italy for thirty years under the Borgias, they had warfare, terror, murder, and bloodshed but they produced Michelangelo, Leonardo da Vinci, and the Renaissance. In Switzerland, they had brotherly love; they had five hundred years of democracy and peace and what did that produce? The cuckoo clock.[6]

The questions that follow are:

- Does Renaissance excuse the gore of the leader?
- Do works of art, howsoever great they are, wipe out the blood splattered on Florentine roads?

- And why blame democracy if the Swiss did not produce a Michelangelo?

A cuckoo clock does not diminish Swiss democracy, even by the tiniest bit. It is a harmless pursuit that hurts no one. That's why among the many qualities that recommend democracy, this stands out.

Overall, though, democracy is not flawless. But then nothing in the world is utterly perfect, and so is the case with democracy.

It is true democracy admits variety and allows criticism. This is the promise. But between promise and performance there can be a gulf. For example, when Augustus became the ruler of ancient Rome, the first impression he gave was of wanting to democratize. As it turned out, it was only a superficial impression. He seduced the army with bonuses, and his cheap food policy was the successful bait for the general population. So far so good. But, as Tacitus noted, he '*gradually pushed ahead and absorbed the functions of the senate, the officials and even the law*.'[7]

It wasn't just Augustus. The norm has been that democracy invariably morphs into dictatorship. But has it never happened the other way round? If we dig deep into times long past, Emperor Ashoka had this transformation, but his was an exceptional case of personality renewal.

Things may change occasionally, new governments may form and democracy may get ushered in again, but history is not erased by change. A basic assumption of political realism is that the international system is ultimately anarchic. That is why it is necessary to recall every so often this warning by Mussolini: '*The liberal state is destined to perish*.'[8]

DEMOCRACY LOSING GROUND

Dictators rise, ever so often, from the ashes of hope that long-lasting democracy will prevail. Towards the end of last century, for instance, there was a glimmer of hope that the time had come for the argument to be settled in favour of democracy. It was claimed then that democracy alone was timelessly human. Consequently, the second half of the twentieth century was the 'age of accountability'. With the exceptions of East Europe and China, democracy seemed to prevail globally. This was especially so in its last decade.

As a result, the last millennium ended on a celebratory note. The Soviet empire had imploded. The Iron Curtain had fallen. There were the Velvet, Orange, Tulip and Rose revolutions. Military dictatorships had lost their mojo. People power seemed to matter. For a brief while, democracy enjoyed a near global victory. But the Cinderella moment that followed was sudden and nasty.

The folding over to a new calendar was accompanied not by a drumroll, but by the grim tidings of a 'millennium horribilis'. Now, in retrospect, it also seems the Cold War was not a final showdown. It was just a confrontation of the moment. The battle of ideas and ideologies carries on. The big difference from the Cold War is that Russia and China are yet to form a supporting bloc of countries, but efforts are on.

Puzzled by its unexpectedness, people began asking what happened to democracy. China and Russia questioned the very concept of democracy propounded by the West, and claimed that its time had passed. China's best-known sci-fi writer, Liu Cixin, commented sharply, '*If China were to transform into a democracy, it would be hell on earth.*'[9]

This doubt is increasingly being expressed by others as well. Is democracy the ideal system for economic reform, or is dictatorship the need when radical change is required?

Opinion on it is divided because China's economic success under communism contrasts with the difficulties of Putin's democracy in Russia.

There is also the other view that even within democracies the success or otherwise of reforms differs. Over the years, direct or indirect, military rule in democratic Pakistan has brought it to economic disaster to such an extent that its Prime Minister Shehbaz Sharif admitted it shamed him to extend his hand to other countries for financial aid.[10] The success of democracies of Central Europe points in the opposite direction.

However, the success or otherwise of societies cannot be measured by the type of governance alone. It is vital but there are other factors as well, ranging from geographical location and natural resources to the fated destiny of a people. A case in point is Afghanistan. Is it the fault of the Afghan people that their land has nearly forever remained the epicentre of the Great Game? Afghans suffer sullenly; their sighs go unheard because every new player of the Great Game carries on regardless.

This is not the first time the battle between liberalism and authoritarianism has become the cause of philosophical angst. The issue was vigorously engaged with during the nineteenth century. It was the original ideological confrontation and has episodically remained so since then.

However, what is new this time, and much more so than during the Cold War, is the global dimension of it, and the fact that China under Xi is unabashed in its pursuit. The militarily ambitious, authoritarian leader is no longer satisfied with his territorial limits. He tries to expand his influence, and his imprint, beyond his country's borders. Xi, who is deeply ideological in his personal commitment to authoritarianism, is a worrying example of this syndrome.

It was alarming enough for US President Biden to remark in February 2021, '...*We're at an inflection point between those who argue that autocracy is the best way forward...and those who understand that democracy is essential...*'[11]

In April, he was even more emphatic in arguing that the world was at a critical stage in determining '*whether or not democracy can function in the 21st century*.'[12]

At the other end of the globe, President Xi was quick to respond, '*China must never follow the path of Western constitutionalism, separation of powers, or judicial independence*.'[13] With this, he gave authoritarians of the world a reference point, and democracies a warning.

After initial hesitancy, driven largely by Chinese inducements and Trump's waywardness, Western European countries too agree that a new phase of struggle against creeping authoritarianism has begun. Already two broad constellations of countries are emerging in the world—one of democracies and the other of autocracies.

Autocrats worry that the free flow of information, the pull of democracy, and economic interdependence will destabilize their regimes. Democrats are concerned that the autocracies led by China will undermine freedom and democracy, pushing international rules in an illiberal direction.

Democrats have a reason to agonize because people are often seduced by illusion, ignoring what stares them in plain sight. The pull of authoritarianism, as an easy cure-all for society's ills, is addictive.

Its appeal is strong enough for someone like Voltaire, who otherwise supported the liberal freedoms of speech and religion, to soothingly tell Catherine the Great, '*Almost nothing great has ever been done in the world except by the genius and firmness of a single man combating the prejudices of the multitude*.'[14]

In this effort to please the Empress, Voltaire was going against his own better judgement. He should have remembered that when institutions weaken, tyranny begins. As history has shown time and again, democracies prevent the worst excesses of a predatory leader because he can be voted out of office. But there are no checks on the predatory power of dictators because:

- No one watches over them and gives an end-of-the-term assessment of their performance through the year.
- Whatever they know is enough for them, once and for all. They don't want to find out about anything else, since that might diminish the force of their arguments.

Charles Bukowski has put the issue succinctly: '*The difference between a democracy and a dictatorship is that in a democracy you vote first and take orders later; in a dictatorship, you don't have to waste your time voting.*'

UNIVERSAL DEMOCRACY: A PIPE DREAM?

Will there ever come a moment when everyone in the world is free of dictators and autocrats? Even if there isn't democracy in its fullest form everywhere, will there come a time when there is at least a semblance of it in every country?

The blunt answer is a big 'no'. Our experience cautions us that hoping for a dictator-free world is a piece of fiction.

Universal democracy will remain a dream for us and for our generations to follow.

However, all is not lost; at least not yet. When all is said and done, the idea of democracy is the ultimate refuge. It is a fragile place in some ways, but an indestructible one. When it is broken, we rebuild it because we need shelter.

One key to strengthening democracy is to give people the freedom of free speech, the right to argue. Argument makes us human; it is the foundation of democracies. A good argument is not just about persuading the other person, it is equally about openness to being persuaded yourself.

But I should add here a note of caution.

Fine words have to be combined with wisdom and a concern for morality. Without these fundamentals, rhetorical flourishes distract rather than enlighten. Argument can also be dangerous. Maliciously used, it can sow divisions and obscure facts rather than reveal the truth. Since argument can work both ways, the future of democracy will depend on rediscovering how to argue well.

Great democracies also acknowledge that great minds don't think in parallel rhymes. They challenge each other to think again. As American writer Walter Lippmann observed, '*Where all think alike, no one thinks very much.*'

That's why the ultimate purpose of debate is not to produce consensus, it is to promote critical thinking. And we must always remember a good debate is not about one person declaring victory, it is about both sides making a discovery.

There are other reasons to hope democracy may still prevail. One of the pressure cooker-style components of a democracy is its parliament. It is a nationally authorized forum where both sides can let off steam to the extent that people can say all is well. Parliament is designed to enable the opposition to have its say and for the government to have its way. If the former is not possible, parliament as a democratic institution cannot survive for long.

Therefore, even as hope lingers, there are signs of concern. That's why heavy-duty governments are being sanctioned by people who feel that Western democracy is falling apart. On the other side, there is the temptation of rulers to encircle parliamentary democracies and subordinate institutions.

The promises they make during elections, of reforms and redemption, are quickly forgotten. Instead dark money, lobbying, patronage and tighter links between government, loyal journalists and the corporate world proliferate. Democracy then begins to mean miserable failure of governance. For all practical purposes, it begins to cede space to the top-down rule by the few of the many. It is because of practices like these that democracies begin to serve as incubators of despotism.

It is this sense of inevitability about creeping authoritarianism, and the feeling of gloom about the state of democracy, that worries people.

Once again, the battle between autocracy and democracy has begun. The tussle promises to be long and hard, and democracy will surely suffer bruises, as will the other side. But people's will and constitutional safeguards give it the strength that an autocrat lacks. In the end, and as was the case with the Cold War, chances are that democracy might prevail.

Indeed, it should prevail because democracy is not a luxury. It is the heart of humanity, the essence of human existence. It has the strength to tell us we can break barriers and be open-minded, that we can tell stories that need to be told.

For a moment, imagine a world without freedom. Will it not be desolate?

22

DEMOCRACY AND DICTATORSHIP

'Just when the gods ceased to be and the Christ had not yet come, there was a unique moment in history, between Cicero and Marcus Aurelius, when man stood alone. Nowhere else do I find that particular grandeur.'[1]

The French writer Gustave Flaubert, who wrote this, was celebrated both as a romantic and a realist. If his idyllic longing for a grand world was reflected in these words, the realistic side of him made him pause reflectively and caution:

The melancholy of the antique world seems to me more profound than that of the moderns...[2]

That comparison with our ancients seems a bit unfair. After all, they too had their tyrants and autocrats. They too suffered like subsequent generations have. But it is not my intention to argue with Flaubert's nostalgic wish. It is merely to say that democracy, too, can be boring if it becomes predictable. It is also to say that not too long after people get bored with democracy and autocracy creeps in, we too whisper wistfully:

I only know that summer sang in me
A little while, that in me sings no more.[3]

Alas, this is the state of the world today. If democracy is timelessly human, autocracies are a child of our times. This, notwithstanding the historical proof that autocracies result in crippling handicaps in innovation and economic growth.

Despite such bitter evidence, dictatorships, monarchies, oligarchies and other forms of authoritarian rule have been the common form of human governance. In comparison, democracies have been mere blips in history. As a generally accepted practice, the democratic form of governance in the world has barely lasted a century so far.

All of a sudden, when it was at the point of prevailing everywhere, democracy started losing ground to autocracy. What caused this abrupt turn? Why should it have happened when the world seemed content? Perhaps it is the fate of man never to be completely at ease; no form of life is fully satisfactory to him. In this churn, illiberal demagogues tend to prevail.

While acknowledging the issue's complexity, let me also focus on the political dynamic of the moment. At present, the debate is not about the gradual eclipsing of democracy by authoritarianism, or the creeping resentment against authoritarian regimes. It is about the helplessness of people and their frustration that all the political systems tried by the world, so far, have fallen short of their promise. It must have been in anticipation of this failure that Aristotle feared democracy would feed on itself and thereby destroy itself.

The term 'democratic deficit' best describes this slide. It is fundamental to an understanding of the rage so evident these days. Paraphrasing Aristotle in the present context might be a way of rationalising this rage. He might have said, in frustration, words to this effect: if democracy is the art of anger management, autocracy, like violence, shutters reality.

Public anger is also about the way it has led to uneven social outcomes. An expression of this anger has been the rise of fearful xenophobia. It has been expertly exploited for personal political gains by populist politicians.

Meanwhile, yet another disappointment was taking hold. The big advantage of liberalism against the other '-isms' was its decentralized approach to decision making. This allowed liberal democracies to out-compete authoritarian states in politics and economics. This had been so till China came along with a blistering economic performance. Fortunately, China is an exception and we are yet to see how long it can maintain its pace.

There is another departure from the past.

The technology that favoured democracy is changing. Social media may still raise its voice in favour of liberal ideas and practices. Idealized youth and left liberals may continue to fume on X against restrictive regimes. But theirs is a short-lived sensation, that too if the tweet catches attention and goes viral.

All along, the authoritarian leader gnaws at the multiplicity of social media. The autocrat wants his voice to drown out dissent. Increasingly, AI will ensure it is so because the autocrat will control the instruments of AI.

There are other ways in which autocrats transform. When they are seeking power, they draw strength from crowds. Once in power, they become distant and reserved. Therefore, the difference between charismatic leadership and the cult of personality is the distinction between democracy and dictatorship.

NARROWING GAP

A charismatic leader draws energy from the crowd; he must be among them and show himself regularly, whether he is campaigning for elections or settled in power. But a dictator promotes the cult of his personality. Almost all such are convinced that their appeal and authority grow on an element of mystique. So, a dictator feels he cannot show himself too often.

This difference between the conduct of a democratic leader in power and that of a dictator is the space between the truth and the image.

A dictator can be omniscient only by being unpredictable. Stalin and Hitler both remained hidden for much of the war. Mao's portraits were everywhere, as were books and pamphlets of his thoughts, but he was rarely seen in public. In sharp contrast, Nehru would gladly plunge into the crowd and so would Clinton, to smilingly pump hands. But a Saddam, Gaddafi or Kim would scoff at the idea.

Moreover, a dictator can be whimsical.

On 29 December 1675, King Charles II issued an edict calling for the suppression of coffee-houses.[4] Three centuries later, during the Emergency imposed on India by his mother, Sanjay Gandhi had New Delhi's famous Coffee House in Connaught Place shut down.[5] The King withdrew his edict a fortnight later in deference to popular outcry, but the Coffee House in India's capital remained shut throughout the period of Emergency.[6]

The decision to shut the coffee house wasn't just whimsical; it was grave in its effect. A dictator discourages conversation as it might pollute people's minds with a different view. Free speech is always, therefore, under attack from intolerant rulers and usurpers. They don't care if their actions hurt the fundamental aspirations of a society and its basic premise that people are essentially plural. And they forget this simple point: if you stifle thought, where do you find the thinker?

This is so at the political level as well. If the government and the opposition are not on speaking terms, democracy cannot be sustained. If people can converse, democracy will be the richer for their talent.

It is, of course, convenient for a leader, be it in a democracy or a dictatorship, to issue edicts and to be obeyed. It is only natural because the State fears that if the rights of the individual are encouraged and promoted, they weaken correspondingly its authority and its ability to set limits for individuals. Still, democracies hesitate in exercising this option freely. In authoritarian States, though, this dilemma is quickly decided by the leader in his favour.

If this is so, it might be fair to conclude that the difference between a democracy and a dictatorship is one of degree.

As the examples of Trump, Erdogan and many others show, the gap between the two is reducing. Their examples lead to the worrying thought that governance of all kinds, be it dictatorial or democratic, is driven by the self-interested effort of a leader to acquire and keep power. In that prism, 'bad behaviour' is also 'good politics'.

Let me view this gap, or rather the narrowing gap, between a democracy and a dictatorship from another angle. It is often said that the Western countries are reasonably dictator-proof.

Till the turn of this millennium, it was largely the case. Now, with rightist leaders in place in some European countries, does it not sound like overstating the issue?

There is another development that is blurring the distinction between an authoritarian leader and a strongman leading a democracy.

The challenge is efficacy of governance. The test here is the delivery, which either sustains leaders and systems or undermines them. Did the leader have a plan for his country's future, and was he able to deliver on its promise? A great leader works to take the country beyond the circumstances he inherited.

A dictator fails that test of imagination; he is distracted by his vision of the possible. If a democrat has a reasonably clear vision for the future of his people, a dictator thinks of the here and now. His vision for the future is tainted by a strong desire for immortality, and shackled by hubris. This is certainly their big difference. But even here there are exceptions; dictators like Xi have a long-term plan for their country.

There is also the matter of style where the distinction between the two is getting blurred.

Many democrats, like dictators, frown at criticism. Rather than shutting down dissenting voices, both types of leaders have learned to harness the democratizing power of social media for their own purposes—jam the signals and sow confusion.

A case from Turkey illustrates this well.

President Erdogan did not take kindly to the reportage by the Dogan Yayin media group. Among its other publications, the group owns the country's widely-read newspaper *Hurriyet*, which had been carrying a series of articles against Erdogan. Finally, the enraged Erdogan gave the nod to the country's tax authorities to go after the Dogan Yayin group for tax evasion. It was all done legally, of course, with apparent investigation and considerable paper work. In the end, the company was fined $2.5 billion.[7] The Dogan group had to sell its major assets to pay the fine. It didn't surprise people that the only companies bidding for these lucrative assets were media groups friendly to the regime.

This case, shocking as it was, left people wondering if there was any shade of democracy in Erdogan's autocratic ways. But Erdogan is not the only one of his kind. The world today is flush with rulers who are arbitrary and whimsical.

THE PROGNOSIS IS DARK

In the spring of 2010, a coalition of opposition groups ousted Kyrgyzstan's dictatorial President Kurmanbek Bakiyev.[8] Watching it from a distance, a group of activists in Africa cheered, '*One coconut down, 39 more to harvest*!'[9]

The activists were only half-right with their simile. Dictators are tough as a coconut, but they are rarely known for a soft inside. To their credit, the activists were on the mark with their numbers, though only for a moment. At that time, there were at least 40 dictators around the world. It was a worryingly big number, which should have decreased over time. Instead, it has increased.

According to the annual survey of freedom conducted by the Freedom House, political rights and civil liberties were diminished in 52 countries between 2023 and 2024.[10] Freedom House defines a dictator as the ruler of a land rated 'Not Free' by it.[11]

The report further states that only 60 per cent of the world's countries are democratic—far more than the 28 per cent in 1950, yet not much more than a majority. Moreover, many of these are not democracies in the true sense of the word. They are ruled by despots in disguise. Some others are a halfway house between democracy and dictatorship.

Another report from the V-Dem (Varieties of Democracy) Institute at the University of Gothenburg in Sweden maintains that by the end of 2022, 72 per cent of the world's population (5.7 billion people) lived in autocracies, out of which 28 per cent (2.2 billion people) lived in 'closed autocracies'.[12] This makes it a very large size of the global population under siege.

It is unlikely that there is an exact, or at least a reasonably informed, count of the damage done to societies by dictators. The very nature of these regimes discourages intrusive outside interest. Still, a broad guess would put the overall loss in material terms, and of human lives, as humongous. Millions of lives have been lost, economies have collapsed, and whole States have failed under brutal repression. What makes it worse is the apathy of a world that has mostly been in denial. Generally, the outside world watches with indifference, leaving people to their fate.

It is natural, then, for people to ask whether the number of dictatorships is going to increase or decrease in future. A decrease does not seem likely because the conditions that give rise to authoritarian rule have not changed. Rather, there will be many more points of crisis in future—Covid-19 and its ill-effects being one such, and economic recession, social strife and war being others. Sadly, we are unlikely to see the end of dictatorship anytime soon. In some measure, the fault lies with people themselves.

Despite the overwhelming historical evidence that dictators only give the illusion of hope, and are in fact destructive of the fundamentals of a society, people are not averse to yet another authoritarian spell. According to a 2017 survey conducted by the Pew Research Center (PEW), autocracy is not universally opposed:

> Roughly four in ten Italians (43%)...and a similar share of the British (42%)...say a strong leader making decisions would be good for their country. Nearly half of Russians (48%) back governance by a strong leader. In Asia, 55% of Indians, 52% of Indonesians and 50% of Filipinos favour autocracy. Such support is particularly intense in India, where 27% very strongly back a strong leader.[13]

But people's views showed a dramatic shift against strong rule in countries that had recently been led by an authoritarian. '*Roughly eight in ten Venezuelans (81%) and 71% of Hungarians opposed* a strong leader.'[14]

Overall, the prognosis warns of hard times. In periods like these, when large parts of the world are under authoritarian regimes, and when most of the world is led by leaders of varying wisdom, pessimism becomes a dark form of realism.

In such times, the weaknesses of democracies may be more evident, but they are less damaging than those of autocracies. In the ultimate sense, then, responsibility rests with people. They must make the prudent choice while selecting their leader. As Octavia Butler wrote,

> Choose your leaders with wisdom and forethought.
> To be led by a coward is to be controlled by all that the coward fears.
> To be led by a fool is to be led by the opportunists who control the fool.
> To be led by a thief is to offer up your most precious treasures to be stolen.
> To be led by a liar is to ask to be told lies.
> To be led by a tyrant is to sell yourself and those you love into slavery.[15]

All this is true and well said by Butler, but she puts excessive faith in the wisdom of people. Therefore a word of caution must be added.

Almost the worst failing of people is the lack of judgement. Had it been otherwise, democracy would not have remained an unfinished project.

23

DICTATOR'S LONGEVITY

The rise to the top is relatively easy for a tyrant or a dictator.

At the most, it may require killing a few. If it is a bloodless coup, it is simpler still; all he needs to do is march up to the palace or the prime ministerial compound and arrest the occupant and his close aides. From then on, he is the ruler.

But even if a dictator seems invincible in power, deep within he remains conscious of two threats—to his life and to his rule. To counter these, the dictator sets up protective rings of associates around him where real decisions are made. Monarchs, for instance, have generally relied on consultative councils for advice. They also appoint family members to head key positions such as defence, internal security and finance. This is the norm in Saudi Arabia and other sheikhdoms in the Gulf States. By co-opting religious leaders as well and keeping the population reasonably happy with extensive subsidies, the rulers in these oil-rich states have had a long and relatively trouble-free run.

There are also cases where a democrat turns a dictator over time. This is so with Erdogan of Turkey who has been in power since 2003, first as Prime Minister and then as

President. In this long stay at the top, once he crushed the military's powerful role as the protector of Turkey's Constitution, there was no limit to his power.

Like him, Putin has had a long stay at the top since 1999. He has not been threatened with a coup, so far. His approval ratings remain high though he has been troubled almost constantly by his political opponents. There are others like Assad in Syria who have somehow carried on governing, but with a constant sense of foreboding.

In most cases of military dictatorship, real power lies with the governing junta. They are usually the former military colleagues of the dictator. This is the way successive military dictators have ruled in Pakistan. Occasionally, they allow the farce of an election and even let a PM be elected. But all that is for show. The PM is a marionette,while the dictator continues to hold all the levers of power.

Yet, all these are at best tactical moves; they do not ensure longevity. What is it, then, that helps a dictator stay on in power? Is there a formula for longevity at top that he can follow?

This seems unlikely. If there were such a guide, it would also prescribe right action and the rule of law—something that a dictator is least likely to follow. The sad reality is that there exists no laid-down set of rules to guide a dictator on this score. Even incompetent dictators can continue to survive, as long as economic shocks are not too large.

Broadly, the dictator's survival at top depends not so much on preventing citizens from expressing their willingness to rebel, but on manipulating public beliefs about the state of the country and the incumbent's type.

Over centuries, various strongmen have attempted different methods, providing insight into strategies to maintain power. Among them, the prime would be:

- The dictator should rely on as small a circle of advisors as possible.
- No aide/advisor should be considered indispensable.
- His supporters must be rewarded for their loyalty, and all potential rivals ruthlessly suppressed.

Above all, dictators survive because they are the strongest as long as they control the security apparatus of the country. They do so by keeping the army and the intelligence services on their side. Dictators like Mobutu Sese Seko, Pervez Musharraf and Idi Amin were army officers themselves who co-opted the military in order to overthrow democracies.

VICTIMS OF THEIR OWN NAIVETY

Once a population comes under a dictator's control, people find it very difficult to dislodge him. As Voltaire noted, the fear of a failed attempt immobilizes them: '*So long as the people do not care to exercise their freedom, those who wish to tyrannize will do so.*'[1]

On his part, a dictator does not seize power in order to cede it. From his point of view, the logic is simple: *he had to dislodge the previous regime because it was incompetent and ruinous for the country*. After taking over, he has been able to set the country on course to development and prosperity.

This may not be so in reality, but this is what he believes. Since a dictator is resistant to reason, he convinces himself that if he were to relinquish power, the country would slide back to its regressive ways under a civilian leader.

These are but excuses to stay on. The widely acknowledged fact is that the desire for power is rooted deep in human nature and is potentially limitless. As George Orwell wrote in *1984*, '*We know that no one ever seizes power with the intention of relinquishing it.*'[2]

But a dictator's desire for power is not enough to keep him there. He needs to broad-base his support beyond the security apparatus. To do so, he has to carry with him as large a section of the population as possible.

While it suits the authoritarian's purposes perfectly, the effectiveness of propaganda in authoritarian regimes is a puzzle. If the citizens know the dictator has an incentive to lie, why do they ever listen?

- They listen because the dictator co-opts them in the web of dreams he weaves.
- He makes them believe that together they can launch a project that will make the nation great and the people prosperous.
- This cadre of his followers and admirers are convinced that his actions reflect their own innermost urges.

In this way, they refuse to give in to reason or evidence to the contrary. These didactic convictions ensure that they, and their leader, remain unchallenged for the most part. Steadily, however, the dictator's rhetoric gets ahead of the policymaking; it raises expectations that everything is going to change.

Consequently, a dictator survives because he convinces people, rightly or wrongly, that he is competent. Beyond the dictator's personal charisma and people's messianic faith, it is also their shared ideological project that cements the bond between him and his followers.

Hitler used symbols from Germany's history to good effect—for example, the use of the colours red, black and white, the colours of imperial Germany. Both Hitler and Mussolini also stressed their link to the glory of the past by commissioning neo-classical government buildings and using symbols from antiquity.

Alongside, a dictator also keeps a stern eye and a strong arm ready because:

- The hostility of masses is free-floating. Knowing this, a dictator does not invite a discussion by people.
- A dictator's rule quickly loses the flexibility and suppleness that informs a democracy.
- The essence of tyranny lies in the absence of constraints or limits. This is so not just in the pursuit and the form of power, but also in the means employed to maintain it. Therefore, the defining mark of a tyrant is impunity in power. He institutionalizes vigilantism, violence and hate into the very core of society.

Ultimately, it is the people who are to blame for a strongman ruling over them. This basic truth may have compelled T.S. Eliot to write: '*If you will not have God (and He is a jealous God), you should pay your respects to Hitler or Stalin.*'[3]

Eliot was reflecting the temper of his times, a declining religiosity in Western societies and the rise of authoritarianism. But if he were to revisit his words today and phrase them in the tempo of the present times of nationalism and religion, he might have said: *You can have a package; God as also a Hitler or a Stalin.*

The result is that people become the victims of their own naivety. As for the dictator, it is the fear of losing power that haunts him.

A RETIREMENT PLAN FOR DICTATORS

Almost immediately after he has taken absolute control, the isolation of the dictator follows. He is confined to his palace—friendless and paranoid. The circle of people around him reduces to a sycophantic few. The dictator, rather than exulting in his triumph, withdraws into fearful seclusion. He begins to view others with suspicion. Everybody is suspect, everyone a schemer against him.

Thereafter, the tough part begins. The problem is one of governance. As Genghis Khan said: '*Conquering the world on horseback is easy. It is dismounting and governing that's hard.*'[4] Genghis Khan will rank close to the top in any list of the world's worst tyrants. He had considerable experience in ruling over a large part of the world he conquered. Given his reputation for cruelty, one might think keeping a conquered population in line was a cakewalk. Surprisingly, it was not so.

Much before Genghis Khan's frustration with governance, the Hindu Gods were confronted with the dilemma of getting rid of a monster they had themselves created.

According to Hindu mythology, the demon Bhasmasura was a devotee of Lord Shiva. Pleased with his devotion (*bhakti*), Shiva granted him a boon. Bhasmasura asked that anyone whose head he touched with his hand should burn and turn to ashes (*bhasma*). Granted this wish, Bhasmasura wished to test it. He wanted to place his hand on the head of Shiva.

Shiva ran away to save his life and prayed to Lord Vishnu for help.

Vishnu appeared before Bhasmasura in the form of the danseuse Mohini. She was so beautiful that Bhasmasura fell in love and asked her to marry him. She told him she would marry him only if he matched her dance moves.

Bhasmasura was smitten, and this test by Mohini seemed harmless and a fun way to marry her. So he readily agreed to the condition and they started dancing. The dance went on for many days. At one point, Mohini struck a pose where she placed her hand on top of her head. As per their agreement, Bhasmasura had to follow this move. The moment he did so,

Shiva's boon came into effect and he was covered by flames till his body turned to ash.

A dictator, therefore, writes his own death warrant either by his incompetence, as Genghis Khan had warned, or by his stupidity, as in the case of Bhasmasura. There are variations to this theme, and many dictators do not fade away quickly. But their longevity is no guarantee that their mind is at rest, or that the crown they wear is free of thorns.

Ultimately, the dictator's stay at the top is a matter of chance and good fortune. He stays in power as long as his luck holds. Once his time is up, and the run of good luck has exhausted itself, it is a cue for him to go. In fact, the countdown starts from the day he grabs power. Even when he seems to be in total control, he and his rule are balanced uncertainly on a razor's edge.

The pattern is usually the same.

Finally, after all the death and brutality that he has imposed, the dictator's own power, and sometimes his life, ends without notice and with remarkable suddenness. The stars turn against him and the dictator loses, as they all do in the end.

The question that follows is this: is there a retirement plan for dictators?

Where do they go when they are alive but no longer in power? Until about 1990, retired dictators tended to buy a home somewhere around Lake Geneva in Switzerland or a townhouse in the posh Belgravia part of London.[5] There, to all outward purposes, they lived a happy life. But the pattern has changed since then. Ninety-two former heads of State or heads of government have been prosecuted since 1990.[6]

Nevertheless, the fear that one day justice will catch up with them has not deterred potential dictators. Rather, their numbers have increased in recent years. In part, this is due to the lacklustre performance of democracies around the world.

One result of it is that even convicted dictators get the benefit of doubt; their sins are then pardoned.

As a rule, criminals should be punished for their crimes without regard for their status. Unfortunately, former strongmen are treated either harshly or leniently based on political expediency. Except for the charge of genocide, everything else is subject to negotiation. Often, all that is required is a guarantee of a quiet life at home, or a foreign bolt-hole.

Suharto, the former strongman of Indonesia, continued to live discreetly in Jakarta. P.W. Botha, who ran South Africa in the last days of apartheid, died unrepentant at his home. Joseph Estrada, the president of the Philippines between 1998 and 2001, was at first jailed for life for taking millions in bribes.[7] But Filipinos are a forgiving people and his successor, Gloria Macapagal Arroyo, pardoned him. It is a different matter that Arroyo's own administration was also accused of corruption.[8] In keeping with such political traditions of the Philippines, Ferdinand Marcos, the corrupt dictator, never faced justice at home for his crimes.

There is clearly a contradiction here. If a dictator is beyond the reach of the law even after he has been unseated, can it truly be said that the society has been set free? Sadly, society continues to rub its eyes in disbelief long after the dictator has faded into retirement. As usual, Machiavelli had a view on this: '*For whoever believes that great advancement and new benefits make men forget old injuries is mistaken.*'

In the end, a dictator leaves a society wounded and in a state of puzzled enquiry long after he has passed. Therefore, a dictator's life should not be celebrated; his death must pass unsung.

As for the dictator, even during a long stay at the top, he should worry about the sequel.

24

FUTURE DICTATORS

In a solemn ceremony in Paris to mark a century after the end of the Great War, President Emmanuel Macron warned the assembly of world leaders, which included believers in nationalism like Donald Trump, Vladimir Putin and Recep Erdogan: '*I know there are old demons which are coming back to the surface. They are ready to wreak chaos and death.*'[1]

On the off chance that they had missed the message, he added, '*History sometimes threatens to take its sinister course again.*'[2]

This was not a rhetorical flourish for a catchy media bite. Nor was it scare-mongering to suit the occasion. Macron was stressing the point that the devil awaits at the national doors, and that it has happened before.

In the post-First World War period, there was a systematic build-up to the worst part. Hitler did not start with the gas chambers from the day he took power. It started gradually. At first, his ministers inflamed the prejudices of the Christian majority in Germany with the message of 'Us' versus 'Them'. This and much else were the essentials of their hate speeches; the intolerance, the denial of basic rights, and the burning of the Jewish synagogues followed. Citizens with a conscience watched it all with sorrow, but turned the other way when they saw a Jewish neighbour being attacked.

Macron warned the assembly of leaders that similar signs were visible again. He could have added, the worst was yet to come. However, even if he had added that touch of drama, would we escape the inevitable?

It seems unlikely, when communism lies defeated and capitalism stands confused. Their imperfections were the cause; both represented a distorted idea of human nature and behaviour. As a result, we are now poised uncertainly at a turn. This could be the catalyst for a new beginning, or a slide into a world without order.

If ours was an ideal world led by able leaders, we would have made the right choice. Alas, we live in a fractious world.

It is, therefore, too much to hope that we will make the prudent choice and that, in this confrontational age, the US, China and Russia will agree to a transformation that transcends '-isms' and dogmas. Ideological uncertainty apart, there is also the concern that in this age of rage, it is idle hope to expect that democracy will prevail universally over dictatorship.

As if this isn't worrying enough, Covid-19 has shattered the assumption that all is well with the world. Further, there are the demons such as conflicts in Ukraine and Gaza, Houthi threats to shipping in the Red Sea, US-led sanctions against twelve thousand-plus entities in the world, religious extremism in many parts of the world, racism in America, and discrimination within societies, to name a few of the ills that divide us.

In fact, ours is one of those times when events unfold with an inexorable historical logic and change becomes inevitable. It is our fault that we fail to see it coming. Therefore, today political life is divided between forms that are democratic and a substance that is often only very partially tied to these forms. One result of this confusion is that our modern age has begun defaulting on its promise of freedom and equality.

There is another change from before.

If the big threat in the past came from within the Western world, this time it is China that threatens. In December 2020, the office of the US Secretary of State issued a policy brief that was bluntly termed *The Elements of the China Challenge*. The first page itself spelt out the US goal: '*In the face of the China challenge, the United States must secure freedom*.'[3]

It was a warning meant to alert the incoming Biden administration that the matter was urgent and serious. It was also a message to the world that 'freedom', so far taken for granted, was now at stake. It was also a reminder that all was not well with Western ways. At a time when China's plans span decades, democracies are struggling to look beyond their next election. Moreover, liberal democracies are constantly struggling with domestic crises, leaving them little energy for longer-term strategic planning. Whether it is the US, the EU or India, democracies are more polarized than ever before. The Pew Global Attitude Survey notes regularly that trust in democratic governments is at an all-time low.[4]

REGRESSION TO TOTALITARIANISM

Like communism, the liberal order, too, has tired the world. An illiberal order is advancing, from the US to Russia, Turkey to Israel, and Hungary to Argentina. This latest form of authoritarianism is still an experiment in the works and, therefore, it is too early to bracket it in a label. But the signs are ominous and, in the coming years, dictators and semi-dictators could lead up to 75 per cent of the world.

This regression to totalitarianism in large parts of the

world can come in unexpectedly early because democracies, and the associated liberal order, are restive. There is increasing anger in the world and there is a philosophical shriek wanting change.

It must be an eerie coincidence that two of the three great powers of today have leaders who are authoritarian by temperament and who want to make their country 'great'. In addition, a number of other countries now have leaders who are authoritarian and nationalistic. And whatever form of democracy the US chooses to practise at home, its interventions abroad have for long been dictatorial in effect. All this is a recipe for fractious coexistence; our flat world is ill-equipped to accommodate so many strong-minded leaders and their ambitious but conflicting agendas.

Let us take the case of the West. Across the EU, democratically elected governments have set out to dismantle the rights enshrined in the Bloc's founding texts. Hungary and, episodically, Poland are leading this 'reactionary revolution', followed closely by Austria and, on occasion, Italy. The electoral successes of these governments are encouraging other European politicians to follow the same path.

They might do some good. Trains may run on time, or big new highways could spring up overnight, and, like Trump, each may have his national version of 'America First'. But this myth-making comes at a cost because all may not go according to the authoritarian leader's claims. After all, populism's drag on the economy is gradual and cumulative. The result is intolerance and the inability and unwillingness of the leader to accept dissent. Ministers and advisers become pliant yes-men and, as things begin to go wrong, the media gets muzzled. Consequently, society suffers and people lose the distinction between real and State-mandated fake news.

This artificial construct cannot be sustained for long

because no authoritarian regime, from a Roman-times Nero to the modern-day Kim of Korea, has ever delivered to society's benefit. As the shortcomings in performance threaten to expose the dictator's flaws, the State tries to divert people's attention. *Panem et circenses* (bread and circuses) was the preferred but futile diversion used by ancient Roman rulers. Variations of it are in practice today.

History is also witness to the fact that nationalism often becomes a convenient ruse to divert people. Angry and aggressive nationalism must not be confused with patriotism. Patriotism has a school-boyish innocence about it involving devotion to a place and a particular way of life, which one does not wish to impose on others. It is defensive both militarily and culturally. Nationalism, in contrast, is didactic in its articulation and aggressive in its practice.

The nationalist aims compulsively to secure more power for his nation, both as an ambition and as the most effective way of blocking the other argument.

Hitler and Mussolini were infamously its most ardent and skilful practitioners. Throughout the last century, there were others who appeared on their national stages briefly, but ultimately disastrously. Theirs was a sporadic and ambition-driven grab of power.

It is different this time.

SLIDE TO NATIONALISM

Nationalism, much more than ever before, is expanding its footprint in the world.

But it is also a fact that nationalism has been lurking around for a long time. So, what is new and worrying this time? The answer may lie in people's disappointment with the democratic experiment and leaders' failure to live up to expectations. For liberals too, as long as it was a project of elites, 'nationalism' was an exciting prospect in the realm of ideas. They reacted with alarm when people joined in; it became less reasonable and often more violent.

It is true that the questions of identity and collective pride become inevitable in a nation-state. But a nation's problems cannot be solved by the collective narcissism of nationalism.

Rarely has the world witnessed such a coincidence where authoritarian regimes have come up around the same time in nearly all the continents. Almost every one of them is whipping up the nationalist agenda and, for the moment, seem to be immensely successful.

When an entire people are emotionally charged, the appeal to reason is ineffective. They get programmed to reject the idea that the other side, the opposition party within the country or a neighbouring State at the border, may also have a point. Conflicts and war become inevitable on this slippery slope.

This slide is worrying the liberal opinion around the world. As President Macron reminded in his address on 11 November 2018: '*Nationalism is a betrayal of patriotism. A withdrawal into isolationism would be a grave error that future generations would very rightly make us responsible for.*'[5]

The slide to nationalism that Macron warned about will impel countries to put up walls around them. Xi is currently busy doing so in China, and this is exactly what a future dictator would want. Such a silo-like condition suits the authoritarian leader. It provides him a sense of security and becomes his safety net against the critical foreign eye. As in the past, the appeal to nationalism is employed by him to good effect.

Totalitarian leaders of the past also sought to influence public beliefs. Some, like Hitler and Stalin, tried to fundamentally reshape citizens' world views by imposing comprehensive ideologies. But the autocrats of the present age are more clinical: they aim only to convince citizens of their competence to govern.

Xi provided a forceful example of it at the celebrations to mark the 100th anniversary of the Chinese Communist Party. Speaking in Tiananmen Square to a frenzied crowd, he said, '*... the Chinese people will never allow any foreign forces to bully, oppress or enslave us. Anyone who dares try to do that will have their heads bashed bloody against a Great Wall of steel forged by over 1.4 billion Chinese people.*'[6]

If there is a message of defiance in it to the outside world, the call within the country is for people to fall in line.

Other dictators, too, are employing variations of this broad theme, but there is a nuanced shift from the past. In this millennium, dictators do not rely merely on censorship, repression and patronage. Instead, as in Hungary and Turkey, they cajole, pressurize and bend the courts, intimidate the press, hamper civil society, and use parliamentary majorities to push through new laws and constitutions. Superficially, everything looks normal: elections take place, people can travel in and out of the country, and the malls are packed. But below the surface, checks and balances that once prevented dictatorship begin to fall away.

New-age dictators also crush separatist rebellions and deploy paramilitaries against unarmed protesters. But, compared to most previous autocrats, they use violence sparingly. They prefer the ankle bracelet to the Gulag. Maintaining power, for them, is less a matter of terrorizing victims than of manipulating beliefs.

As a raging narcissist, an authoritarian leader functions as a distorted mirror to many, in which they see their own fantasies reflected back at them. Unfortunately, the number of such unquestioning faithfuls has become immense.

THE HYBRID DICTATOR

The world and its future generations will have to prepare for an altogether different type of dictatorship—a technological dictatorship or a 'hybrid dictatorship', where AI is the backseat driver that makes the decisions to be implemented by a figurehead.

The reach of this hybrid dictatorship need not be confined to national boundaries.

Just think what will happen to developing economies once it is cheaper to produce textiles or cars in Detroit than in Dhaka. Think also of what will happen to politics in a country when somebody in Beijing or Moscow knows the entire medical and personal history of every politician, every general and every journalist in that country, including all their corrupt dealings and their sexual escapades. Will it still be an independent country? It is likely that such a country could very quickly become a data-colony. When this happens, an AI system that understands people better than they understand themselves can manipulate their feelings and decisions.

This is the critical point because the power to hack humans will give rise to the worst kind of dictator the world has known so far.

Imagine a State where everybody has to wear a biometric bracelet that constantly monitors your blood pressure, your heart rate, your brain activity and your emotions. With this, freedom of choice will be the first to go. At a not-too-distant date in the future, algorithms might tell us where to work, who to marry and when to raise a family. In this way:

- People will lose control over their lives and over the ability to understand public policy.
- Hybrid dictatorship will take over. A machine will

then make decisions but with a token front-man as the dictator.

- There will be no scope for a rebellion against such a system because people's power to think and act independently will have been taken away by AI.

Worse still is the reminder that all the earlier revolts and revolutions were fed by ideas, with philosophers being the driving force. In contrast, this millennium is notable for the lack of the big idea. There is nothing worthwhile to excite and incite.

That we should be numbed to resigned acceptance is only natural. When AI takes over people's thought process, and their emotions become a uniform standard, there is hardly any chance that a philosopher can rise from amongst us with the cry of 'liberty, freedom'. People's life under such a hybrid dictator will be dark and dreary.

There will be no hint, not even a glimmer, of light at the end of that long, depressing tunnel.

Part 7: THE END GAME

25

THAT BURST OF ANGER

Every living being, be it from the animal kingdom or from amongst us, aspires for more. When that aspiration meets with superior resistance, there are two broad options available to that person or a body of people. They can sit back and sulk, or take their grievance to the next level and challenge the superior force. This has been the general pattern from the earliest times. Palace coups, assassinations of kings, revolts and intrigues were all a manifestation of that aspiration for more.

But dictators are least likely to spread a welcome mat for those plotting against them.

Generally, dictators are short on patience. They do not pursue ambition with the discipline of a person climbing a long flight of stairs. They know the slightest hint of procrastination on their part will be seen as a sign of weakness. So, chances are they will act swiftly to crush a protest. As George Orwell wrote, '*One does not establish a dictatorship in order to safeguard a revolution; one makes the revolution in order to establish the dictatorship.*'[1]

Therefore, a revolt against a regime has to contend with sharp and forceful reaction. Moreover, compared to the vast options available to the State, violence as a medium of challenge is mostly a privilege of the powerful or a sudden burst of anger in the sullen.

This sense of sullenness seems to be on the rise and there is pervasive panic in the world, resembling the centralized fear that comes from despotic power. Partly in reaction, the world seems steadily angrier and there is a global surge in protest. There have been over 700 anti-government protests in the world since 2017.[2]

An individual is unlikely to challenge the dictator on his own, but he is more likely to join a crowd because it offers him the benefit of anonymity. As novelist and playwright Elias Canetti writes in his book *Crowds and Power*:

> In the crowd, the individual feels that he is transcending the limits of his own person. He has a sense of relief.[3]

On a cautionary note, he adds: '*A crowd resembles a besieged city, subject to the pressures of defection from within and hostility from without.*'[4]

Moreover, the masses do not readily take to arms. For them, the written word has been a powerful medium of protest. It offers them the safety of being the nameless author. It is, therefore, no surprise that graffiti has long been an effective way of spreading the message ever since people could scribble. It was the most iconic symbol in medieval Rome, against the State and sometimes against the Pope as well. The intent, however, was to lampoon them and their acts, rather than rebel.

In India, in the 1980s, Khalistani cadres plastered the walls around New Delhi Railway Station with the words 'Raj Karega Khalsa'. It served as a recruitment tool to attract new followers as well as a public statement signalling the presence of an issue and a resolve to address it, regardless of any flaws in the pursuit of that ambition.

Words written on banners, signs on the city walls, on clothes, bodies and faces have been central in social movements. These writings remind us that social movements are not solely spaces for speeches and gestures; they are also stages for the written word.

In recent years, with the evolution of social media, the force and form of such writing is increasing: slogans and protest writings are becoming more individualized and personalized. They are also increasingly aimed at an ever-wider, potentially global audience. Some slogans have played a central role in the international diffusion of many social movements. For instance, the slogan '*The personal is the political*' was an important catalyst of the feminist movement.[5] As an aside, it should be mentioned that protest need not be only against a regime or society. It can be against another nation and may also have a message for yet another country. This happened during the presidential election campaign in the Maldives in 2023. Mohamed Muizzu, who later became the President, had the words '*India Out*' printed on his T-shirt.[6] It was a blunt message to India as also a signal to China for closer relations.

POWER OF PROTESTS

A question that intrigues is this: why are so many protests happening in our times? After all, humankind has never before had it so good, and on such a large scale. We stand at the high point of technological advancement. Widespread famine is a rarity. The world is experiencing an unparalleled era of prosperity. Social media gives immense scope for letting off steam. Yet people seem sullen. Why are they still raising their fist to pump the air?

There are good reasons for it.

In formally democratic countries, the public becomes disappointed by corruption, incompetence and lacklustre economic results. All these are powerful triggers for protests. When people take courage to gather in masses and protest, they do so knowing their survival is at stake. Then, there are no unbreakable laws or boundaries that limit what should be done to survive and win.

On the other hand, an autocrat's challenge is to repress political opponents, but not so much that it sparks a backlash. Repression is a costly and blunt tool; it cannot solve the problems that generate opposition. It can also backfire. But authoritarian regimes, by their nature, forget that legitimacy—not repression—is the strength of a resilient power.

Either way, a society without legitimate governance does not function well. People can be forced to comply, but it is harder to coerce enthusiasm. Eventually, people take to the streets. These protests are a signal to the authorities that people are restive.

But do protests work?

Opinion on it is divided. On their own, street marches do not hold any particular power beyond their ability to frame questions for society. Still, and at the very least, protests attempt to force a conversation about the issue they are focussed on. The few successful protests are the ones that win that conversation. In the short term, it does seem protests are a failure. Yet, much of the power of protests lies in their long-term effects.

Unfortunately for people, repression works quickly and more often. Howsoever brave protesters may be, a State often possesses a much greater capacity to inflict costs than the protesters have the stamina to withstand. If this is so, why doesn't the State increase repression till people give up? Why does it sometimes give in to a protest movement?

The clue to this mystery lies in understanding the long-term power of social movements.

They are powerful because they successfully influence the minds of people. Such protests, even when they are not immediately successful, are potentially potent. They succeed in planting the seed of revolt. Moreover, by raising a doubt against the regime, they undermine the most important pillar of power: legitimacy. Two recent examples of this kind were the protests, in 2022, in Sri Lanka and then in China. Neither was successful, but they were not a failure either. Both badly shook the glum assumptions of the powers-that-be in their countries.

Somewhat similar was the experience earlier, in the second decade of this millennium, when there were a series of protests in the world:

> In early 2011, the Arab Spring surprised the world—as well as the autocrats that these movements targeted. Toward mid-decade, massive demonstrations took place in Brazil, Turkey, Ukraine, and Hong Kong. On January 21, 2017, the largest number of demonstrators ever—five million of them—massed on the streets of American cities for the Women's March...Several million citizens mobilized around the globe in 2019, crowding into streets and squares from Ecuador to Tehran, Santiago to Beirut, Delhi to Paris, and beyond. In Hong Kong alone, as many as 1.7 million citizens demonstrated on a single day...[7]

These were mostly spontaneous movements and they kept the world spellbound with their enormity. But taking out street marches without a clear plan for what follows often leads protests to lose momentum. Or they succumb to State power, as they did in Hong Kong in 2019–20 and in Myanmar in 2021. These leaderless protests do not know how to keep protesters engaged and integrated in the political process. Some of the principal weaknesses in such protests include loose leadership and organization, lack of control over media image, and the absence of an inspiring ideology.

Before social media became popular, protests were planned in secrecy. The intricate work required to evade the authorities helped build infrastructure for protests, as also the strategies for sustaining momentum. Now, protest movements rush past that effort. Consequently, they crumble quickly when government forces confront them.

As the country limps back to life as before, the masses retreat to lick their wounds and to count their losses. They also make the sorry discovery that their protest hardly brought about any change. In some cases where the leadership of the government changed, it was mostly a cosmetic arrangement. Previous leaders were still around, sitting on the sidelines to manipulate the strings of power. On the other hand, the instigators of the protest find themselves jobless, and often in jail.

Sitting in a prison cell they ponder over the fact that a burst of anger, without an endgame, is futile fluff.

26

SAYING NO

Whether it is a putsch, insurrection, uprising, mutiny, coup d'etat, resistance, rebellion, revolt or revolution, all involve opposition to the ruler. In each case, there is extra-constitutional rejection of government authority. The label given to the act symbolizes the means used to achieve the goal of overthrowing the government.

Let me single out 'putsch' for a brief mention because of Hitler's association with it. The dictionary meaning of 'putsch' is a violent attempt to overthrow a government. It is secretly plotted and suddenly executed, and the term derives from the Swiss-German root for 'knock' or 'push'. It was in troubled Germany between the two wars that journalists started using this word to describe many attempts at a violent overthrow of government. These included the Kapp Putsch in 1920, an attempt to overthrow the Weimar government in Berlin, and the more famous Hitler's Beer Hall Putsch in Munich in 1923, in which the fledgling Nazi party attempted a failed takeover of the Bavarian government.

When the ultimate objective of a putsch or any of the other acts of defiance against the government is the overthrow of a regime, then why must we give different labels to the act? After all, what is there in a name?

It is true that the name is not indicative of the result; it only reflects the path taken, each different in its method and result. But once the endgame is in sight and success near, the substance takes over. It is the result that makes the difference. Measured on that matrix, a rebellion, a coup and a revolution can be as different as chalk is from cheese.

This distinction is important to bear in mind as it represents a graded expression of anger and its relative success, or failure. Beginning from the bottom, in this gradation, a 'protest' is limited to the satisfaction of a stated objective. 'Rebellions', too, rarely become revolutions. But a military 'coup' changes the government to install the coup-maker in power. In most cases, a coup is negative in its long-term effect. In sharp contrast, a 'revolution' can be transformative in a fundamental manner.

Successful, major revolutions have changed the social and political structures of societies.

There have been five major revolutions in recent centuries: the English Revolution (1688), the American Revolution (1776), the French Revolution (1789), the Russian Revolution (1917) and the Chinese Revolution (1949). Each one of these was fundamentally transformative for the State and its people. As against these, most modern-day, anti-government movements, despite colourful labels such as the Orange, Purple and Tulip revolutions, will not qualify as revolutions.

Most revolutions, with rare exceptions like that of Mahatma Gandhi, have been brought about at the point of a spear or through the barrel of a gun. Given its extreme nature, a revolution is the turning over of an established order by changing the form of government: a monarch, for example, is ousted to be replaced by a parliament.

Unlike a revolution, both a protest and a rebellion are temporary in nature. Rebellions are political uprisings that may or may not be violent. They do not call for revolutionary transformation. Instead, rebellions demand reform within the existing order. To put a practical note to this difference, a politician who talks of revolution usually has in mind a minor rebellion whose aim is to provide him victory in the next election.

A real, large-scale rebellion, more famously known as the Indian Mutiny, happened in 1857 when Indian soldiers rose against the British. They were joined by the rulers of Indian princely states and thousands of ordinary people in a struggle that threatened to destroy British colonial power on the Indian subcontinent. Among many reasons, poor pay and the cultural and racial insensitivity of British officers contributed to the discontent among the Indian soldiers. The immediate trigger for the mutiny were rumours that cartridges for a new rifle were greased with pig and cow fat—anathema, respectively, to Muslim and Hindu soldiers. This spontaneous rebellion was crushed by the determined colonizer.

The writer Albert Camus did not have the Indian Mutiny in mind, but he was speaking for every such act of injured pride when he wrote, '*Every act of rebellion expresses a nostalgia for innocence and an appeal to the essence of being*.'[1]

Camus sought an ideal world, but the everyday reality is that the world is far from innocent. While it is relatively risk-free for people to revolt against a democratically elected government, rising up to confront any type of an authoritarian regime can be hazardous. Consequently, people living under an authoritarian regime are afraid of the consequences of a failed protest. What if they are unsuccessful? It is the fear of participating in an unsuccessful revolt that makes people hesitate.

Add to this the fact that in recent times, fear has begun to pervade our societies to an extent, and in ways that were not so earlier. Protest has been smothered to an odd whimper. Within populations, particularly among youth, there is a sense of fatalism. Very few are ready to sacrifice everything to rebel.

Yet, pushed to desperation, people rise up as a last resort. So why do people rise up in anger, why do they come out on streets to protest, and when do revolutions start?

The broad experience is that these begin when people get over the fear of saying no. That is the tipping point. On a somewhat similar note, Camus had asked, '*What is a rebel?*' Answering his own question, he said, '*A man who says no.*'[2] While a man overcoming his fear to say no might be the trigger for a rebellion, it need not always be successful.

As regards the critical point when people become desperate enough to say no, Aristotle described the following as major issues leading to resentment:

> ...In democracies, demagogues encourage public discontentment by attacking the rich either individually or collectively.
>
> ...In oligarchies, discontent sprouts when masses are treated harshly by officials.
>
> ...In an aristocracy, resentment begins to build up when the circle of people around the ruler narrows to a small number of advisors. The result is disequilibrium in the balance of the constitutional authorities.[3]

While Aristotle's prescription remains largely valid, others ask: what is the alternative? As John Milton wrote in 'Paradise Lost', '*Awake, arise or be for ever fall'n.*'[4]

It is the promise of a new beginning, and frustration with the existing arrangement, that makes people break free. Even then, even at a seminal moment in a revolution, protests do not come in neatly spaced intervals. These spring up in a bewildering cascade. Such a protesting crowd is the most primitive human response to oppression.

REBELLION TO REVOLUTION

Rebellions, resistance, revolt are all essentially a part of the same genome, the result of a people's desperation. Let me, therefore, use these terms interchangeably to describe a society's angst, anguish and eventually anger.

Whether it is a carefully planned revolution or a spontaneous rebellion, it usually follows a similar course.

The first steps in a rebellion are the most critical. An early indicator is the slow shift in the largest part of the population from 'neutrality' to widespread but unorganized and unarmed resistance. Activities during this phase involve writing anti-regime graffiti on public walls, surreptitiously distributing anti-regime literature, the spontaneous singing of anti-regime songs in private gatherings, and participating in demonstrations against the regime.

It is often assumed that only the majority population of a country can bring about a revolution. That may generally be the case, but there can be exceptions. A minority population can also influence the majority community to come around to its view, and together they can bring about change. However, a critical mass of the minority is necessary to convince the majority. That tipping point is generally at 25 per cent.

If 25 per cent of the total population is convinced of the rightness of its cause, chances are that these contrarians may then be able to 'convert' a majority of their respective groups. Some put this figure as high as 72 to 100 per cent of the population as converts to the cause that the minority had started with.

The second phase usually means coming out in the open

and starting protests against the regime. It is still largely peaceful. This phase of a potentially successful rebellion begins to gather form when people decide to join in. This means the masses, as distinct from the leaders opposed to the regime. These ordinary people will drive or walk up to a few hundred metres of a demonstration to see if there are enough people for them to join in as well. Their chief concern in making that strategic decision about joining in is the apprehension of being the sole participant. There should be a large crowd already because there is safety in numbers.

During the rebellions of the late 1980s in Eastern Europe, people looked for two signs: the level of student involvement and the presence of workers. In more recent cases, the role of social media has been powerful because it spreads the message at lightning speed, influencing people's mood. The social dynamics of rebellion against authoritarian regimes, therefore, serve as a critical case study, demanding careful consideration from the planners of a revolt.

The third phase must follow quickly if the rebellion is to succeed.

As mentioned already, the second phase is mostly peaceful; it is the third phase that is generally balanced precariously. A single spark can steer it towards violence. But whatever happens, regardless of how the regime tries to suppress it, the revolting public must maintain its momentum if it wishes to succeed.

Many of the successful rebellions have a focal point, the case of an individual that becomes a cause célèbre, whether it was the Romanian priest László Tökés in 1989, Mohamed Bouaziz the fruit seller from Tunisia who set himself on fire in 2010, or Khaled Said, who was murdered by the police in Egypt the same year. Each one became a rallying call for activists against the regime.

After a successful revolt, reports in the media have a vital role to play in spreading the message. The euphoric moments are condensed to catchy slogans by the crowd and vivid narratives of the crimes of the fallen regime. All through, social media offers an easy, quick and almost cost-less form of communication.

But communication, or lack of it, can cut both ways. Revolts have failed because the government in power seized the initiative, as seen during the July 2016 coup attempt in Turkey where Erdogan retrieved a seemingly impossible situation.

While the Turkish case exemplified the power of communication, an earlier Russian case demonstrates how confidence and gumption can influence the media to favour the government's narrative. In the failed coup against the Russian government in 1991, the rebels had much more power than Yeltsin's loyalists, but eventually that didn't matter. What mattered ultimately was the bluster of Yeltsin and his confidence in the battle of communication. Yeltsin was more adept at manipulating the media.

Through an extensive misinformation campaign, Yeltsin and his aides convinced the establishment and people that the rebels were decrepit, elderly generals without support, and that officers and soldiers were leaving them in great numbers. This greatly undermined the confidence of the junta. They hesitated when they should have taken the final step and launched their attack on Parliament. But they were afraid their troops would not obey them. The coup crumbled soon thereafter.[5]

The leaders of this coup slipped up because they failed to recognize that in a military coup ideology does not matter. Their supporters join them in the belief the coup is likely to be successful. Therefore, astute leadership is the key. It must be nimble enough to tailor its message in tune with the shifting wind. Accordingly, unpopular rebels may succeed, while popular rebels may fail. In this case, a quick-thinking Russian government won.

RAM RAJYA FOR THE WORLD

Who wins and which side loses is not so material as the cause of dissatisfaction. Since a sense of denial and a feeling of injustice are at the heart of a revolution, the ruler must pay attention to these. In other words, if the cause of upheaval is inequality, people must see practical steps being taken in their favour.

Aristotle listed some methods to prevent a revolution.[6] He advised rulers to always obey laws, the slightest transgression of which would, sooner or later, result in total disrespect and violation of laws. Moreover, if people, like their leaders, start breaking laws, the entire social order will be at stake.

He added that a ruler should not discriminate between the officer and common citizen, between the governing and the governed. Every citizen must be given a chance to express opinion about the government and the tenure of the officials must be short-term. This way, oligarchies and aristocracies would not fall into the hands of some families.

Aristotle believed a ruler can avoid a revolution if he prevents extremes of poverty and wealth, because such disparity leads to conflicts. A ruler must be seen to be loyal to the State's Constitution. He should be competent and should be seen to be just and good by people. The quality of his advisors too is critical to prevent a revolution.

All these are the type of qualities that were also prescribed for *Ram Rajya* in the epic *Ramayana*. Much later, Chanakya's celebrated work *Arthashastra* contained, largely, the same prescription. In fact, most major works of the world would counsel along similar lines. Alas, they have mostly remained an ideal that the potential rulers swear by but discard in the swoon of power.

That's the reason for the continual ferment and frequent *cri de cœur* by people, about great expectations betrayed. Had successive generations of rulers followed even some of these prescriptions, there might not have been much scope for resentment. Consequently, many of the rebellions and revolutions might not have taken place.

But a ruler's memory is selectively short. Once seated in the highest chair, the ruler has little time to think of the people who once rose up by his side to say 'no' to the previous regime.

As for the country, the effect of an autocrat or a dictator's rule is like the passage of a hurricane. When the dictator is gone, and the dust of his terror has settled, the country he once ruled looks like no real place at all.

It seems an elaborate alibi.

27

PRIDE BEFORE THE FALL

Historians do not always ponder over the past to make a list of the nice and the naughty.

Still, there are exceptions like the Roman historian Suetonius who wrote *The Twelve Caesars*. As with his candid portrayal, a historian of dictators might observe that the ruins of monuments are witness to the pride that comes before the fall.

The historian would be right on both scores—the dictator's pride and his eventual fall. That fall is as certain as death because no dictator comes with immortality as his warranty.

Many strongmen make catastrophic short-term mistakes in governance—the errors that are usually avoided in democratic systems. They hear only from sycophants and invariably get bad advice. Entrapped by their honeyed words, they do not remember the Greek philosopher Xenophon's advice: '*...plots against tyrants spring from none more than from those who pretend to love them most.*'[1]

But why blame the advisors? They, too, are victims of the system the dictator created. Their personal priority would be survival. Those who repeat his absurd claims without blinking are deemed loyal. To be trusted, advisers must lie on behalf of the regime. Anyone who hesitates is considered suspect.

This test applies to the population as well. To stay in power, a despot has to worry about more than just advisers and hangers-on. A dictator has to win over, intimidate, or coerce the population too.

As an illustration, consider this quote from the Auschwitz-Birkenau State Museum about Nazi Germany:

> It didn't start with gas chambers. It started with one party controlling the media. One party deciding what is truth. One party censoring speech and silencing opposition. One party dividing citizens into 'us' and 'them' and calling on their supporters to harass them. It started when good people turned a blind eye and let it happen.[2]

Look around, and you will note most dictatorships follow some variation of this script.

Despite all the power he thus gets through absolute control, a dictator lacks the subtlety of a political leader who has been through the grind for decades. He does not fit into either of these categories—the visionary boldness of the prophet or the far-sighted pragmatism of the statesman.

Dictators tend to view the world around them in stark tones of black and white. As a result, the style of dictators may vary but the substance of their governance remains the same—absolute power and complete control. By and large, they opt for the rough and ready as policy. Some among them may do a few good acts. Many remain devoted to their family; others may have a romantic side.

Yet, almost all dictators commit great atrocities. There is for instance the case of Saddam Hussein. Six days after replacing Ahmed Hassan al-Bakr as President of Iraq, Saddam convened a meeting of Baath Socialist Party leaders on 22 July 1979. Following his instructions, this meeting was videotaped so the proof of what followed exists.

> Seated on stage, Saddam announced that sixty-six party leaders had been uncovered as traitors and comprised a fifth column. As each name was read out, guards grabbed a baffled man from his seat in the audience and forced him out of the auditorium. At the end of this process, those still seated, white with both fear and relief, spontaneously leaped to their feet shouting undying loyalty to Saddam. Of the sixty-six named, twenty-two were quickly ordered executed by firing squads. Wider purges followed that autumn. The country now was literally Saddam's. He had achieved total fear.[3]

ROUGH AND READY

A fine Urdu saying maintains, '*Tamaddun se pehle ka tasanno.*' It translates as: '*Snobbery has arrived, but culture, not yet.*' This subtle suggestion is one of the many reasons why dictators tend to be crude and crass. As a broad generalisation, it could also be added that there are two types of dictators in our present-day world—the 'totalitarians', who maximize power, and the 'tinpot' dictators, who maximize their own consumption subject to a minimum power constraint.

On the other hand, democracies are generally an open book. A strong democracy guarantees that the government figures are critically evaluated by experts and political opponents. As Orwell put it, '*If liberty means anything at all, it means the right to tell people what they do not want to hear.*'[4]

The moral responsibility to reflect reality extends to issues such as the state of the economy. Although the incentive to exaggerate economic performance is ever-present, a well-functioning democracy can rein in, to some extent, the impulse to manipulate official statistics.

This is not the case with dictatorships. By one estimate, the yearly GDP growth is inflated in most authoritarian regimes by a factor of 1.15 to 1.3.[5] Broadly speaking, countries led by autocrats have disappointing economic outcomes as compared to democracies. And it is not just on economic growth that dictators fail to deliver. They also fall short on employment, health and education spending, and government debt. There is plenty of evidence in this regard from dictator-led countries across the world. However, the case of Pakistan should be illustrative enough. When it was carved out of India in 1947, it was its most prosperous part—so much so that it was quoted in parts of Southeast Asia as an economic model to follow. Yet, continual direct or indirect military rule reduced it to a near basket case!

An assessment done by Stephanie Rizio and Ahmed Skali of 133 countries from 1858 to 2010 contradicts the view that some dictators have done well for their country. Using annual data on economic growth, political regimes and political leaders, they document that growth-positive autocrats happen only by chance. In contrast, growth-negative autocrats are found far more frequently. They also assert that growth under supposedly growth-positive autocrats is not the complete picture. They suggest that even the infrequent growth-positive autocrats largely 'ride the wave' of a previous government's success.[6]

Though it is rare for a dictator to be shown the mirror, it has sometimes happened. One such occasion was when Iranian President Mahmoud Ahmadinejad came to Columbia University in 2007 to address students. In his introductory remarks Lee Bollinger, President of the University, said, '*Mr. President, you exhibit all the signs of a petty and cruel dictator.*'

As if that was not enough, Bollinger added, '*Ahmadinejad's denial of the Holocaust suggested he was either brazenly provocative or astonishingly uneducated.*'[7]

It is necessary to enter a caveat here. Bollinger was showing Ahmadinejad the mirror in the safety of the US. It wouldn't have been possible for any Iranian or, for that matter, even for Bollinger to dare badmouth him in Iran.

Still, this encounter between a democrat such as Bollinger and an autocrat like Ahmadinejad triggers an intriguing thought. What would Ahmadinejad have thought of this encounter? Or, more generally speaking, what is the autocrat's view of democracy? It may not be far off the mark to say that for an autocrat, a democrat is a man with no centre who moves as the wind moves.

DAY OF RECKONING

A question often asked is this: is there no hope for people? Are they doomed to suffer in silence under a dictatorship? To be correct, however, it must be added that such display of stoicism by people is not only under a dictator, but also under a leader who instils fear with his words.

Sometimes, though, the public or its representative has been known to gather courage and rouse itself. This happened on 9 June 1954, when Senator Joseph Nye Welch rose to speak during the Army-McCarthy hearings in the Senate Subcommittee on Investigations. The proceedings were being watched by over 20 million anxious Americans on TV. '*Have you no sense of decency, Sir,*' Senator Nye asked Senator Joseph McCarthy, the notorious persecutor of communists in America.[8] This sharp rebuke was the cue for the print and TV media to come down heavily on McCarthy, effectively ending his political career as also his hate campaign.

It isn't just the dictatorship, or the dictatorial types like

McCarthy, that must be resisted and told 'enough is enough'. There comes a time when a democratic government, too, needs to be told its time is up. This happened in the spring of 1940 when British forces in Norway were overwhelmed by the Nazis. On May 7, Prime Minister Neville Chamberlain faced a critical motion by the Labour opposition in the House of Commons. His Conservatives had a big majority, but a respected Conservative backbencher, Leopold Amery, rose to repeat the words to Chamberlain that 300 years earlier Cromwell had spoken in the Long Parliament: '*You have sat too long here for any good you have been doing. In the name of God, go*!'[9]

Three days later, Chamberlain resigned. Winston Churchill became the new PM and went on to inspire victory in the Second World War against the Germans.

But these cases are exceptions to the rule that once installed, dictators do not easily give up power, as was the case with Hitler, Mao, Stalin and Pol Pot.

Yet, despite their omnipotence these dictators suffered from excessive anxiety, mostly a paranoid fear of assassination or an uprising by people. This inner turmoil of a dictator is neither widely known, nor discussed often. But it was once given form by a sculptor, Emmanuel Michel, who won the commission in France to make yet another sculpture of Napoleon. He must have pondered long about the inner core of his subject so he could bring him alive in stone. What he found was an insecure and tormented man. Emmanuel's articulation of it in stone was the validation of this reality,

> I tried to make him (Napoleon) as I think he was: very tormented, introspective, never satisfied...I didn't want to make him a conqueror, but rather someone very lonely.[10]

Such hidden angst was not unique to Napoleon; many other dictators are suspected to be very vulnerable inside.

On the other hand, there is this rare case of Xi, who, along with his father, had suffered the wrath of a dictator. Yet, when he himself became the dictator, he began to hero-worship the tormentor. Obviously, the world does not know if President Xi still carries the scars of ill-treatment by Mao. But occasionally, when he is alone and in a pensive mood, the bitterness of those times must distress him:

> (Xi)'s father Xi Zhongxun was a revolutionary hero-turned-vice premier...But when Xi Zhongxun was purged by Mao and targeted during the Cultural Revolution, '(Xi Jinping) and his family were traumatised'...His status vanished overnight, and the family was split up. One of his half-sisters is reported to have killed herself because of the persecution...
>
> At just 15, Xi was ordered to the countryside in central China where he spent years hauling grain and sleeping in cave homes.
>
> 'The intensity of the labour shocked me,' he later said.
>
> He also had to take part in 'struggle sessions' in which he had to denounce his father.
>
> 'Even if you don't understand, you are forced to understand,' he said. 'It makes you mature earlier.'[11]

Under similar circumstances, a democratic leader would want to ensure that he does not repeat what he had to endure. Whatever be his inner struggles, Xi chose differently.

Despite the veneer of confidence, a dictator is restless. The day of reckoning worries him. Finally, when that last hour arrives, as it inevitably does, most dictators have the look of a hunted animal.

It was so when the Pakistani dictator Pervez Musharraf was handing over the military chief's baton to his successor, General Ashfaq Pervez Kayani. The video of this event shows him hesitate, as if he is having second thoughts about it. Without the power of the military chief's baton, his presidential post is going to lack absolute authority. That possibility is reflected in his moment of hesitation, and more visibly in the slight, but noticeable, twitch of his lips as if he is about to say, let's leave it for another day. But Kayani nods in assurance and artfully squeezes the baton from under Musharraf's arm. That assurance lasted less than one year. Other dictators have fared even worse. Both Gaddafi and Saddam were plucked out, dishevelled, from the holes they were hiding in.

BROKEN AND BRUISED

Going by these examples and even those of democratic leaders, the question to ask is: do emotions pull leaders in a hawkish or dovish direction? This is tough to comment on conclusively. Even in normal times, it is hard to determine how much influence emotions have on a leader's decision making. It is far more difficult to do so when times are tough. Leaders, especially dictators, become irrationally unpredictable then.

Despite his inner struggles, his personal demons, his insecurities, and an overwhelming sense of personal gloom, the authoritarian leader puts up a bold façade. For the country, he is a compulsive control freak. It is, in part, a functional necessity and driven by his domineering instinct. But the result for society is all-pervasive fear and atrocities. The barbarism of a dictator is discussed in hushed tones in comfortable homes, but their distance from the horrors does not disconnect them from what is happening in the country. No one is immune and no one is spared the dictator's wrath.

In the end, both the absolute ruler and the absolutely ruled end up broken and bruised.

The natural question, then, is: if a dictator is fragile within, if like the people he too is gripped by fears, can he not be cured? After all, who is responsible for enabling a dictator? There is no one-size-fits-all answer to an issue of such historical precedence and complexity. While it is easy to vilify dictators, we must also acknowledge that people are the ones enabling them. After all, a dictator cannot function without followers.

Can people then prevent dictators from assuming power?

That, theoretically at least, is what democracy is about. In a sound democracy, people are tolerant of different points of view and they are able to manage differences. Such a democracy is sustained by a voting population that is knowledgeable, mobilized and engaged—a population that cares for liberty and takes responsibility for it. Equally, the government, the legislature, the courts and the media should be independent. But this combination seems in the realm of ideas. In our present age, institutions bend to suit the dictator's whims.

When such submission happens, that moment represents a national humbling.

If this is the reality of our times, then do people have the means and the ability to prevent the rise of a dictator? Charlie Chaplin gave his opinion on it in the 1940 film *The Great Dictator*: '*You, the people, have the power to make this life free and beautiful, to make this life a wonderful adventure...*'[12]

In case people do not exercise their choice wisely, Chaplin also had a warning for them: '*Dictators free themselves but they enslave the people...*'[13]

28

SUMMARY JUSTICE

When he was the absolute ruler of Haiti, Baby Doc Duvalier put up a poster that read:

> I should like to stand before the tribunal of history as the person who irreversibly founded democracy in Haiti.

It was signed 'Jean-Claude Duvalier, president-for-life.'[1]

The irony of the message may have amused the wider world, but for Haitians it conveyed a life sentence. Like Baby Doc, once they grab power, dictators and autocrats hang on to it. They are more likely to die of old age or disease than at the hands of an enraged population or an assassin. An analysis by Matthew White found that 60 per cent of oppressors lived long in power.[2] Spain's Francisco Franco died at 82, China's Mao was 83 when he died, North Korean dictator Kim Il-sung was 82 when he died.[3] Stalin, Kim Il-Sung, Mao Zedong, Francisco Franco, Enver Hoxha and Hafez al-Assad, all died in power.

A study by Erica Frantz and Andrea Kendall-Taylor found that dictators have tenures lasting an average 16 years, compared to just seven years for leaders who leave power through means other than death.[4]

Longevity in office enables these leaders to portray themselves as indispensable to the political system. However, this apprehension about instability is often misplaced. In fact, their study found that in 87 per cent of the cases where the strongman died in office, or was otherwise done away with, the transition to a new leader was smooth.[5]

That is why this cautionary tale must be told. It should be told even if there is hardly any chance of holding a potential dictator back, or of people not succumbing yet again.

WHEN ANGER SUPERSEDED PRUDENCE

Let me start with a case where, exceptionally, a dictator received summary justice. The graphic account below is based on my conversations when I had gone to Târgoviște to receive the title of honorary professor from the city's university:

> The courtroom was empty now; except for the two of them, an edgy soldier and the very cold draught from a door the jury had not bothered to close after them. A slight film of wetness in Nicolae's eyes gave away his only emotion, showing resentment and betrayal.
>
> 'Please,' the soldier said, pointing his righthand halfway across his body towards the door.
>
> But Nicolae and Elena kept looking abstractedly ahead.
>
> They were thinking of the previous 72 hours, the viciousness of those three long days and even longer nights. Elena and Nicolae Ceausescu remembered every single slight of those 72 hours. They had resented the discomfort and snapped at the discourtesies. But the insults did not trouble them as much as the humiliation of trial; the insolence of it and the judge's barbs.

'Please!' The soldier repeated, a lot more firmly this time.

Nicolae screwed his eyes tight and turned sharply towards the soldier. For a moment, there was a flash of temper across his face. He clenched both his hands forming two angry fists, but in a sober afterthought, he unclenched them slowly. Then, he nudged Elena forward.

Before they walked out of the courtroom into the courtyard, the soldier stepped forward to roughly pull Elena's hands behind her back. She didn't have the time to react to this indignity because in a flash he had tied her hands together with a piece of cord. He repeated the procedure with Nicolae. Then, they were led past the generals and a line of soldiers to a wall on the opposite side of the courtyard.

A slight wind was beginning to stir, adding bite to the chill. Occasionally, the leafless branches of trees swayed in the breeze to shake off another layer of snow. That powdery accumulation floated down to spread itself uniformly over the soldiers and the metal barrels of their AK-47s.

It must have been a coincidence that Elena was dressed for death. Her flower-patterned dull-grey frock left her neck and a part of her arms uncovered. Elena shivered as they passed through the open courtyard but Romania's first lady did not complain, neither to the weather Gods nor to the soldier who had tied her hands.

They had barely reached the wall on the other side of the courtyard when two soldiers marched up noisily to stand next to them, one on either side.

Soon, a Major stepped forward and asked Nicolae: 'Do you want a blindfold?'

Nicolae turned to look away.

'Should I ask them to cover your eyes?' The Major asked again.

'No,' Nicolae replied calmly.

The Major stepped sideways to stand in front of Elena.

'Should they...'

'Nooooooo!' Elena shrieked, even before the Major could finish his offer.

'No! No! No!' She wailed again.

Her 'nos' reverberated inside the compound, knocking futilely against the stone walls.

The State, and its new system, looked on mutely.

'Nooooo!' Elena shouted one final time at the Major.

Then, she turned to the soldiers who had taken up the firing position.

'Why!' She appealed. 'How can you do this? I recruited you.'

'Get set.' The Major shouted from a safe corner of the courtyard.

The soldiers bent down mechanically in response. One knee touched the ground, the hunched other knee cradled their AK-47. They had barely got into this position when the Major shouted his next command, 'ready'.

Forty soldiers responded with robot-like efficiency. No one raised an enquiring eyebrow in doubt, nor was there any sigh of disbelief at what they were about to do. All forty looked up to point their AK-47s at the bull's eye—just as they had been taught in the endless training sessions at the shooting range. The lessons there had involved mock targets, whose bullet-ridden holes were a testimony to their proficiency. This time, they would not be walking up to the targets to see if they had hit the bull's eye. Blood would be their proof.

Twenty soldiers aimed their guns at Nicolae Ceausescu, the President of Romania; the other twenty pointed their AK-47s at the power behind the dictator, his wife Elena Ceausescu.

'Don't,' she wailed again. 'Please don't. You were my children.'

'Fire!' The Major ordered in a baritone.

Forty AK-47s spewed fire relentlessly.

The Ceausescus must have felt the first few bullets piercing their bodies. Then, the pain of bullets and the sting of a thousand scorpions would have taken them beyond the threshold of suffering.

But the soldiers kept firing. They kept firing dutifully till their magazines had emptied out.

Suddenly, it was very quiet in the courtyard. Then sluggishly, as in a slow-motion replay, the bullet-blown bodies of the Ceausescus fell against the wall making a soft thud. The impact would have hurt the living. The corpses did not complain.

Their blood kept oozing out to spread over the snow-covered floor. Those two large patches of red, in an expanse of pure white, were a sign for the omen-conscious Romania; that communism had bled to nothingness.

This happened in December 1989. Legally speaking, Ceausescu was still the President of Romania when he was shot dead by his soldiers after a mock trial lasting a few hours. He was the only East European dictator to be summarily executed. Many Romanians regret so blatant and so brutal a denial of justice.

This was not the only instance where, in the hurry to

get rid of the dictator, anger superseded prudence. Among many factors compelling people towards a shortcut is the fear of retribution in case the overthrown dictator makes a comeback.

29

HANG HIM!

Ceausescu was put to death on Christmas day by his closest aides. Julius Caesar's death on 15 March immortalized the date as the '*ides of March*'. But other dictators were not killed on similarly remarkable dates such as 25 December or 15 March. Nor were many killed in a conspiracy by their aides.

Rather, it has often happened quite the other way, with the aides trying to prolong a dictator's rule. This is only to be expected where absolute power is wielded, because those who owe their position to the dictator want to maintain their influence by somehow keeping the leader functional—even past the point of death—while they try and find an alternative.

Stalin's death is a case in point.

In the days before he died, it was clear to those around him that the end was near. But even in his frail condition, the hands of doctors treating him shook with fear. His inner circle, hovering nearby, kept praying desperately for recovery. The KGB chief Lavrenti Beria instructed Stalin's servants, '*Don't tell anyone about Comrade Stalin's illness.*'[1]

Stalin was the source of this cabal's power. Without him, those around him feared they would lose their influence and privileges.

On 1 March 1953, after a late-night dinner and movie with some of his political colleagues, Stalin went to bed in the early morning. His guards, under orders not to disturb the leader, were worried when he did not come out of his room till late in the afternoon. But they were too scared to disturb him. It wasn't until about 10 p.m. in the night that some officials gathered enough courage to check on him. He was lying on the floor, soaked in urine, having suffered a major stroke.[2] A watch lying on the floor had stopped at 6:30 in the morning. Stalin struggled between life and death till 5 March 1953.[3]

His daughter Svetlana describes his death in this manner:

> ...at the last moment he suddenly opened his eyes...It was a horrible look—either mad, or angry and full of fear of death...Suddenly he raised his left hand and sort of either pointed up somewhere, or shook his finger at us all...The next moment his soul, after one last effort, broke away from his body.[4]

Like Stalin, a few other dictators have also died in office. But execution or unnatural death is the more likely fate of dictators. There are some dictators who can sense the coming change. Benito Mussolini was one such. By the beginning of 1945, he seemed to know the end was near and he told an interviewer, '*Seven years ago I was an interesting person. Now I am a corpse.*'[5]

Mussolini was removed from government in July 1943 when Italy's prospects of victory in World War II began to sour. He was imprisoned in Hotel Campo Imperatore in central Italy up to September, when German paratroopers rescued him. He was thereafter taken to Germany, and then brought back to Lombardy in northern Italy. From there, in April 1945, Mussolini and his mistress Clara Petacci were trying to escape to Spain when they were caught by communist partisans, taken hostage and shot.[6] Their bodies were carried to Milan's *Piazzale Loreto* and hung upside-down from a lamp-post. Passersby spat and pelted stones on their dead bodies.[7]

Hitler had heard of Mussolini's death and the desecration of his corpse. He didn't want to suffer a similar humiliation and ordered that his body be burned. This was during the last days of World War II, with the Russian Army closing in on Berlin. Hitler was staying then in a bunker under the Reich Chancellery building.[8]

As bad news began to pour in from all fronts, Hitler made preparations for his suicide. He married Eva Braun and, on 30 April 1945, Hitler and Braun went into a lower room in the bunker. There Braun took a cyanide pill, while Hitler shot himself in the temple. Both corpses were put to flames, but the burning was not thorough. The Russian army discovered the bodies and destroyed what was left of that bunker to prevent Hitler's grave from becoming a place of pilgrimage.[9]

ONE MAN'S HERO, ANOTHER MAN'S VILLAIN

But dictators don't easily fade away from public memory.

Often, they leave behind some sort of a calling card that keeps haunting people long after they have gone. One such account concerns Taimur (Tamerlane), who typifies the quote '*one man's villain is another man's hero*'. He was responsible for the death of over 17 million people, yet he remains a national icon in Uzbekistan.[10] Interestingly, his story brings together a confluence of four of the most terrible tyrants of history. This legend also associates Hitler's invasion of Stalin's Soviet Union with him and his curse.

Taimur died in 1405 when he was on his way to invade China. His body was brought back to be buried in 'Gur-e

Amir' (Persian for 'Tomb of the King').[11] This grand monumental complex of Samarkand, with its azure dome, was the architectural inspiration for Humayun's Tomb in Delhi and to some extent the Taj Mahal as well.

Taimur had left warnings that he should not be disturbed in death. Therefore, an inscription in his tomb reads, '*When I rise from the dead, the world shall tremble*.'[12]

But reigning dictators seldom pay heed to dire warnings.

The first such misadventure took place in the eighteenth century. The Persian dictator Nader Shah took a fancy to the precious stone that was used to cover the fake grave that is usually kept at the ground-floor level of mausoleums of such importance, the actual grave being at a level below. In 1740, Nader Shah took this stone away to Iran where it was unfortunately broken into two parts. It is said that Nader Shah's misfortunes began after this. It was only when he returned the stone to Taimur's coffin that fortune began to favour him again.[13]

Like Nader Shah, Stalin was also headstrong. Two centuries later, in 1941, he sent a group of anthropologists led by Mikhail Gerasimov to exhume Taimur's body in order to do a scientific study of it, and to create a replica of what he might have looked like in real life.[14] The people of Samarkand warned the anthropologists that there was a terrible curse attached to Taimur's grave. But the anthropologists dismissed it as superstitious mumbo-jumbo. However, they took the precaution of conducting their operation in the dead of night so as not to offend local sensitivities.

On the night of 19 June 1941, they broke open the grave.[15]

The air around them was instantly filled with the strong odours of frankincense, rose, camphor and resin. At first, the team was terrified; they thought the dictator had risen from the dead. A little later, as the air inside slowly returned to its normal musty smell, they realized that the fragrance was the smell of oils used for embalming.[16]

The anthropologists also found a curse inscribed inside the tomb. The wording of the curse translated approximately as:

> Whomsoever opens my tomb
> shall unleash an invader
> even more terrible than myself.[17]

The anthropologists dismissed this curse as medieval superstition and removed Taimur's body to take it back to Moscow.

Three days later, on 22 June 1941, Hitler launched his attack on Russia. That invasion took nearly 30 million lives. The legend also maintains that the German retreat began only after Taimur's body was brought back from Moscow and reinstalled in his grave.[18]

In a strange way, four dictators intersect in these two episodes: Taimur, Nader Shah, Hitler and Stalin. Each one of them was more brutal than the other, each responsible for millions of deaths, each reviled, but each remembered long after he had gone.

It seems strange that four dictators should have connected in this manner in Samarkand. This, however, is not the only instance. There are other accounts of an admiration society of sorts among dictators. Thus, Stalin used to read about Nader Shah and admired him, calling him, along with Ivan the Terrible, a teacher! Napoleon, too, used to read about and admire Nader Shah. He considered himself the new Nader and, in his later years, was indeed called a European Nader Shah.[19]

Genghis Khan is another tyrant who continues to be revered by Mongolians as a great national hero. But legend maintains that his end was not heroic. His hands and legs must have lost their strength, for the Mongolian tyrant simply fell off his horse. It was an embarrassing end for one of the most powerful conquerors the world has known. Slaves and warriors escorted the ruler's body, wrapped in a white felt blanket, to its final resting place. Slivers of fragrant sandalwood were placed in the grave to prevent insects from gnawing at the body of the Great Khan.[20]

Till date, however, no one knows where exactly he was buried. Was it in Mongolia, Russia or China? The search goes on, as do claims and counter-claims.[21]

How long a dictator lives, and rules, should normally be the concern of the country and of the people he rules. But matters got a bit tangled when, in mistaken zeal, some Western countries led by the US felt that the outside world (meaning largely they) had a '*responsibility to protect*'. This concept was given the formal stamp of a UN resolution in 2005 at the UN World Summit.[22] Having armed themselves with this legal instrument, they were quick to sally forth and slay.

Saddam Hussein's hanging took place shortly thereafter.

Mowaffak al-Rubaie was Iraq's National Security Adviser (NSA) when Saddam was hanged. According to him, Saddam's execution was set in motion after a video conference between Iraqi Prime Minister Nouri al-Maliki and then US president George W. Bush, who asked:

> 'What are you going to do with this criminal?'
> Maliki replied: 'We hang him.'
> Bush gave him a thumbs up, signalling his approval.[23]

With that brief conversation, a judgement was delivered and a responsibility discharged. So it was thought then.

After a summary trial, Saddam was condemned to be executed on 30 December 2006. Rubaie said he pulled the lever to hang Saddam but it did not work. Another person then pulled it a second time, killing him. According to eyewitnesses, Saddam remained calm till the end; he did not ask for mercy or forgiveness.[24]

A few years later, Muammar Gaddafi became the next major Arab leader to be summarily dispatched. In October 2011, a US drone over Libya alerted NATO of a fleeing 80-car convoy. A group of French fighter jets responded with an airstrike, which took out two of the vehicles. Thereafter, Gaddafi and his guards left the convoy to hide in the drainage nearby. This is where the rebels seized him. This frenzied mob was quick to grab him, propping him up and pummelling him while he looked dazed. He was bleeding profusely all this while. Finally, the gun shot that killed Gaddafi was fired by a young man wearing a baseball cap with a Yankees logo.[25]

The US Secretary of State Hillary Clinton was in Afghanistan when she was given the news of Gaddafi's death. She responded with an ecstatic 'wow'.[26]

Thus, in a strange way, the US exulted in its ability to protect a population that had neither sought protection, nor wished such a humiliating end to its ruler. But in its confidence that it had the license to act as per its determination, the US forgot one of the fundamental tenets of democracy—that it is better to debate than destroy.

The US also forgot that the smell of blood pollutes debate, consuming argument.

Long years after Saddam's hanging and Gaddafi's bloody end, the Iraqis and the Libyans continue to wonder how, and if, they have been 'protected' while a civil war continues to rage around them and their once prosperous countries lie in tatters.

In both these executions, it was the American desire for what it thought was quick justice that prevailed over prudence. In both cases, the local population continues to feel that its leader was wronged. Moreover, general opinion in the larger Arab world was that Saddam and Gaddafi had provided stability to their part of the world. But America had thought otherwise.

Whatever be the sanctity of the fig leaf provided by the UN resolution on 'responsibility to protect', the widely held conviction in the region is that these executions did not protect people, nor were they necessary. Moreover, they have done more harm than good to their societies. Even when these executions are viewed in the context of America's domestic law, there is doubt whether the US had acted with due propriety. After all, President Gerald Ford had signed in 1976 an executive order stating: '*No employee of the United States government shall engage in, or conspire in, political assassination.*'[27]

Despite this, the US has not abandoned its strategy of selective elimination. It has simply changed the terminology from assassination to targeted killings, from aerial bombing of presidents to drone attacks on alleged terrorist leaders. Its earlier aerial bombing attempts on leaders have included those on Gaddafi in 1986, Slobodan Milosevic in 1999, and Saddam Hussein in 2003.[28] Some of the more recent and successful killings have included those of Osama bin Laden in May 2011 in Pakistan, the Iranian General Qasem Soleimani in January 2020 in Iraq, and Ayman al-Zawahiri in Kabul in July 2022.

The US is not alone in targeting those it does not like. Other countries ranging from Russia to China, Pakistan, North Korea and Saudi Arabia, too, opt for the easier course. There have been nearly 300 serious assassination attempts on leaders worldwide since 1875 up to the beginning of this millennium. Of these, 60 succeeded.[29] It means a well-planned assassination attempt has almost a 20 per cent chance of success. It is also true that assassination attempts need not be from external sources only. It can also be the work of a rival aspirant to power.

Moreover, all dictators do not get assassinated. Some are forced out of office after they have lost an election or failed to secure majority in a referendum. Others are unseated in a coup or following public protests.

THE ILL EFFECTS LINGER

Do dictators regret the death and destruction caused during their rule? The full answer to it remains in the iffy category of doubt, but some anecdotal evidence reveals that they remain unconvinced till the very end that they had erred. Gaddafi, for instance, had shouted at his captors, '*Shame on you, you know no sin.*'[30]

After the mock trial that Ceausescu knew would condemn him to death, he said, '*I don't deserve it.*'[31]

Whether a dictator regrets or repents does not bother people. What matters to them is a sense of instant relief, and the fact that at long last they are free. Therefore, towards the end, all that is left with a dictator is an almost operatic cast of figures. Besides the isolated ruler himself, there are the treacherous courtiers, the money-grabbing agents, and the audacious pretender—each acting according to a script repeated over and over again in history, and each busy conjuring an alibi to distance himself from the dictator and his rule.

A Russian account provides us a glimpse of what happens after the dictator has died and the transition is not smooth. Russians call this period *Smuta* ('times of trouble'). It lasted from 1604 to 1613 but the cause of it was the brutal rule of

Ivan the Terrible, who died in 1584. He had exhausted his people and the country's finances by fighting endless wars in the Baltic:

> He (Ivan) decimated the Russian elite in a paranoid orgy of executions as he tried to consolidate absolute power. And in a fit of rage, he killed the son who could have succeeded him, transforming the throne into an object of fierce competition among elite clans.
>
> What followed was a period of economic decline, famine, and conflict—including between an ambitious courtier named Boris Godunov, who occupied the throne from 1598 until 1605, and an adventurous young man who claimed to be Ivan's son. The Pretender, or 'False Dmitry', enjoyed the backing of Polish-Lithuanian rulers, who coveted Russia's resources...Godunov's death in 1605 quickly led to the triumph of False Dmitry, who... declared himself tsar—only to be killed along with his Polish retinue the following year by a disillusioned mob.
>
> Civil war and economic crisis engulfed Russia as the Smuta intensified. External enemies moved in: the Swedes came from the north; the Crimean Khanate... raided the south; and Polish troops ended up occupying the Kremlin.[32]

The Russian period of *Smuta* is not exceptional. In the end, once he is gone, the dictator may be the unseen thing that everybody is trying to ignore. But there is doubt that people are able to live down that monstrosity. The ill effects linger.

LIGHT OF EVERLASTING HOPE

For all of them, be it the terrible dictator or the pretenders who follow him, poet W.H. Auden builds an utterly persuasive image in his short poem *Epitaph on a Tyrant*.

The poem was probably based on Hitler's dystopian odyssey. But its narrative echoes the journey of other dictators as well. The final, harrowingly poignant line measuring death by the tyrant's tears is as much a mourning for the dying children as a warning to the tyrant that one day all, including the all-powerful dictator, must turn to dust:

> Perfection, of a kind, was what he was after,
> And the poetry he invented was easy to understand;
> He knew human folly like the back of his hand,
> And was greatly interested in armies and fleets;
> When he laughed, respectable senators burst with laughter,
> And when he cried the little children died in the streets.[33]

Enveloped thus in gloom, people under a dictatorship would be right to ask: *Quo Vadis* ('where are you going')?

There are no easy answers to this because, historically, exceptional leaders have been the exception. Therefore, in future, too, people's salvation, or ruination, may seem conveniently possible through charismatic individuals. Add to this the fact that there is no such thing as absolute freedom within a society, and we come back to the question we started with: Quo Vadis?

Once again, history does not provide us comfort. It simply gives these summary verdicts; dictatorship is messy, democracy is an attempt at clarity, but people have a chaotic mind. This combination often leads to stasis, where contentment and despondency confusedly merge into each other.

We started on a note of despair by quoting Brecht. Our journey through these pages does not hold out the promise of a liberal and democratic future. Still, our many-splendoured world urges us not to give up.

As the poet Faiz Ahmed Faiz wrote,

Dil nā-umīd to nahīñ nākām hī to hai
Lambī hai ġham kī shaam magar shaam hī to hai
(The heart has not lost hope, merely suffered a setback
The night of suffering is long, but it is just a night)[34]

The poet Sahir Ludhianvi dreams of a sequel to this wish:

वो सुबह कभी तो आएगी
इन काली सर्दियों के सर से जब रात का आँचल ढलकेगा
जब दुख के बादल पिघलेंगे जब सुख का सागर छलकेगा
जब अम्बर झूम के नाचेगा जब धरती नग्में गाएगी
वो सुबह कभी तो आएगी

One day, that dawn will come,
When after centuries of darkness, the veil of night slips,
When the clouds of sorrow melt, when the ocean of contentment is immense,
When sky begins to dance with joy, when the earth sings songs,
Surely, there will be that dawn

Perhaps, one morning, the world might wake up in such a dawn!

ACKNOWLEDGEMENTS

Every time I finish writing a book, I promise myself—'never again'. But the spirit is weak. Once more a dream begins to take shape, gradually overwhelming me and my thoughts to become an all-consuming presence. And the grind begins, yet again.

It would have been easier if I had followed the trend of employing a researcher. But manufactured writing is easy to spot.

My chosen route is the old-fashioned way of blood, sweat and tears. It means living enveloped in my dream as the book begins to take shape. For days, months and years it becomes my entire existence, the provoker of agony when words become scarce and the giver of ecstasy when they pour out in an inspired torrent.

It also means a slog of 14 hours a day, and at least ten readings of the final text. The effort drains me physically. Sometimes I ask myself whether the enormity of the effort is worth it. But the words that I have chiselled over and over again implore me to carry on. I know then, my dream has taken the form to cherish.

Still, if I hesitate, Rupa's Managing Director Kapish Mehra gently prods, '*by when should I expect the manuscript*?' And the proverbial moving finger resumes its pace.

This is when the editor takes over to snip here and mould there. It is my good fortune that Yamini Chowdhury has edited five of my latest books. She prudently wields her pen, to strike out the extra word. Her suggestions have invariably been useful.

Equally, I am grateful to the senior team of Rupa, especially

Padma Pegu, Harshita Sabharwal and Geetu Martolia, for being generous with their time, advice and help.

A writer's anxiety begins when the book is ready to go to the printer. This is the critical moment. Until then, the book was his zealously guarded, and precious, private affair. At the printer the *purdah* is taken off.

The book is now in public space—everyone's purchasable commodity, and open to anyone's gaze. The critics and the reading public become the jury and the judge. A glowing review is life-enhancing, a critical comment stings.

The support of family and friends is critical then. I remain indebted to my grandchildren Maanas Swarup and Anaia Swarup, who lead my cheer team.

ENDNOTES

CHAPTER 1: BRAINWASHING

1 Aizenman, Hannah, 'Daniel Borzutzky's Poems Channel Cacophony in an Age of Calamity', *The New Yorker*, 31 March 2021, https://tinyurl.com/yv6u6c25. Accessed on 14 May 2024.

2 Hill, Matthew, David Campanale and Joel Gunter, 'Their goal is to destroy everyone: Uighur camp detainees allege systematic rape', *BBC*, 3 February 2021, https://tinyurl.com/muvvu5jr. Accessed on 15 May 2024.

3 https://tinyurl.com/23s9znjx. Accessed on 10 May 2024.

4 Freedom House, 'Freedom in the World 2021', Democracy under Siege, http://tinyurl.com/ysmj425t. Accessed on 28 February2024.

5 https://tinyurl.com/4wrzwwh7. Accessed on 15 May 2024.

6 Svolik, Milan W., Elena Avramovska, Johanna Lutz and Filip Milacic, 'In Europe, Democracy Erodes from the Right', *Journal of Democracy*, January 2023, http://tinyurl.com/mrxte2ux. Accessed on 28 February 2024.

7 Schmitz, Rob, 'Poland's judiciary was a tool of its government. New leaders are trying to undo that', *NPR*, 26 February 2024, https://tinyurl.com/mv93xh9z. Accessed on 15 May 2024.

8 https://tinyurl.com/57vbjv6m. Accessed on 10 May 2024.

9 Carothers, Thomas, and Benjamin Feldman, 'Examining U.S. Relations with Authoritarian Countries', Carnegie Endowment for International Peace, 13 December 2023, http://tinyurl.com/4aj6vjfz. Accessed on 28 February 2024.

10 Machiavelli, Niccolo, *The Prince*, Reader's Library Classics, 2021.

CHAPTER 2: POMERIUM

1 http://tinyurl.com/bdduf8bv. Accessed on 29 February 2024.
2 http://tinyurl.com/3jcmjhtc. Accessed on 29 February 2024.
3 http://tinyurl.com/4byryuzd. Accessed on 29 February 2024.
4 http://tinyurl.com/3mwzwhfc. Accessed on 29 February 2024.
5 Orwell, George; *1984*; Signet Classic (1961).
6 ANI, 'First wife softened Stalin's heart!', *Hindustan Times*, 22 August 2013, http://tinyurl.com/899eazx8. Accessed on 29 February 2024.
7 Moraes, Dom, *Indira Gandhi*, Little, Brown, 1980.
8 Edison, Thomas Alva, 'The Philosophy of Thomas Paine by Thomas Edison', The Thomas Paine National Historical Association, 7 June 1925, http://tinyurl.com/ycyym6p7. Accessed on 29 February 2024.
9 Dockery, Tim, 'The Rule of Law Over the Law of Rulers: The Treatment of De Facto Laws in Argentina', *Fordham International Law Journal*, Volume 19, Issue 4, 1995, http://tinyurl.com/3y9jf62b. Accessed on 29 February 2024.
10 Boutrous, Theodore J., Jr., 'President Correa's Libel Suit and the Fraud Against Chevron', *Forbes*, 6 March 2012, http://tinyurl.com/mr3v8u6z. Accessed on 29 February 2024.
11 'A Zambian opposition leader fights treason charges for not stopping his car', *The Economist*, 24 June 2017, http://tinyurl.com/4tezwp5b. Accessed on 29 February 2024.
12 Janjevic, Darko, 'Erdogan purges army after failed coup', *DW*, 17 July 2016, http://tinyurl.com/5yk2yrdu. Accessed on 29 February 2024.
13 http://tinyurl.com/3jwxn2v7. Accessed on 29 February 2024.
14 Mo Ibrahim Foundation, http://tinyurl.com/ydp3nxf6. Accessed on 29 February 2024.
15 Laërtius, Diogenes, 'The Lives and Opinions of Eminent Philosophers', http://tinyurl.com/3ht8y9c8. Accessed on 29 February 2024.

CHAPTER 3: MUSKETS ARE BETTER

1 https://tinyurl.com/yck88cfu. Accessed on 14 March 2024.

2 A Dictionary of Greek and Roman Antiquities, 1890, https://tinyurl.com/y9mufupv. Accessed on 22 March 2024.

3 Hobbes, Thomas, *Leviathan*, https://tinyurl.com/32phndke. Accessed on 21 March, 2024.

4 'Thomas Hobbes: Solitary, Poor, Nasty, Brutish, And Short', Yale University Press, London, https://tinyurl.com/53at864d. Accessed on 21 March 2024.

5 Alighieri, Dante, *Divine Comedy*, Penguin USA, 2003.

6 Machiavelli, Niccolò, *Discourses on Livy*, University of Chicago Press, First Edition, 1998.

7 Gibbon, Edward, *The Decline and Fall of the Roman Empire*, Everyman's Library, 1993.

8 https://tinyurl.com/2nvkfkbx. Accessed on 14 March 2024.

9 Manifesto Issued by Empress Catherine II of Russia, 22 July 1763.

10 Villa La Pietra, NYU Florence, https://tinyurl.com/47myydah. Accessed on 14 March 2024.

11 'Hannah Arendt on the State', *The Core Centennial*, 27 September 2019, https://tinyurl.com/3vbfbwh5. Accessed on 14 March 2024.

12 Treisman, Daniel, and Sergei Guriev, 'The new authoritarianism', *VoxEU*, 21 March 2015, https://tinyurl.com/2s3n662c. Accessed on 14 March 2024.

13 'Ukraine Gongadze murder: Ex-President Kuchma charged', *BBC*, 24 March 2011, https://tinyurl.com/2mh2t6uh. Accessed on 15 May 2024.

14 Tandon, B.N., *PMO Diary-I: Prelude to the Emergency*, Konark Publication, 2002.

15 Fitzgerald, F. Scott, *The Great Gatsby*, original 1925 Edition.

16 Constitution of the People's Republic of China, The State Council of the People's Republic of China, https://tinyurl.com/yc236b3n. Accessed on 14 March 2024.

17 Schorske, Carl E., 'Totalitarian Dictatorship and Autocracy. By *Carl J. Friedrich* and *Zbigniew K. Brzezinski*. (Cambridge, Mass.:

Harvard University Press. 1956. Pp. xii, 346.)', *The American Historical Review*, Volume 63, Issue 2, January 1958, pp. 367–368, https://doi.org/10.1086/ahr/63.2.367. Accessed on 10 July 2024.

18 https://tinyurl.com/6f55ytky. Accessed on 14 March 2024.

CHAPTER 4: BORN BAD

1 https://tinyurl.com/278x9r44. Accessed on 4 March 2024.

2 Tenorio, Rich, 'What were Hitler, Stalin, Mao, like as kids? Early years of 6 dictators...plus Putin', *The Times of Israel*, 26 April 2022, https://tinyurl.com/zpkuu88j. Accessed on 10 May 2024.

3 Sandgruber, Roman, *Hitler's Father: Hidden Letters – Why the Son Became a Dictator*, Frontline Books, 2022.

4 Ibid.

5 Ibid.

6 Levin-Areddy, Adaam James, '13 Facts about Benito Mussolini', Mental Floss, 1 November 2018, https://tinyurl.com/mk5auh7h. Accessed on 10 May 2024.

7 Matsolo, Vuyiswa, 'A Psycho Biographical Study of Joseph Stalin', April 2019, https://tinyurl.com/yhrv4wds. Accessed on 10 May 2024.

8 Boddy-Evans, Alistair, *Biography of Idi Amin, Brutal Dictator of Uganda*, Thought Co, https://tinyurl.com/5n6we32y. Accessed on 10 May 2024.

9 'Saddam's Roots an Abusive Childhood', *The Washington Post*, https://tinyurl.com/4e8jk3ex. Accessed on 10 May 2024.

10 Ibid.

11 Stevens, Jane Ellen, 'How Vladimir Putin's childhood is affecting us all', *Aces too High*, 2 March 2022, https://tinyurl.com/msyt48kf. Accessed on 4 March 2024.

12 Lockett, Jon, 'THE YOUNG UN Kim Jong-un was dubbed "the little dictator" as childhood of excess groomed him for tyrannical rule', *The Sun*, 26 April 2020, https://tinyurl.com/nherecsb. Accessed on 10 May 2024.

13 'Vladimir Lenin and his lust for power', *History Extra*, https://tinyurl.com/4wp3cr7e. Accessed on 4 March 2024.

14 Ibid.

15 Niiler, Eric, 'How Dictators Keep Control', *NBC News*, 21 December 2011, https://tinyurl.com/43w9xkwy. Accessed on 4 March 2024.

16 Orwell, George, *Animal Farm*, Harcourt, Brace and Company, First American Edition,1946.

CHAPTER 5: DESTINY PLAYS A PART

1 Uhlman, Fred, *Reunion*, Farrar, Straus and Giroux, 1997.

2 The Great Depression, *Alpha History*, https://tinyurl.com/k7v3ewxs. Accessed on 7 March 2024.

3 Range Peter Ross, 'Hitler's Quest for Power Was Nearly Derailed Multiple Times. But the System Enabled His Rise', *Time*, 31 August 2020, https://tinyurl.com/23nczats. Accessed on 7 March 2024.

4 Kershaw, Ian, *Hitler: 1889-1936 Hubris*, WW Norton & Co, 1999.

5 'Vladimir Lenin and his lust for power', *History Extra*, 9 April 2021, https://tinyurl.com/4wp3cr7e. Accessed on 8 March 2024.

6 'How the 1999 Pakistan coup unfolded', *BBC*, 23 August 2007, https://tinyurl.com/p74vntjv. Accessed on 8 March 2024.

7 https://tinyurl.com/mrpyh6hm. Accessed on 7 March 2024.

8 https://tinyurl.com/5xm7n6zz. Accessed on 21 May 2024.

9 https://tinyurl.com/mrnjbz2k. Accessed on 7 March 2024.

10 Csaky, Zselyke, 'Capturing Democratic Institutions: Lessons from Hungary and Poland', *Freedom House*, 3 November 2021, https://tinyurl.com/5b893ck9. Accessed on 8 March 2024.

11 Bonhoeffer, Dietrich, 'BONHOEFFER: On stupidity', *North State Journal*, 3 December 2021, https://tinyurl.com/45awvnua. Accessed on 7 March 2024.

12 'The Life and Death of Julius Caesar', https://tinyurl.com/29rjczb5. Accessed on 21 May 2024.

CHAPTER 6: A FIRM HAND AND A CLEAR EYE

1 https://tinyurl.com/yttf6b8d. Accessed on 6 March 2024.

2 Greenblatt, Stephen, 'Shakespeare's Close Call with Tyranny', *The*

New Yorker, 4 May 2018, https://tinyurl.com/3s4utyr6. Accessed on 6 March 2024.

3 Orwell, George, '"The fixed vision of a monomaniac": George Orwell's 1940 review of Hitler's "Mein Kampf"', Scroll.in, 14 September 2019, https://tinyurl.com/47t3wbj7. Accessed on 21 May 2024.

4 Mehta, Pratap Bhanu, 'The Age of Cretinism', *Open*, 9 August 2018, https://tinyurl.com/mv9vsc7z. Accessed on 6 May 2024.

5 Nietzsche, Friedrich Wilhelm, *The Dawn of Day*, https://tinyurl.com/4r3hs3hn. Accessed on 6 May 2024.

6 Maccoby, Michael, 'Narcissistic Leaders: The Incredible Pros, the Inevitable Cons', *Harvard Business Review*, January 2004, https://tinyurl.com/2xe7zp5m. Accessed on 6 May 2024.

7 Khrushchev's Secret Speech, 'On the Cult of Personality and Its Consequences', Delivered at the Twentieth Party Congress of the Communist Party of the Soviet Union, 25 February 1956, *Wilson Center*, https://tinyurl.com/22mucper. Accessed on 6 May 2024.

8 Dallek, Robert, *Lone Star Rising: Lyndon Johnson and His Times, 1908-1960,* Vol. 1, Oxford University Press, First Edition, 1991.

9 *Ain-i-Akbari*, Vol. II, p.3.

10 Habib, Irfan, *Akbar and His India*, Oxford University Press, 1997.

11 Machiavelli, *History*, 9 January 2020, https://tinyurl.com/53u4y7ap. Accessed on 15 March 2024.

12 Friedman, Uri, 'How the Media's Covered Qaddafi's Clothing Through the Years', *The Atlantic*, 26 February 2011, https://tinyurl.com/5uvhzcdm. Accessed on 15 March 2024 .

13 Lepore, Jill, 'The Last Time Democracy Almost Died', *The New Yorker*, 27 January 2020, https://tinyurl.com/yey8k379. Accessed on 6 March 2024.

14 'Top 10 U.N. General-Assembly Moments', *Time*, https://tinyurl.com/bdcn9zbt. Accessed on 16 May 2024.

15 'Gadaffi crowned "King of Kings" as he seeks to create "Africa govt"', *The East African*, 12 October 2008, https://tinyurl.com/5n8ub46p. Accessed on 16 May 2024.

16 Gilson, Dave, 'The CIA's Secret Psychological Profiles of Dictators

and World Leaders Are Amazing', *Mother Jones,* 11 February 2015, https://tinyurl.com/53unfmf. Accessed on 16 May 2024.

17 Ibid.

18 Ibid.

19 Akihiko, Tanaka, 'Abe Shinzo talks about Japan's diplomacy during the seven years and eight months he was in office: Reinforcing the Japan-US alliance, the foundation of Japan's revitalization', *Discuss Japan,* https://tinyurl.com/3642bh49. Accessed on 15 March 2024.

20 Ibid.

21 Ibid.

22 Fallon, James, 'The Mind of a Dictator', *Psychology Today,* 11 November 2011, https://tinyurl.com/mpwsa6xe. Accessed on 15 March 2024.

23 Ibid.

24 Ibid.

25 Ibid.

26 Pappas, Stephanie, 'Could You Become a Dictator?' *Live Science,* 12 February 2011, https://tinyurl.com/zea7ydck. Accessed on 7 May 2024.

27 Shakespeare, William, *Henry IV,* Part Two, https://tinyurl.com/47k3vrht. Accessed on 8 May 2024.

28 https://tinyurl.com/4zjetw6s. Accessed on 6 March 2024.

29 Guha, Ramachandra, 'It's about the Dear Leader', *The Indian Express,* https://tinyurl.com/3embdcbc. Accessed on 6 March 2024.

CHAPTER 7: CYROPAEDIA

1 Rattini, Kristin Baird, 'Who was Cyrus the Great?', *National Geographic,* 6 May 2019, https://tinyurl.com/5ezdhetn. Accessed on 12 March 2024.

2 Gandhi, Mahatma, 'What Swaraj Means To Me', https://tinyurl.com/dz5az9kh. Accessed on 13 March 2024.

3 'The Modern Review Special: Rashtrapati', *Indian History Collective,* https://tinyurl.com/ysrue3bh. Accessed on 12 March 2024.

4 Chrysopoulos, Philip, 'The Ancient Greek Tyrant Who Ruled Athens Three Times', *Greek Reporter*, 20 December 2023, https://tinyurl.com/3dhjw9n8. Accessed on 12 March 2024.

5 https://tinyurl.com/32d589fb. Accessed on 12 March 2024.

6 Kleinfeld, Rachel, 'Benevolent Dictatorship Is Never the Answer', Carnegie Endowment for International Peace', https://tinyurl.com/yeyfp9cs. Accessed on 12 March 2024.

7 Simha, Rakesh Krishnan, 'Why Lee Kuan Yew Believed Democracy Was A Drag', *Swarajya*, 28 March 2015, https://tinyurl.com/3t4bbj6s. Accessed on 10 May 2024.

8 https://tinyurl.com/2rcxbvsc, Accessed on 12 March 2024

CHAPTER 8: FIELD GUIDE TO TYRANNY

1 Prideaux, Sue, 'The great performers: How image and theatre give dictators their power', *New Statesman*, 20 September 2019, https://tinyurl.com/bddr68ad. Accessed on 7 March 2024.

2 Ibid.

3 Dikötter, Frank, *Dictators*, Bloomsbury Publishing, 2020.

4 https://tinyurl.com/yc633xbp. Accessed on 7 March 2024.

5 https://tinyurl.com/384heduv. Accessed on 7 March 2024.

6 Langworth, Richard M., 'Greatest Law Giver: The Truth behind Churchill's Mussolini Bouquets', Hillsdale College Churchill Project, https://tinyurl.com/mvyezpzv. Accessed on 7 March 2024.

7 Fireside Chat, Franklin D. Roosevelt, 24 December 1943, https://tinyurl.com/4ee759rx. Accessed on 7 March 2024.

8 Heer, Jeet, 'A brief history of American presidents praising dictators', *The New Republic*, 12 June 2018, https://tinyurl.com/2d7c7nru. Accessed on 7 March 2024.

9 Chandrasekhar, K.M., 'Democracy isn't enough to deter autocracy', *The New Indian Express*, 1 October 2023, https://tinyurl.com/2kh2hsv7. Accessed on 8 March 2024.

10 Madhav, Ram, 'How Xi Jinping went from China's Gorbachev to a combination of Mao and Stalin', *The Print*, 19 March 2024, https://tinyurl.com/3v6s92ce. Accessed on 24 April 2024.

11 Ibid.

12 O'Toole, Fintan, 'Why George Bernard Shaw Had a Crush on Stalin', *The New York Times*, 11 September 2017, https://tinyurl.com/3bb28m8r. Accessed on 24 April 2024.

13 Ibid.

14 Prideaux, Sue, 'Dictators: The Great Performers', *The New Statesman*, 18 September 2019, https://tinyurl.com/ycw3hsst. Accessed on 24 April 2024.

15 Ibid.

16 'The Big Con Pankaj Mishra on Modi's India and the New World Order', *London Review of Books*, May 2023, https://tinyurl.com/5ymxas3z. Accessed on 24 April 2024.

17 'U.S. CEOs on the Chinese Menu', *Wall Street Journal*, 16 November 2023, https://tinyurl.com/wa2fjeer. Accessed on 7 March 2024.

18 https://tinyurl.com/4fkns7y5. Accessed on 6 March 2024.

CHAPTER 9: DICTATORIAL WAYS

1 Person, Robert, 'Soviet Union Is Gone, But Lenin Stuck Around', *The Moscow Times*, https://tinyurl.com/3srxutjb. Accessed on 8 March 2024.

2 Macdonald, Julien, 'Designs on Cheryl', *British Vogue*, 23 October 2009, https://tinyurl.com/3f82wppr. Accessed on 8 March 2024.

3 Rawi, Maysa, 'Dictator chic: How celebrities are taking fashion inspiration from the world's most notorious tyrants', *Daily Mail*, 9 April 2010, https://tinyurl.com/sjvwdnkt. Accessed on 13 May 2024.

4 Goraya, G.S., *The Great Game: Afghanistan, British India and the Hundred Year War for India's Northern Frontier*, Independently published, 2019.

CHAPTER 10: TOO SALTY

1 Associated Press, 'One of Hitler's 15 Food Tasters Finally Tells Her Story', *The Denver Post*, 27 April 2013, https://tinyurl.com/3b2xuwt3. Accessed on 13 May 2024.

2 Lucullus, https://tinyurl.com/mrxwufxu. Accessed on 20 March 2024.

3 Sam Wollaston, 'Hitler's Hidden Drug Habit, Downton Abbey review – high Hitler, and hang Bates', *The Guardian*, 20 October 2014, https://tinyurl.com/29rujyy6, Accessed on 13 May 2024.

4 Musharbash, Von Yassin, 'The End of a Tyrant', *Spiegel International*, 20 October 2011, https://tinyurl.com/yy36ketm. Accessed on 13 May 2024.

5 Walsh, John, 'What the World's Worst Dictators Liked to Eat More Than Anything Else', *indy100*, https://tinyurl.com/xthubpua. Accessed on 20 March 2024.

6 Demick, Barbara, 'The Way to Understand Kim Jong-il Was Through His Stomach', *Daily Beast*, 14 July 2017, https://tinyurl.com/3zyju345. Accessed on 13 May 2024.

Demick, Barbara, 'The Unpalatable Appetites of Kim Jong-il', *The Telegraph*, 8 October 2011, https://tinyurl.com/39xaza7k. Accessed on 13 May 2024.

7 'Last outpost of the Khmer Rouge', *The Guardian*, 26 March 2000, https://tinyurl.com/572wdfvj. Accessed on 20 March 2024.

8 Szabłowski, Witold, *How to Feed a Dictator: Saddam Hussein, Idi Amin, Enver Hoxha, Fidel Castro, and Pol Pot Through the Eyes of Their Cooks*, Penguin Books (2020).

9 'The Fitness of the 10 Most Notorious Dictators', *Health Fitness Revolution*, 24 March 2021, https://tinyurl.com/5xf7jfve. Accessed on 13 May 2024.

10 'What Do Dictators Like To Eat?' *BBC*, 5 December 2014, https://tinyurl.com/ycyhbxbe. Accessed on 13 May 2024.

11 As told to the author by a Romanian Minister.

12 Garcia-Navarro, Lulu, '"How To Feed A Dictator" Spills The Beans On 5 Strongmen', *Texas Public Radio*, 26 April 2020, https://tinyurl.com/4jwsmjfw. Accessed on 20 March 2024.

13 Szabłowski, Witold, *How to Feed a Dictator: Saddam Hussein, Idi Amin, Enver Hoxha, Fidel Castro, and Pol Pot Through the Eyes of Their Cooks*, Penguin Books (2020).

14 'One of Hitler's 15 Food Tasters Finally Tells Her Story, *The Denver*

Post, 27 April 2013, https://tinyurl.com/563s2eur. Accessed on 22 March 2024.

15 'What Do Dictators Like to Eat?', *BBC*, 5 December 2014, https://tinyurl.com/ycyhbxbe. Accessed on 13 May 2024.

16 'Putin Says Grandfather Cooked for Stalin and Lenin', *Reuters*, 11 March 2018, https://tinyurl.com/3src2z6u. Accessed on 21 March 2024.

17 Zubacheva, Ksenia, 'What Were Stalin's Hobbies?', *Russia Beyond*, 24 January 2020, https://tinyurl.com/29ad7hap. Accessed on 21 March 2024.

18 Plokhy, Serhii, 'Vodka Shots with Stalin: On the Dinner That Changed the War', *Literary Hub*, 20 November, 2019, https://tinyurl.com/4betx879. Accessed on 20 March 2024.

19 'Rich French Food May Have Killed Napoleon, *ABC News*, https://tinyurl.com/mrx9zr7u. Accessed on 13 May 2024.

20 'The Fitness of the 10 Most Notorious Dictators', *Health Fitness Revolution*, 24 March 2021, https://tinyurl.com/5xf7jfve. Accessed on 13 May 2024.

21 Clark, Victoria, and Melissa Scott, 'Dining with the Devil: The Eating Habits of the World's Most Evil Dictators', *Express*, 2 March 2015, https://tinyurl.com/23e9ee7m. Accessed on 13 May 2024.

22 https://tinyurl.com/mszj8625. Accessed on 20 March 2024.

23 Surewicz, Anita, 'Dictators With Strange Eating Habits', *Mashed*, 22 May 2023, https://tinyurl.com/5ehdukvx. Accessed on 13 May 2024.Clark, Victoria, and Melissa Scott, *Dictators' Dinners: A Bad Taste Guide to Entertaining Tyrants*, Gilgamesh Pr Ltd, 2014.

24 https://tinyurl.com/ycm4hf69. Accessed on 20 March 2024.

CHAPTER 11: TIGER'S TEETH

1 de Vries, Manfred F.R. Kets, 'In Praise of Dictators: A Satire', *Insead*, https://tinyurl.com/bdf2hbjy. Accessed on 26 March 2024.

2 Bileta, Vedran, 'Caligula: 18 Facts on the "Mad" Roman Emperor', *The Collector*, 16 August 2023, https://tinyurl.com/yrkpsf8y. Accessed on 13 May 2024.

3 'Assassination of Caligula', *Italy on this Day*, 24 January 2019,

https://tinyurl.com/yzp7zprc. Accessed on 13 May 2024.

4 Historicalhysteria, 'According to Chairman Mao's Doctor, Mao Didn't Believe in Brushing His Teeth. Instead he Rinsed with Green Tea. By the End of His Life This Had Stained His Teeth Green. When Dr Li Zhisui Recommended Brushing Mao Responded "A Tiger Does Not Brush Its Teeth"', *Reddit*, https://tinyurl.com/2att2ck3. Accessed on 26 March 2024.

5 Oliver, Mark, '10 Filthy Facts about the Private Life of Chairman Mao Tse-Tung', *Listverse*, 1 March 2017, https://tinyurl.com/n2rnptkf. Accessed on 26 March 2024.

6 Stevens, Christopher, 'Mussolini the Insatiable: He Was a Violent Lover Who Demanded Sex Constantly and Only Truly Cared for One Woman...the Beautiful Heiress Doomed to Die Alongside Him', *The Daily Mail*, 24 February 2017, https://tinyurl.com/bdk6jhfu. Accessed on 13 May 2024.

7 'Ne Win: The Dictator Who Bathed in Dolphin Blood', *History Answers*, 8 January 2015, https://tinyurl.com/3mymkkr9. Accessed on 26 March 2024.

8 Ibid.

9 Ibid.

10 Geiger, Abigail, 'Awaiting the Enemy That Never Came: The Bunkers of Albania', *Atlas Obscura*, 10 October 2013, https://tinyurl.com/3mjtbd4a. Accessed on 26 March 2024.

11 Fevziu, Blendi, *Enver Hoxha: The Iron Fist of Albania*, I.B. Tauris, London, 2016.

12 Ibid.

13 Morton, Ella, 'Golden Statues and Mother Bread: The Bizarre Legacy of Turkmenistan's Former Dictator', *Slate*, 6 February 2014, https://tinyurl.com/5asbw72s. Accessed on 26 March 2024.

14 Cathill, Paul, 'Interesting Histories: Saparmurat Niyazov—The Real General Aladeen', *Medium*, 26 September 2018, https://tinyurl.com/497eysyp. Accessed on 26 March 2024.

15 Ibid.

16 Ibid.

17 Smith, David, 'Where Concorde Once Flew: The Story of President

Mobutu's "African Versailles"', *The Guardian*, 10 February 2015, https://tinyurl.com/4rzeja6v. Accessed on 13 May 2024.

18 Cheung, Helier, 'The Dictator: Why Do Autocrats Do Strange Things?', *BBC*, 15 May 2012, https://tinyurl.com/4c6cumd4. Accessed on 13 May 2024.

19 As told to the author.

20 Quammen, David, 'The Bear Slayer', *The Atlantic*, July-August 2003, https://tinyurl.com/4vmte9ft. Accessed on 13 May 2024.

21 Walker, Shaun, 'Romania Comes to Terms with Monument to Communism 30 Years After Ceausescu's Death', *The Guardian*, 22 December 2019, https://tinyurl.com/f7y9tp8w. Accessed on 13 May 2024.

22 Cheung, Helier, 'The Dictator: Why Do Autocrats Do Strange Things?', *BBC*, 15 May 2012, https://tinyurl.com/4c6cumd4. Accessed on 13 May 2024.

23 Tamara, Karlus, 'No, Bolsonaro's Brazil Is Not a Dictatorship. It's Worse', *The Globe Post*, 3 April 2020, https://tinyurl.com/3tmbct3u. Accessed on 26 March 2024.

24 'Dictatorial Passions', *Bangalore Mirror*, 12 September 2011, https://tinyurl.com/ry9ff4rz. Accessed on 13 May 2024.

25 Philips, Matthew, 'China Regulates Buddhist Reincarnation', *Newsweek*, 15 August 2007, https://tinyurl.com/yv8mrh5h. Accessed on 26 March 2024.

26 Based on author's personal interaction in Albania.

27 'The Psychology of Dictators: Power, Fear, and Anxiety', *Anxiety.org*.

28 Kissinger, Henry, *Leadership: Six Studies in World Strategy*, Allen Lane (UK), 2022.

CHAPTER 12: COLONIZERS AS TYRANTS

1 Stevis-Gridneff, Matina, 'Crude Comments from Europe's Top Diplomat Point to Bigger Problems', *The New York Times*, 17 October 2022, https://tinyurl.com/45n23k2u. Accessed on 17 April 2024.

2 Williamson, Lucy, 'Napoleon's Incendiary Legacy Divides France

200 Years On', *BBC*, 5 May 2021, https://tinyurl.com/4u8hzykj. Accessed on 17 April 2024.

3 Tremlett, Giles, 'Lost Document Reveals Columbus as Tyrant of the Caribbean', *The Guardian*, 7 August 2006, https://tinyurl.com/mv5p3nkc. Accessed on 17 April 2024.

4 Conrad, Joseph, *Heart of Darkness*, https://tinyurl.com/ytrac8ru. Accessed on 17 April 2024.

5 Sullivan, Dylan, and Jason Hickel, 'How British Colonialism Killed 100 Million Indians in 40 Years', *Al Jazeera*, 2 December 2022, https://tinyurl.com/ynv8x233. Accessed on 18 April 2024.

6 Ibid.

7 Malik, Kenan, 'Colonialism by Nigel Biggar Review – A Flawed Defence of Empire', *The Guardian*, 20 February 2023, https://tinyurl.com/5x7rnu76. Accessed on 18 April 2024.

8 Orwell, George, 'Shooting an Elephant', https://tinyurl.com/3yj6up35. Accessed on 18 April 2024.

9 'Responsibility to Protect', *United Nations | Office on Genocide Prevention and the Responsibility to Protect*, https://tinyurl.com/2cz8vk82. Accessed on 18 April 2024.

10 Thomas, Mariah, '50 Inspirational Barack Obama Quotes on Life, Hope and Change', *Reader's Digest*, 25 February 2024, https://tinyurl.com/2f2zv76s. Accessed on 21 May 2024.

CHAPTER 13: SOFT CORE

1 Ramm, Benjamin, 'Why Tyrants Love to Write Poetry', *BBC*, 25 October 2017, https://tinyurl.com/48mna5an. Accessed on 27 March 2024.

2 Walsh, Michael, '"What an Artist Dies in Me!"', *The Pipeline*, 23 October 2022, https://tinyurl.com/4s73c2vv. Accessed on 27 March 2024.

3 Rickett, Oscar, 'Famous Last Words? Say Them Now, Before It's Too Late', *The Guardian*, 2 August 2015, https://tinyurl.com/yrk8vwcp. Accessed on 27 March 2024.

4 Ramm, Benjamin, 'Why Tyrants Love to Write Poetry', *BBC*, 25 October, 2017, https://tinyurl.com/48mna5an. Accessed on 27

March 2024.

5 Ganji, Akbar, 'Who Is Ali Khamenei? The Worldview of Iran's Supreme Leader', *Foreign Affairs*, September/October 2013, https://tinyurl.com/mtycp7e8. Accessed on 27 March 2024.

6 'Saddam Hussein Had Qur'an Written in His Blood', *AllGov*, https://tinyurl.com/yc78ye4k. Accessed on 27 March 2024.

7 Kalder, Daniel, '10 Things I Learned From Reading Terrible Books Written by Dictators', *PW*, 16 March 2018, https://tinyurl.com/eybs5kwa. Accessed on 27 March 2024.

8 Kalder, Daniel, 'Daniel Kalder: The Nervous Breakdown Self-Interview', 7 March 2018, https://tinyurl.com/yjbzhw3d. Accessed on 27 March 2024.

9 Hussein, Saddam, *Zabiba and the King*, Virtualbookworm Publishing, 2004.

10 Ibid.

11 Bo Gu, 'China's New Mandatory Curriculum Focuses on "Xi Thought"', *VOA*, 25 August 2021, https://tinyurl.com/4kckyz5w. Accessed on 27 March 2024.

12 Dikötter, Frank, *How to Be a Dictator: The Cult of Personality in the Twentieth Century*, Bloomsbury Publishing, New York, 2019.

13 Ibid.

14 *Quotations From Chairman Mao Tse-Tung*, Foreign Language Press, Peking, 1966.

15 Li Liandi, 'Changsha Cultural Bookstore: A Secret Revolutionary Point', *Changsha Kaifu*, 7 January 2021, https://tinyurl.com/ydbte6kb. Accessed on 13 May 2024.

16 Dikötter, Frank, *The Cultural Revolution: A People's History, 1962—1976*, Bloomsbury Press, 2017.

17 'Book Burnings in Germany, 1933', *American Experience*, https://tinyurl.com/2ey7mw2y. Accessed on 27 March 2024.

18 Flynn, Joseph, 'Perspective: The Right to Read', *Northern Public Radio*, 29 March 2023, https://tinyurl.com/ustu23ra. Accessed on 27 March 2024.

19 Dikötter, Frank, *How to Be a Dictator: The Cult of Personality in the Twentieth Century*, Bloomsbury Publishing, New York, 2019.

20 Gopnik, Adam, 'The Field Guide to Tyranny', *The New Yorker*, 16 December 2019, https://tinyurl.com/4u72k6sw. Accessed on 27 March 2024.

21 Ibid.

22 Ibid.

23 Festa, Paul, '"Mussolini," by R.J.B. Bosworth', *Salon*, 9 July 2002, https://tinyurl.com/yc4n2zhu. Accessed on 13 May 2024.

24 'Dictators and Their Favourite Pastime', *The Economic Times*, 28 May 2015, https://tinyurl.com/4r76mbym. Accessed on 13 May 2024.

25 Carney, Scott, and Jason Miklian, '"Just kill 20,000 Bengalis": Zulfikar Bhutto's Advice to Yahya Khan before 1971 War', *The Print*, 27 May 2022, https://tinyurl.com/mtsfrxw6. Accessed on 27 March 2024.

26 Castro, Fidel, and Ignacio Ramonet, *Fidel Castro: My Life: A Spoken Autobiography*, Illustrated Edition, Scribner, New York, 2009.

27 Munro, Cait, 'From Jimmy Carter to Hitler, 10 Politicians Who Tried Their Hands at Art', *artnet*, 25 April 2014, https://tinyurl.com/mpcvh79a. Accessed on 27 March, 2024.

28 'My Dad Idi Amin...', *Mumbai Mirror*, 15 January 2007, https://tinyurl.com/b2bc9xtd. Accessed on 27 March 2024.

29 Pruitt, Sarah, 'When Hitler Tried (and Failed) to Be an Artist', *History*, 13 September 2019, https://tinyurl.com/448yb586. Accessed on 27 March 2024.

30 Kalder, Daniel, *Dictator Literature: A History of Bad Books by Terrible People*, Simon and Schuster, 2018.

31 Gopnik, Adam, 'The Field Guide to Tyranny', *The New Yorker*, 16 December 2019, https://tinyurl.com/mr88462s. Accessed on 13 May 2024.

32 Zulueta, Lito, and Totel V. De Jesus, 'Mario Vargas Llosa at UST: "Dictators Are Afraid of Literature"', *Lifestyle.INQ*, 14 November 2016, https://tinyurl.com/27dpn3ze. Accessed on 27 March 2024.

33 Popova, Maria, 'JFK on Poetry, Power, and the Artist's Role in Society: His Eulogy for Robert Frost, One of the Greatest Speeches of All Time', *The Marginalian*, https://tinyurl.com/3dn7kbmp. Accessed on 27 March 2024.

34 'Afghans Have Broken "Shackles of Slavery": Pakistan PM Imran

Khan', *The Hindu*, 16 August 2021, https://tinyurl.com/2xvky7fj. Accessed on 27 March 2024.

35 Angelou, Maya, 'Caged Bird', *Poetry Foundation*, https://tinyurl.com/teu3b62h. Accessed on 27 March 2024.

CHAPTER 14: CHARISMA

1 Roy, Anita, 'On the Shelf. The Charismatic Light-eaters', *The Hindu Businessline*, 10 March 2018, https://tinyurl.com/529ew9v3. Accessed on 27 March 2024.

2 'Wellington and Napoleon', *Wellington Collection*, https://tinyurl.com/3eu2wbks. Accessed on 27 March 2024.

3 'Back to Basics: The Two Tasks of Effective Leadership', *Process Excellence Network*, 29 May 2012, https://tinyurl.com/r6r77atw. Accessed on 27 March 2024.

4 Money-Kyrle, Roger Ernle, 'The Psychology of Propaganda', *Welcome Collection*, https://tinyurl.com/2fua2naa. Accessed on 13 May 2024.

5 Ibid.

6 Sharif, Ikraam, 'Understanding Tony Blair's and the 2003 Iraq Invasion', *Rock* and *Art*, 24 July 2023, https://tinyurl.com/2f2j5pe6. Accessed on 27 March 2024.

7 Rees, Laurence, *The Dark Charisma of Adolf Hitler*, Ebury Press, London, 2013.

8 Kissinger, Henry, *Leadership: Six Studies in World Strategy*, Allen Lane, New York, 2022.

9 Muo, Comicus, 'Nietzsche – To Live Is to Suffer, to Survive Is to Find Some Meaning in the Suffering', *The Stand Up Philosophers*, 7 November 2023, https://tinyurl.com/mrxdzdkz. Accessed on 13 May 2024.

CHAPTER 15: DICTATOR'S WIFE

1 https://tinyurl.com/2652brex. Accessed on 22 March 2024.

2 Luzer, Daniel, 'The Lives of Dictators' Wives', *Pacific Standard*, 3 May 2017, https://tinyurl.com/3rst5s86. Accessed on 22 March 2024.

3 Ibid.
4 Ibid.
5 Ibid.
6 Ibid.
7 Evans, Sophie Jane, 'Wives of Luxury: Inside the Lavish Lives of Dictators' Wives from £75k Shopping Sprees and 1,200 Pairs of Shoes to Mid-air Plane U-turns to Buy Some Cheese', *The Sun*, 17 September 2019, https://tinyurl.com/5h2nr7d4. Accessed on 22 March 2024.
8 'What Marcoses Brought to Hawaii after Fleeing PHL in '86: $717-M in Cash, $124-M in Deposit Slips', *GMA New Online*, 25 February 2016, https://tinyurl.com/4hztj7v4. Accessed on 22 March 2024.
9 Pakula, Hannah, *Elena Ceausescu: The Shaping of an Ogress*, August 1990, https://tinyurl.com/24yze9ma. Accessed on 13 May 2024.
10 Ibid.
11 Ibid.
12 As narrated to the author.
13 Chenoweth, Erica, and Zoe Marks, 'Revenge of the Patriarchs', *Foreign Affairs*, 8 February 2022, https://tinyurl.com/mwvw32z9. Accessed on 13 May 2024.
14 'Dictators' Wives: How the West is Wooed by the Pretty Faces of Tyranny', *The Sydney Morning Herald*, 29 February 2012, https://tinyurl.com/uakr74pz. Accessed on 13 May 2024.
15 Betts, Hannah, 'Leila Trabelsi: Imelda Marcos of the Arab world', *The Telegraph*, 19 January 2011, https://tinyurl.com/3ym58ku5. Accessed on 13 May 2024.
16 Taylor, Jerome, 'The Exile Factor: Wives of Deposed Dictators', *The New Zealand Herald*, 22 January 2011, https://tinyurl.com/s6z7nphm. Accessed on 13 May 2024.
17 'Marie-Antoinette', *100 Women, Encyclopædia Britannica*, https://tinyurl.com/ze4yu77n. Accessed on 13 May 2024.

CHAPTER 16: MESMERIZE WITH WORDS

1 Library of Congress, https://tinyurl.com/yak6whs9. Accessed on 29 March 2024.

2 'Politics, by Aristotle', https://tinyurl.com/2m8dbbz6. Accessed on 29 March 2024.

3 Trollope, Anthony, *The Warden*, Penguin Classics, Reprint edition, 1984.

4 Scharre, Paul, 'How AI Became "The Autocrat's New Toolkit"' [BOOK EXCERPT], *Breaking Defense*, 28 February 2023, https://tinyurl.com/mtvfwbp7. Accessed on 13 May 2024.

5 Browne, Ryan, 'Elon Musk Warns A.I. Could Create an "Immortal Dictator from Which We Can Never Escape"', *CNBC*, 6 April 2018, https://tinyurl.com/34myxk29. Accessed on 29 March 2024.

6 Katatikarn, Jasmine, 'Animation Market Statistics: The Ultimate List in 2024', *Academy of Animated Art*, 11 January 2024, https://tinyurl.com/2bz5prct. Accessed on 13 May 2024.

7 McClintock, Pamela, 2023 Box Office: Global Revenue Clears Estimated $33.9B in 31 Percent Gain Over Prior Year', *The Hollywood Reporter*, 4 January 2024, https://tinyurl.com/bdda3b2u. Accessed on 13 May 2024.

CHAPTER 17: SPIN DOCTORS

1 Torossian, Ronn, 'Hitler's Nazi Germany Used an American PR Agency', *Observer*, 22 December 2014, https://tinyurl.com/3p6a7pfn. Accessed on 10 April 2024.

2 Zaveri, Mihir, 'Massachusetts High School Apologizes after Nazi Quote Is Printed in Yearbook', *The New York Times*, 16 June 2018, https://tinyurl.com/3rjbse5e. Accessed on 13 May 2024.

3 Torossian, Ronn, 'Hitler's Nazi Germany Used an American PR Agency', *Observer*, 22 December 2014, https://tinyurl.com/3p6a7pfn. Accessed on 10 April 2024.

4 Faherty, Anna, 'Political Brilliance and the Power of Self-promotion', *Wellcome Collection*, https://tinyurl.com/yckv5wew. Accessed on 13 May 2024.

5 Hanley, Wayne, 'News from the Front: Bonaparte's Dispatches and the Press', *The Genesis of Napoleonic Propaganda, 1796–1799*, https://tinyurl.com/44xe7nny. Accessed on 13 May 2024.

6 Kundera, Milan, *The Book of Laughter and Forgetting*, Harper

Perennial Modern Classics, 1999.

7 Olmsted, Kathryn S., *The Newspaper Axis: Six Press Barons Who Enabled Hitler*, Yale University Press, New Haven, 2022.

8 Sen, Somdeep, 'Big Money Is Choking India's Free Press—And Its Democracy', *Al Jazeera*, 6 January 2023, https://tinyurl.com/ywtvxs4r. Accessed on 11 April 2024.

9 'How to Remove Negative Articles from Google', *Otter PR*, https://tinyurl.com/2xb48spd. Accessed on 13 May 2024.

10 Ibid.

11 Carlisle, Johan, 'Public Relationships: Hill & Knowlton, Robert Gray, and the CIA', *Covert Action Quarterly*, No. 44, Spring 1993, pp. 19–25, https://tinyurl.com/4cnx3cv2. Accessed on 13 May 2024.

12 Somaiya, Ravi, 'P.R. Firm for Putin's Russia Now Walking a Fine Line', *The New York Times*, 31 August 2014, https://tinyurl.com/ye23rkk8. Accessed on 11 April 2024.

13 Pilger, John, 'Silencing the Lambs. How Propaganda Works. John Pilger, His Legacy Will Live', *Global Research*, 2 January 2024, https://tinyurl.com/4h3j2mxr. Accessed on 1 April 2024.

14 Ibid.

15 Fu, Eva, 'China's Huawei Pays Tony Podesta $1 Million for White House Lobbying', *The Epoch Times*, 22 January 2022, https://tinyurl.com/3v2dek7v. Accessed on 1 April 2024.

16 Holtz, Shel, 'PR for Dictators: Where Should We Draw the Line?', *Shel Holtz | Communicating at the Intersection of Business and Technology*, https://tinyurl.com/2szkx969. Accessed on 11 April 2024.

17 Ingram, Haroro, 'A Brief History of Propaganda During Conflict: Lessons for Counter-Terrorism Strategic Communications', International Centre for Counter-Terrorism - The Hague (ICCT), June 2016, ICCT-Haroro-Ingram-Brief-History-Propaganda-June-2016-LATEST.pdf.

18 Gilbert, Jack, 'PR Firms in Britain Are Spinning Stories for Foreign Dictatorships, *Vice*, 29 July 2014, https://tinyurl.com/3buc2cp7. Accessed on 13 May 2024.

19 Michel, Casey, 'Details of Tony Blair's Dealings with Kazakhstan Leaked', *The Diplomat*, 25 April 2016, https://tinyurl.com/2277pdc7. Accessed on 11 April 2024.

20 Polgreen, Lydia, 'A Journalist in India Ends Up in the Headlines', *The New York Times*, 3 December 2010, https://tinyurl.com/3mfwkyzs. Accessed on 11 April 2024.

21 Olmsted, Kathryn S., *The Newspaper Axis: Six Press Barons Who Enabled Hitler*, Yale University Press, New Haven, 2022.

22 Eppes, Tom, 'Can Ethical PR Practitioners Represent Dictators?', *PRsay*, https://tinyurl.com/2xxkw67x. Accessed on 11 April 2024.

23 Corporate Europe Observatory, *Spin Doctors to the Autocrats: How European PR Firms Whitewash Repressive Regimes*, 20 January 2015, https://tinyurl.com/suxk4maf. Accessed on 11 April 2024.

24 'Public Relations for Terrorists & PR Report on Working in PR for Dictators', *Everything PR News*, 23 January 2015, https://tinyurl.com/yvwye4sn. Accessed on 11 April 2024.

25 'Public Relations for Dictators', *On the Media*, 15 June 2012, https://tinyurl.com/3axx6jas. Accessed on 13 May 2024.

26 Guriev, Sergei, and Daniel Treisman, *Spin Dictators: The Changing Face of Tyranny in the 21st Century*, Princeton University Press, Princeton, 2022.

CHAPTER 18: CRUEL DICTATOR

1 'The Living Mahabharata', *Languagehat*, 17 December 2020, https://tinyurl.com/atrmsrrf. Accessed on 6 May 2024.

2 Rizvi, S.A.A., 'Ibn Sina's Impact on the Rational and Scientific Movements in India', *Indian Journal of History of Science*, Vol. 21, No. 3, 1986, pp. 276–84, https://tinyurl.com/3dyn39x5. Accessed on 12 July 2024.

3 Agarwal, Manjul K., 'From Bharata to India: Volume 2: The Rape of Chrysee', iUniverse, Bloomington, 2012.

4 'Armenian Genocide', *Oxford Reference*, https://tinyurl.com/4cdjfzvk. Accessed on 29 March 2024.

5 Haven, Cynthia, 'Stalin Killed Millions. A Stanford Historian Answers the Question, Was It Genocide?', *Stanford Report*, 23

September 2010, https://tinyurl.com/bdhrx7a7. Accessed on 29 March 2024.

6 Ibid.

7 Branigan, Tania, 'China's Great Famine: The True Story', *The Guardian*, 1 January 2013, https://tinyurl.com/5evcv8d8. Accessed on 13 May 2024.

8 Ibid.

9 De Witte, Melissa, 'China's Cultural Revolution Was a Power Grab from within the Government, Not from Without, Stanford Sociologist Finds', *Stanford Report*, 29 October 2019, https://tinyurl.com/y3bhyzun. Accessed on 29 March 2024.

10 'Idi Amin Buried in Jeddah', *Al Jazeera*, 16 August 2003, https://tinyurl.com/sp6s8kwv. Accessed on 29 March 2024.

11 '7 Steps to Becoming a Dictator: A Manual for Strengthening Your Power Position as Elected Leader', *Professor Mark van Vugt*, https://tinyurl.com/4kzktmzm. Accessed on 29 March 2024.

12 Fevziu, Blendi, *Enver Hoxha: The Iron Fist of Albania*, I.B. Tauris, London, 2016.

13 Bezati, Valbona, 'How Albania Became the World's First Atheist Country', *Balkan Transitional Justice*, 28 August 2019, https://tinyurl.com/mwfzb2ch. Accessed on 29 March 2024.

14 'A Tyrant and a Saint from the Same Small Country', *Sacred Windows*, 24 September 2021, https://tinyurl.com/25877cck. Accessed on 13 May 2024. Wilkinson, Chris, 'Suspicious Minds – Enver Hoxha & Albania: A Cult of Capriciousness', *LinkedIn*, 28 June 2020, https://tinyurl.com/dyu4e4zb. Accessed on 13 May 2024.

15 Arreseigor, Juan José Sánchez, 'Vlad the Impaler's Thirst for Blood Was an Inspiration for Count Dracula', *National Geographic*, 28 October 2021, https://tinyurl.com/mr22eenp. Accessed on 29 March 2024.

16 Lallanilla, Marc, 'Vlad the Impaler: The Real Dracula Was Absolutely Vicious', *NBC News*, 31 October 2013, https://tinyurl.com/43w5yh6v. Accessed on 13 May 2024.

17 Arreseigor, Juan José Sánchez, 'Vlad the Impaler's Thirst for Blood

Was an Inspiration for Count Dracula', *National Geographic*, 28 October 2021, https://tinyurl.com/mr22eenp. Accessed on 29 March 2024.

18 Rivero, Nicolas, 'When Vlad the Impaler Repelled an Invasion with a Forest of Corpses', *Mental Floss*, 14 July 2017, https://tinyurl.com/bdf9uzsf. Accessed on 13 May 2024.

19 Ramesh, Randeep, 'India's Secret History: "A Holocaust, One Where Millions Disappeared..."', *The Guardian*, 24 August 2007, https://tinyurl.com/mr2492v7. Accessed on 13 May 2024.

20 Ibid.

21 Taibbi, Matt, 'The Great American Bubble Machine', *Rolling Stone*, 5 April 2010, https://tinyurl.com/5bhx4ny3. Accessed on 29 March 2024.

22 'Joseph Stalin 1879–1953: Soviet Dictator', *Oxford Reference*, https://tinyurl.com/5n8sjsxv. Accessed on 29 March 2024.

23 'Quotes by Democritus', *The Best Quotations*, https://tinyurl.com/y96a5477. Accessed on 29 March 2024.

24 Bhattacharyya, Sujay, 'Mein Kampf: Hitler's Bestseller Book of Hate', *India Today*, 21 July 2021, https://tinyurl.com/bddx5c9w. Accessed on 29 March 2024.

25 Dalrymple, William, 'Robert Clive Was a Vicious Asset-stripper. His Statue Has No Place on Whitehall', *The Guardian*, 11 June 2020, https://tinyurl.com/37hbsxcf. Accessed on 29 March 2024.

26 Ibid.

27 Pitogo, Heziel, 'Is This the End of Hitler's Bloodline?', *War History Online*, 1 January 2016, https://tinyurl.com/3jd4f9ay. Accessed on 13 May 2024.

28 Pearce, Joseph, 'Henry VIII Was Indeed a "Horrible, Horrible Person"—But Should We Cancel Him For It?', *National Catholic Register*, 4 January 2023, https://tinyurl.com/2j8k65ck. Accessed on 29 March 2024.

CHAPTER 19: COUP

1 Grzymala-Busse, Anna, 'Paths to Power: The Rise and Fall of Dictators', *Foreign Affairs*, 10 December 2019, https://tinyurl.

com/8d3a4bup. Accessed on 1 April 2024.

2 Chitty, Tom, 'Why Does Thailand Have So Many Coups?', *CNBC*, 20 August 2019, https://tinyurl.com/3tn7xsvp. Accessed on 13 May 2024.

3 Anderson, Kenneth, 'A Dissertation on the Strategic Logic of Military Coups', *Lawfare*, 15 July 2016, https://tinyurl.com/3cvxxnck. Accessed on 13 May 2024.

4 Desilver, Drew, 'Despite Apparent Coup in Zimbabwe, Armed Takeovers Have Become Less Common Worldwide', *Pew Research Centre*, 17 November 2017, https://tinyurl.com/yw9j977p. Accessed on 1 April 2024.

5 'Fact Sheet: Military Coup in Niger', *ACLED*, 3 August 2023, https://tinyurl.com/26b687c4. Accessed on 13 May 2024.

6 Ndiloseh, Melvis, and Alexander Hudson, 'The New Model of Coups d'état in Africa: Younger, Less Violent, More Popular', *International IDEA*, 19 December 2022, https://tinyurl.com/3uuzmy3r. Accessed on 13 May 2024.

7 'Imran Khan Loses No-confidence Vote after Day of High-octane Developments; Shehbaz Sharif May be New PM', *National Herald*, 10 April 2022, https://tinyurl.com/ykuuny8e. Accessed on 1 April 2024.

8 Nord, Marina, et al., 'When Autocratization is Reversed: Episodes of Democratic Turnarounds since 1900', *V-Dem Institute*, January 2024, https://tinyurl.com/5at9z29s. Accessed on 13 May 2024.

9 Gajdzis, Krystian, 'The Greatest Comeback in Byzantine History', *Medium*, 7 August 2022, https://tinyurl.com/4sktx2jn. Accessed on 1 April 2024.

10 Liamfoley63, 'Circa February 15, 706: Byzantine Emperor Justinian II Executes His Predecessors', *European Royal History*, 15 February 2022, https://tinyurl.com/mr46f5c9. Accessed on 20 May 2024.

11 Gajdzis, Krystian, 'The Greatest Comeback in Byzantine History', *Medium*, 7 August 2022, https://tinyurl.com/4sktx2jn. Accessed on 1 April 2024.

12 Ibid.

13 https://tinyurl.com/42hx5mt7. Accessed on 1 April 2024.

14 'Étienne de la Boétie, Discourse of Voluntary Servitude (1576)', *The Online Library of Liberty*, https://tinyurl.com/2xsx9e7m. Accessed on 20 May 2024.

15 As narrated to the author.

16 Ibid.

17 'The Jasmine Revolution', *Brittanica*, https://tinyurl.com/yv9vwumc. Accessed on 13 May 2024.

18 Lageman, Thessa, 'Remembering Mohamed Bouazizi: The Man Who Sparked the Arab Spring', *Al Jazeera*, 17 December 2020, https://tinyurl.com/5z38fpup. Accessed on 1 April 2024.

19 Moore, Pete W., 'The Bread Revolutions of 2011: Teaching Political Economies of the Middle East', *PS: Political Science and Politics*, Vol. 46, No. 2, 2013, pp. 225–9, https://tinyurl.com/ycxfsku9. Accessed on 20 May 2024.

20 'National Dialogue Quartet: Facts', *The Nobel Prize*, https://tinyurl.com/y588vw77. Accessed on 1 April 2024.

21 Human Rights Watch, *A Blank Check*, 25 October 2016, https://tinyurl.com/2xvekbwb. Accessed on 13 May 2024.

22 'Jefferson Quotes & Family Letters', *Thomas Jefferson Foundation*, https://tinyurl.com/53ctkbm4. Accessed on 1 April 2024.

23 Barry, John, 'How Dictators Maintain Their Grip on Power', *Newsweek*, 20 February 2011, https://tinyurl.com/55cv8bnu. Accessed on 1 April 2024.

24 Roychowdhury, Adrija, 'Four Reasons Why Indira Gandhi Declared Emergency', *The Indian Express*, 25 June 2018, https://tinyurl.com/27td2dby. Accessed on 1 April 2024.

25 De Bruin, Erica, 'Do Democracies Need to Worry about Coups?', *Cornell University Press*, https://tinyurl.com/37hxub5r. Accessed on 13 May 2024.

26 Ibid.

27 Montefiore, Simon Sebag, 'Dictators Get the Deaths They Deserve', *The New York Times*, 26 October 2011, https://tinyurl.com/2r6xmc7z. Accessed on 13 May 2024.

CHAPTER 20: ILL WINDS

1 Alighieri, Dante, *Inferno*, Harper Press, UK Edition, 2011.
2 https://tinyurl.com/2hnnum48. Accessed on 21 March 2024.
3 Plato, *The Republic*, https://tinyurl.com/mu2endum. Accessed on 21 March 2024.
4 Ambedkar, B.R., 'Why BR Ambedkar's three warnings in his last speech to the Constituent Assembly resonate even today, *Scroll.in*, 26 January, 2016, https://tinyurl.com/4nt8jxsa. Accessed on 21 March 2024.
5 Rand, Ayn, *Atlas Shrugged*, Signet, New York, 1996.
6 Orwell, George,*1984*, Signet Classic, New York, 1961.
7 'Why is Zimbabwe Using Scraps of Paper as Currency?', *Read On*, 28 March 2023, https://tinyurl.com/22hfxffm. Accessed on 22 May 2024. Coles, Stuart, 'Poaching in Zimbabwe "out of control"', *The Telegraph*, 10 July 2007, https://tinyurl.com/3mczs7aa. Accessed on 22 May 2024.
8 Kissinger, Henry, *Leadership*, Allen Lane (UK), 2022.
9 'Hitler Forecasts No Reich Overturn In Next 1,000 Years; Proclamation To Nazi Congress Says Movement Won't Yield No Matter What Happens', *The New York Times*, 6 September 1934, https://tinyurl.com/mpdtynvj. Accessed on 22 March 2024.
10 Barry, John, 'How Dictators Maintain Their Grip on Power', *Newsweek*, 20 February 2011, https://tinyurl.com/46umuj3d. Accessed on 17 May 2024.

CHAPTER 21: A CASE FOR DEMOCRACY

1 Guerra, Lenin Cavalcanti, '"Does Not Tyranny Spring from Democracy?" How Plato's 380 BC Philosophy Is Truer Than Ever Today', *Scroll.in*, 14 November 2019, https://tinyurl.com/ymhm9kw5. Accessed on 12 April 2024.
2 'Quotations about Democracy, Politics and Government, and Related Matters', *Center for Civic Education*, https://tinyurl.com/32d589fb. Accessed on 12 April 2024.
3 Soni, Mallika, 'Old Interview: Donald Trump's First Wife Said He

Kept Hitler Speeches beside Bed', *Hindustan Times*, 19 December 2023, https://tinyurl.com/yeypefyt. Accessed on 12 April 2024.

4 'Locke's Political Philosophy', *Stanford Encyclopedia of Philosophy*, 6 October 2020, https://tinyurl.com/2s3kbvza. Accessed on 12 April 2024.

5 Kagan, Robert, 'Opinion Readers Had Questions about My Essay on the Rise of Strongmen. Here Are the Answers', *The Washington Post*, 20 March 2019, https://tinyurl.com/2pr6pxcs. Accessed on 12 April 2024.

6 Pines, Jonathon, and Iain Hagan, 'The Renaissance or the Cuckoo Clock', *The Royal Society Publishing*, 27 December 2011, https://tinyurl.com/78j6kayh. Accessed on 12 April 2024.

7 Tacitus, *The Annals of Imperial Rome*, Penguin Classics, 2003.

8 Lepore, Jill, 'The Last Time Democracy Almost Died', *The New Yorker*, 27 January 2020, https://tinyurl.com/yey8k379. Accessed on 12 April 2024.

9 Chen, Heather, 'Pandemics and Aliens: Sci-Fi Writer Liu Cixin Says the Dystopian Future Is Now', *Vice News*, 16 November 2020, https://tinyurl.com/tc435adv. Accessed on 12 April 2024.

10 PTI, 'Asking for More Loans from Friendly Countries Is Embarrassing: Pakistan PM', *Business Standard*, 15 January 2023, https://tinyurl.com/4zj8m2b6. Accessed on 12 April 2024.

11 'Remarks by President Biden at the 2021 Virtual Munich Security Conference', *The White House*, 19 February 2021, https://tinyurl.com/mrymrmxn. Accessed on 12 April 2024.

12 Ward, Alex, 'Joe Biden Wants to Prove Democracy Works—Before It's Too Late', *Vox*, 29 April 2021, https://tinyurl.com/mryk7u4h. Accessed on 12 April 2024.

13 Gao, Charlotte, 'Xi: China Must Never Adopt Constitutionalism, Separation of Powers, or Judicial Independence', *The Diplomat*, 19 February 2019, https://tinyurl.com/yzjmc7mn. Accessed on 12 April 2024.

14 Hendricks, Scotty, 'Why Socrates Hated Democracy, and What We Can Do about It', *Big Think*, 7 October 2017, https://tinyurl.com/yeyu7apc. Accessed on 12 April 2024.

CHAPTER 22: DEMOCRACY AND DICTATORSHIP

1 'Gustave Flaubert in a Letter to Madame Roger Des Genettes (*c.* 1861)', *tumblr*, https://tinyurl.com/kbt7bhzk. Accessed on 12 April 2024.
2 Ibid.
3 Millay, Edna St. Vincent, 'What Lips My Lips Have Kissed, and Where, and Why', *Poetry Foundation*, https://tinyurl.com/5czcpatd. Accessed on 10 May 2024.
4 Ukers, William Harrison, *All About Coffee*, The Tea and Coffee Trade Journal Company, 1922.
5 'Indian Coffee House, Connaught Place', *Atlas Obscura*, 7 August 2019, https://tinyurl.com/a8dbss4h. Accessed on 24 April 2024.
6 Ibid.
7 Arsu, Sebnem, and Sabrina Tavernise, 'Turkish Media Group Is Fined $2.5 Billion', *The New York Times*, 9 September 2009, https://tinyurl.com/czuzejwr. Accessed on 12 April 2024.
8 Ayittey, George B.N., 'The Worst of the Worst', *Foreign Policy*, 15 June 2010, https://tinyurl.com/bdtevjez. Accessed on 10 May 2024.
9 Ibid.
10 *Freedom in the World 2024*, Freedom House, February 2024, https://tinyurl.com/3p7k345x. Accessed on 24 April 2024.
11 'Current World Dictators', *PlanetRulers*, https://tinyurl.com/5ub7r2pp. Accessed on 24 April 2024.
12 *Democracy Report 2023: Defiance In the Face of Autocratization*, V-Dem Institute, 2023, https://tinyurl.com/5rezp54r. Accessed on 10 May 2024.
13 Wike, Richard, et al., 'Democracy Widely Supported, Little Backing for Rule by Strong Leader or Military', 16 October 2017, *Pew Research Center*, https://tinyurl.com/4hyf2fkp. Accessed on 24 April 2024.
14 Ibid.
15 Popova, Maria, 'Octavia Butler on How (Not) to Choose Our Leaders', *The Marginalian*, https://tinyurl.com/m2jezhze. Accessed on 10 May 2024.

CHAPTER 23: DICTATOR'S LONGEVITY

1 'Selected Political Writings of Voltaire', https://tinyurl.com/yxx62yt6. Accessed on 18 April 2024.

2 Orwell, George,*1984*, Signet Classic, New York, 1961

3 T.S. Eliot Quote, https://tinyurl.com/3xzx73uj. Accessed on 18 April 2024.

4 '"Conquering the world on horseback is easy. It is dismounting and governing that's hard." – Genghis Khan', *Newstalk*, 10 November 2015, https://tinyurl.com/59u5j929. Accessed on 19 April 2024.

5 Here and Now, 'Retirement for Deposed Dictators: Where Do They Go?', *The World*, 15 August 2013, https://tinyurl.com/bdddrhan. Accessed on 14 May 2024.

6 Ibid.

7 Mydans, Seth, 'Former Philippine President Jailed on Corruption Charges', *The New York Times*, 26 April 2001, https://tinyurl.com/u3cs2rex. Accessed on 14 May 2024.

8 'Philippines Charges Gloria Arroyo with Corruption', *Associated Press*, 18 November 2011, https://tinyurl.com/42anhjsh. Accessed on 19 April 2024.

CHAPTER 24: FUTURE DICTATORS

1 Liptak, Kevin, 'Macron Rebukes Nationalism as Trump Observes Armistice Day', *CNN*, https://tinyurl.com/mpv4hn76. Accessed on 22 April 2024.

2 Ibid.

3 Office of the Secretary of State, 'The Elements of the China Challenge', November 2020 (Revised December 2020), https://tinyurl.com/2knsjduu. Accessed on 22 April 2024.

4 Wike, Richard, Janell Fetterolf, Maria Smerkovich, Sarah Austin, Sneha Gubbala and Jordan Lippert, 'Representative Democracy Remains a Popular Ideal, But People Around the World Are Critical of How It's Working', Pew Research Center, 28 February 2024, https://tinyurl.com/bddmr65m. Accessed on 22 April, 2024.

5 Miller, Nick, 'Nationalism is a Betrayal of Patriotism: France's President Lectures the Powerful', *The Sydney Morning Herald,* 11 November 2018, https://tinyurl.com/mvuzx6h8. Accessed on 23 April 2024.

6 Crawshaw, David, and Alicia Chen, '"Heads bashed bloody": China's Xi Marks Communist Party Centenary with Strong Words for Adversaries', *The Washington Post,* 1 July 2021, https://tinyurl.com/5xevc6ad. Accessed on 23 April 2024.

CHAPTER 25: THAT BURST OF ANGER

1 Orwell, George, *1984,* Books&Coffe, 1949.

2 Global Protest Tracker: Carnegie Endowment for International Peace, https://carnegieendowment.org/features/global-protest-tracker?lang=en. Accessed on 15 July 2024.

3 Canetti, Elias, *Crowds and Power,* Continuum, New York, 1981.

4 Ibid.

5 Gupta, Rahila, 'The Personal is Political: The Journey of a Feminist Slogan', *Open Democracy,* 13 April 2015, https://tinyurl.com/hz5mvhjn. Accessed on 25 April, 2024.

6 Geeta Mohan, 'Maldives had Proposed President Muizzu's Visit to India in December 2023: Sources', *India Today,* 10 January 2024, https://tinyurl.com/yv9spp5a. Accessed on 25 April 2024.

7 Aytaç, S. Erdem, and Susan Stokes, 'Why Protest?', *The Wilson Quarterly,* Winter 2020, https://tinyurl.com/mu3ckkfb. Accessed on 25 April 2024.

CHAPTER 26: SAYING NO

1 https://tinyurl.com/yckf35ys. Accessed on 26 April 2024.

2 Popova, Maria, 'Albert Camus on What It Means to Be a Rebel and to Be in Solidarity with Justice', *The Marginalian,* https://tinyurl.com/3c8z8adc. *Accessed on 26 April 2024.*

3 'Aristotle's Theory of Revolution: Causes and Methods to Prevent Revolution', *Your Article Library,* https://tinyurl.com/4w844fkc. Accessed on 14 May 2024.

4 Milton, John, *Paradise Lost: Book 1* (1674 version), Poetry

Foundation, https://tinyurl.com/5n8brnvz. Accessed on 26 April 2024.

5 Orbach, Danny, 'The Not-So-Secret Ingredients of Military Coups', *War on the Rocks*, 27 July 2017, https://tinyurl.com/ya93eyt7. Accessed on 14 May 2024.

6 'Aristotle's Theory of Revolution, Causes and Prevention', *yoopery*, https://tinyurl.com/4rumfedf. Accessed on 14 May 2024.

CHAPTER 27: PRIDE BEFORE THE FALL

1 Klaas, Brian, 'Vladimir Putin Has Fallen Into the Dictator Trap', *The Atlantic*, 16 March 2022, https://tinyurl.com/4497dp3a. Accessed on 2 May 2024.

2 'Disney Fans Slam Susan Sarandon for Posting Same Quote as Fired Gina Carano', *Newsweek*, 25 October 2022, https://tinyurl.com/4fwmf5be. Accessed on 2 May 2024.

3 Kaplan, Robert D., 'Xi Jinping: An Echo of Saddam? Center for New American Security', 27 October 2022, https://tinyurl.com/32k8fzzd. Accessed on 2 May 2024.

4 12 essential George Orwell quotes about freedom, 1 November 2018, https://tinyurl.com/mvxd7yxa. Accessed on 2 May 2024.

5 Martinez, Luis R., 'How Much Should We Trust the Dictator's GDP Estimates?', https://tinyurl.com/mv42vz5b. Accessed on 2 May 2024.

6 Rizio, Stephanie M., and Ahmed Skali, 'How Often Do Dictators Have Positive Economic Effects? Global Evidence, 1858–2010', *The Leadership Quarterly*, Volume 31, Issue 3, June 2020, https://tinyurl.com/5n8fdjex. Accessed on 2 May 2024.

7 Wright, Robin, and Willaim Branigin, 'Ahmadinejad Met with Protests, Criticism at Columbia University', *The Washington Post*, 23 September 2007, https://tinyurl.com/9a4pj53j. Accessed on 2 May 2024.

8 Durant, David, '"Have you left no sense of decency": The Army-McCarthy Hearings 60 Years Later', Cold War & Internal Security (CWIS) Collection, https://tinyurl.com/yc4y54j3. Accessed on 2 May 2024.

9 '"In the name of God, go": The history of a speech that has brought down parliament and a prime minister', *The Conversation*, 20 January 2022, https://tinyurl.com/32khf5dd. Accessed on 2 May 2024.

10 Williamson, Lucy, 'Napoleon's incendiary legacy divides France 200 years on', *BBC*, 5 May 2021, https://tinyurl.com/47amdwwv. Accessed on 2 May 2024.

11 AFP, 'At 15, Xi Was Sent To Countryside. He Slept In Cave Homes For Years', *NDTV*, https://tinyurl.com/4bz3mnsr. Accessed on 14 May 2024.

12 Chaplin, Charlie, 'The Final Speech from The Great Dictator', https://tinyurl.com/n4k4pxx7. Accessed on 2 May 2024.

13 Ibid.

CHAPTER 28: SUMMARY JUSTICE

1 Menand, Louis, 'The Devil's Disciples', *The New Yorker*, 20 July 2003, https://tinyurl.com/2jz3prjh. Accessed on 14 May 2024.

2 White, Matthew, *The Great Big Book of Horrible Things: The Definitive Chronicle of History's 100 Worst Atrocities*, W. W. Norton & Company, New York, 2011.

3 Pappas, Stephanie, 'Dictator Deaths: How 13 Notorious Leaders Died', *Live Science*, 17 August 2022, https://tinyurl.com/5n7kzsjv. Accessed on 29 April 2024.

4 Frantz, Erica, and Andrea Kendall-Taylor, 'When ailing dictators die in office, what happens next?', *The Washington Post*, 1 December 2016, https://tinyurl.com/y42jdv6v. Accessed on 29 April 2024.

5 Ibid.

CHAPTER 29: HANG HIM!

1 Faria, Miguel A., 'Stalin's mysterious death', National Library of Medicine, https://tinyurl.com/5ea6df4h. Accessed on 29 April 2024.

2 Ibid.

3 Ibid.

4 James, Ben, 'Fear of Joseph Stalin's wrath contributed to his death',

The Daily Telegraph, 26 March 2018, https://tinyurl.com/bddajkje. Accessed on 29 April 2024.

5 Pappas, Stephanie, 'Dictator Deaths: How 13 Notorious Leaders Died', *Live Science*, 17 August 2022, https://tinyurl.com/5n7kzsjv. Accessed on 29 April 2024.

6 Klein, Christopher, 'Benito Mussolini's Final Hours', *History.com*, 3 August 2023, https://tinyurl.com/jpzxuys9. Accessed on 14 May 2024.

7 Pappas, Stephanie, 'Dictator Deaths: How 13 Notorious Leaders Died', Live Science, 17 August 2022, https://tinyurl.com/5n7kzsjv. Accessed on 29 April 2024.

8 Ibid.

9 Ibid.

10 Gaskill, Matthew, 'Tamerlane Wiped Out Perhaps 17 Million People With Just Fire & Swords', *War History Online*, 3 February 2019, https://tinyurl.com/3a6cy9c3. Accessed on 14 May 2024.

11 'How Conqueror Timur Continues To Scare Many After His Death', *News 18.com*, 23 December 2016, https://tinyurl.com/2fk8c3bc. Accessed on 29 April 2024.

12 'Tamerlane, the last greatest nomadic conqueror and his cursed tomb', https://tinyurl.com/4x6hh9d3. Accessed on 29 April 2024.

13 'How Conqueror Timur Continues To Scare Many After His Death', *News 18.com*, 23 December 2016, https://tinyurl.com/2fk8c3bc. Accessed on 29 April 2024.

14 Ibid.

15 Alikhan, Anvar, 'The curse of Taimur that gave Joseph Stalin grief', *daily O*, 24 December 2016, https://tinyurl.com/2zrsv2cf. Accessed on 29 April 2024.

16 Ibid.

17 Ibid.

18 Ibid.

19 Axworthy, Michael, *The Sword of Persia*, I.B. Tauris & Co Ltd (2016), https://tinyurl.com/3cyp4ts5. Accessed on 14 May 2024.

20 'Path of a Tyrant: Uncovering Genghis Khan's Lost Legacy', *ABC News*, 7 September 2013, https://tinyurl.com/bdebym7j.

Accessed on 14 May 2024.

21 Jacobs, Frank, 'Mongolia's 'Forbidden Zone' Is Guarding an 800-Year-Old Secret', *Atlas Obscura*, 28 July 2023, https://tinyurl.com/yc2mj2p3. Accessed on 14 May 2024.

22 Responsibility To Protect, Office on Genocide Prevention and the Responsibility to Protect, https://tinyurl.com/nhj9n548. Accessed on 1 May 2024.

23 'Man who oversaw Saddam hanging recalls dictator's end', *AFP*, 27 December 2013, https://tinyurl.com/4e7xpyhy. Accessed on 1 May 2024.

24 Ibid.

25 'Moammar Gadhafi Dead: How Rebels Killed the Dictator', *ABC News*, 21 October 2011, https://tinyurl.com/ys3fpbfc. Accessed on 1 May 2024.

26 Shaw, Lucas, 'Hillary Clinton Reacts to Gaddafi's Death' (Video), *The Wrap*, 20 October 2011, https://tinyurl.com/5n9aaw5p. Accessed on 1 May 2024.

27 MacAskill, Ewen, 'The CIA has a long history of helping to kill leaders around the world', *The Guardian*, 5 May 2017, https://tinyurl.com/5h4pjrvz. Accessed on 1 May 2024.

28 Ibid.

29 Jones, Benjamin F., and Benjamin A. Olken, 'Hit or Miss? The Effect of Assassinations on Institutions and War', https://tinyurl.com/4ymkrtds. Accessed on 14 May 2024.

30 Sellmagical, 'What were the last words of famous dictators', *Medium*, 14 February 2022, https://tinyurl.com/m48d3z2h. Accessed on 1 May 2024.

31 As told to the author.

32 Zubok, Vladislav, 'Russia's New Time of Troubles', *Foreign Affairs*, 28 June 2023, https://tinyurl.com/ycx9ucs3. Accessed on 1 May 2024.

33 'Another Time' by W.H. Auden, published by Random House. Copyright © 1940 W.H. Auden, renewed by The Estate of W.H. Auden. Used by permission of Curtis Brown, Ltd.

34 https://tinyurl.com/mtt2d9y8. Accessed on 1 May 2024.

INDEX